Edwin Abbott Abbott

Hints on Home Training and Teaching

Edwin Abbott Abbott

Hints on Home Training and Teaching

ISBN/EAN: 9783337168544

Printed in Europe, USA, Canada, Australia, Japan

Cover: Foto ©Paul-Georg Meister /pixelio.de

More available books at **www.hansebooks.com**

RECENT ENGLISH PEDAGOGY.

HINTS

ON

HOME TRAINING AND TEACHING

BY

EDWIN A. ABBOTT, D.D.,

Head Master of the City of London School.

REPRINTED BY PERMISSION OF AUTHOR,

With Lectures by Canon Farrar, Professors Huxley, Quick, Laurie, and Meiklejohn,
and the Contents of other recent Pedagogical Treatises.

AMERICAN JOURNAL OF EDUCATION.
HARTFORD—28 MAIN STREET.
1884.

CONTENTS.

	PAGE
MEMOIR OF AUTHOR,	5
PREFACE TO LONDON EDITION,	7

PART I.—MORAL TRAINING.

	PAGE			PAGE
1.	HABITS IN GENERAL,	9	10. DUTY,	16
2.	THE FORMATION OF HABITS,	9	11. THE APPETITES,	16
3.	HABITS FORMED BY IMITATION,	10	12. THE WILL,	17
4.	THE HABIT OF ATTENTION,	11	13. OBEDIENCE,	18
5.	OBSERVATION,	12	14. KINDNESS AND HELPFULNESS,	21
6.	MEMORY,	13	15. TRUTHFULNESS,	21
7.	EXACTNESS,	14	16. SIMPLICITY,	23
8.	IMAGINATION,	15	17. REVERENCE,	25
9.	ORDER,	16	18. PUNISHMENTS,	26

PART II.—MENTAL TRAINING.

19.	REGULARITY,	28	39.	MULTIPLICATION OF FRACTIONS,	59
20.	EXACTNESS,	28		DIVISION OF FRACTIONS,	59
21.	ADAPTATION AND VARIATION,	29	40.	MODERN RULE OF THREE,	61
22.	TRANSITION FROM PLAY TO WORK,	30		METHOD OF UNITY,	61
23.	INTRODUCTION AND GUIDANCE,	31	41.	DECIMAL FRACTIONS,	63
24.	READING,	32	42.	GENERAL CAUTIONS,	64
25.	QUESTIONING ON READING,	36	43.	ENGLISH COMPOSITION,	65
26.	WRITING,	37		A NATURAL STYLE,	65
27.	DRILLING, SINGING, DRAWING,	38	44.	CONVERSATION AND COMPOSITION,	65
28.	SPELLING,	38	45.	USE OF LETTERS IN COMPOSITION,	66
29.	PUNCTUATION,	40	46.	USE OF TALES IN COMPOSITION,	66
30.	NUMBERS,	40	47.	TYPICAL SENTENCES,	67
31.	FIGURES,	42	48.	ENGLISH GRAMMAR,	68
32.	TABLES,	42	49.	IRREGULARITIES OF IDIOM,	74
33.	FIRST FOUR RULES APPLIED,	45	50.	MEMORY,	75
	NUMBERS ABOVE A HUNDRED,	45	51.	REPETITION OF POETRY,	78
34.	THE TRANSITION TO FRACTIONS,	51	52.	FRENCH,	82
35.	FRACTIONS,	53	53.	LATIN,	84
36.	FRACTIONAL EXPERIMENTS,	54	54.	GEOGRAPHY,	92
37.	ADDITION OF FRACTIONS,	56	55.	HISTORY,	96
38.	THE VALUE OF A FRACTION,	58	56.	GEOMETRY,	103

PART III.—RELIGIOUS INSTRUCTION.

57. RELIGIOUS INSTRUCTION,	113	58. HOME INFLUENCE ON THE CHILD AT SCHOOL,	120

HINTS ON HOME TRAINING AND TEACHING.

BY EDWARD A. ABBOTT, D.D.

Head Master of City of London School.

MEMOIR.*

The Rev. Edward A. Abbott, D.D., author of *Hints on Home Training and Teaching*, for the use of parents, governesses, and teachers, was born in London, in 1838, and having received his preparatory course in King's College School, was educated at St. John's College, Cambridge, attaining his degree of Bachelor of Arts, with the rank of seventh Senior Optime, and first class in classics, in 1861, and becoming Fellow in the same year. From 1862 to 1865 he was assistant master in King Edward's school, Birmingham, where he displayed such fine scholarship and efficient management as to secure the appointment of Head Master of the City of London School. The City of London School, resting on an ancient foundation, the bequest of John Carpenter in 1442, to the City of London, for the education of four boys, has been elevated into great prominence, under Dr. Abbott's mastership and twenty assistants, by recent endowments in scholarships and exhibitions by city merchants and bankers, and now educates 620 boys, all day scholars, between the ages of seven and fifteen years, who are admitted on the nomination of a member of the corporation, and the payment of £9 per annum, with the exception of those who obtain some of the numerous scholarships and exhibitions, viz.:

Eight Carpenter Exhibitions of 11*l*. per ann. at School, and 25*l*. at Oxford, Cambridge, or London. One Tegg Exhibition of 22*l*. per ann., tenable at Oxford, Cambridge, or London. One *Times* Exhibition, at Oxford or Cambridge, of 30*l*. per ann. Four Beaufoy Exhibitions of 50*l*. per ann. each, tenable at Cambridge. One David Salomons Exhibition, of 50*l*. per ann., at Oxford, Cambridge, or London. One Travers exhibition of 50*l*. per ann., at University of London. One Lambert Jones Exhibition of 49*l*. 8*s*. 9*d*. per ann., at Oxford, Cambridge, or London. One S. Thomas Medical Exhibition, of 30*l*. per ann., at S. Thomas's Hospital, for 3 years. One Goldsmiths' Exhibition, of 50*l*. per ann., at Oxford or Cambridge. Two Grocers' Exhibitions of 50*l*. per ann., at Oxford or Cambridge. One Masterman Exhibition of 30*l*. per ann., at any University, all tenable for 4 years (when not otherwise stated) at the Universities. One David Salomons Exhibition, of 31*l*. 10*s*. per ann., tenable at the School. One Jews' Commemoration Exhibition, of 40*l*. per ann., tenable for 3 years at School or University College, London.

---

* For the principal facts we are indebted to Rentledge's "*Men of the Time (Eleventh Edition)*" and "*Our Schools and Colleges*," by Simpkin, Marshall & Co.

Two William Tite Exhibitions, of 25*l.* and 20*l.* per ann. each, at the School. One Lionel Rothschild Exhibition, of 60*l.* per ann., tenable for 4 years at an English or Foreign University. One W. Stormes Hale Scholarship of 43*l.* 17*s.* 6*d.* per ann., at the School, and afterwards at Oxford, Cambridge, or London University.

Dr. Abbott has been very successful in making the English language both a profitable and interesting study, and his manuals for beginners, "How to tell the Parts of Speech" and "How to Write Clearly," are admirable specimens of condensed directions for the use of teacher and pupil. Grammar ceases to be mere formal drudgery, but is evolved almost unconsciously out of its correct and pleasing use in actual conversation and composition.

Dr. Abbott has published the following theological works: "Bible Lessons," 1872; "Cambridge Sermons," 1875; "Through Nature to Christ," 1877. His other works are, a "Shakespearian Grammar," 1870; an edition of "Bacon's Essays," 1876; "Bacon and Essex," 1877; and an "English Grammar." Dr. Abbott is also the author of two religious romances, published anonymously: "Philochristus: Memoirs of a Disciple of our Lord," 1878; and "Onesimus: Memoirs of a Disciple of St. Paul," 1882.

PREFACE TO LONDON EDITION.

THESE Hints on Home Training and Teaching (although it is hoped they may be of use to governesses and private tutors) are addressed also to parents.

The increased educational opportunities now afforded to girls and women justify the belief that in the next generation mothers will take a large part in the teaching and training of the young, at all events in the middle classes; and, even where parents have not the leisure or the desire to superintend in detail the studies of their children, they can go far to form in them those habits which constitute the foundation of their intellectual as well as their moral future, and can assist the day-school or the private tutor by an influence always most valuable, when wise. To enable parents thus to contribute to the training of their children, is one of the objects of this treatise.

It need scarcely be said that the following pages make no claim to be called an exhaustive book. They contain little more than the results of the Author's observation in the training of his own children, supplemented by experience in class-teaching and in the examination of pupils of every age. During a long professional career many books on education have been of course studied and assimilated, such as the instructive and stimulating works on "Educational Reformers" and "Practical Educationalists" by Mr. Quick and Mr. Leitch, and the suggestive though uneven treatise by Mr. Herbert Spencer. To these and others the Author doubtless owes unconscious debts, but more especially to Stowe's "Training System." In spite of many exaggerations and some mistakes (inevitable for every enthusiast), that book is likely to retain for many years a very great value for all teachers. The interesting work by the Baroness Marenholtz-Bülow on Froebel's system, and the valuable Lectures delivered by Mr. Fitch before the University of Cambridge, were not studied until after the composition of the rough draft of the book; but the former has helped to put some old truths in a new light; and to the latter the

Author is indebted for several hints about the teaching of special subjects — obligations which will be found duly acknowledged as they occur.

Partly to save the space that must otherwise have been devoted to transitions and introductions, and partly to give the book the appearance of being what it really is, viz., a collection of hints, and not a continuous or complete treatise, the Author's remarks are set down disconnectedly, and perhaps in some cases abruptly, the main object being to say as briefly and clearly as possible no more than needed to be said.

Some apology may seem to be required when a single teacher presumes to give even hints on the teaching of so many subjects. But in supervising the miscellaneous curriculum of a large school, the Author has been forced to consider in detail both the theory and practice of many departments of instruction; and hence the area of these "hints," wide though it be, is very little wider than the Author's perhaps too wide circle of professional experiences; which are here set down in the hope that they may enable others to avoid some of the mistakes that he made, and improve on the successes that he thought he had achieved.

EDWARD A. ABBOTT,
City of London School.

LONDON, 1883.

I. MORAL TRAINING.

1. HABITS IN GENERAL.

MAN has been described as a bundle of habits; and Bacon tells us that, whatever may be our sentiments and professions, it is habit that dictates our actions: "Men's thoughts are much according to their inclination; their discourse and speech according to their learning and infused opinions; but their deeds are after as they have been accustomed."

The business of the trainer of children is to mould them for right action by creating in them good habits.

2. THE FORMATION OF HABITS.

Habits are formed by the repetition of actions; and therefore in deciding whether this or that action is good for children, we must constantly ask ourselves not only, "Is the action good in itself?" but also, "Suppose this action, by repetition, to develop a habit; will the habit be a good one?"

It is a pleasure to healthy children to move and to act; and it must be the trainer's object not to suppress action, but to regulate it with a view to producing good habits.

As Nature supplies a plant with influences from earth, sun, and air, all tending to growth, so Nature supplies a child with sights, sounds, objects of touch and taste, inciting him to act, to experimentalize, to attend, observe, and remember, thus stimulating both bodily and mental development.

Put a child to roll on the sea-beach. With the sand to shape at his pleasure, the shells, pebbles, and sea-weed, all close at hand and suggesting countless observations and experiments, he cannot be in a better school. Shut up the same child within the four walls of a room, and his growth will be retarded, because you have deprived him of Nature's gifts.

All children bred up in towns are to some extent thus imprisoned; and they require a kind of interpreter to represent Nature, as it were, to them, and to supply them with substitutes for the gifts from which they are excluded. Even for children in the country Nature does not always suffice without the intervention of some kind selecting hand. The gifts of Nature are sometimes too vast, too distant, too complex, and too similar to come within the compass of a child's observation and discrimination. Nature gives, but it is the business of the trainer to select such of her gifts as may be near, distinct, and suggestive.

What is called the system of Froebel is based upon the recognition of the importance of Nature's influence in the training of the young, and upon the part which may be played by the trainer in the selection of her "gifts." For example, he lays it down—and the precept seems in accordance with common sense—that children should first be presented with opposites, *e. g.* yellow and blue, treble and bass, rough and smooth, hard and soft, because contrast naturally appeals most powerfully to the infant perception. Afterwards he would present the intermediate objects which connect these opposites, showing the child, for example, the different colors of the rainbow which lie between the yellow and blue, and, as it were, unite and reconcile them so as to exhibit what he calls the Law of Reconciliation. For details of Froebel's gifts the reader is referred to special works upon his system; but it must be borne in mind that no toys of this kind, and no system of any kind, can supply a substitute for common sense and observation of Nature's rules on the part of the trainer.

3. HABITS FORMED BY IMITATION.

It is well known that children will imitate irrational objects of every kind, from ducks to steam-engines; but few recognize the very great extent to which they unconsciously imitate their elders in voice, manner, temper, and in a thousand other minute matters which go towards the formation of habits.

Where parents undertake the training of their children there is a special likelihood of imitation, because, in many cases, the latter will have a physical predisposition for the habits of the former. Those, therefore, who are hasty, careless, unobservant, slovenly, hot-tempered, and the like, ought not to be surprised if these habits are reproduced in their children. To come to a smaller matter as an instance, no amount of scolding or teaching is likely to induce a child to attach sufficient importance to writing legibly and carefully, if he constantly sees his father or mother producing an illegible scrawl.

It is in part for this reason that children taught in a school are, for the most part, more orderly and neat in their handwriting and school-work than those who are taught at home. At school there is generally a supply of methodical, orderly pupils, whose work can serve as a pattern for the rest, and the less methodical are more influenced by the sight of what is actually done by their school-fellows than by general exhortations about order and neatness. Another reason is, that parents—and, in a less degree, governesses and private tutors—because they are in sympathy with their pupils and "understand what they mean"—often pass too indulgently over omissions, slips, and slight errors of eccentricity, which would be more wholesomely and justly criticised if contrasted with the better work of other children of their own age.

Although, therefore, there are very great advantages in early home training where it can be given regularly and thoroughly, yet parents and private tutors will do well to be on their guard against the special dangers of inexactness and slovenly incompleteness.

4. THE HABIT OF ATTENTION.

Of all habits, the most valuable, both intellectually and morally, is the habit of attention.

In their religious rites the Romans, the conquerors of the world, were wont to enforce attention by saying to bystanders, "Do this"—meaning, "Do what you are doing, and nothing else"; and it is by the habit of *doing what one is doing*, or, in other words, by attention, that worlds and difficulties are conquered. This habit can be encouraged even in the very youngest; but it is too often discouraged, especially in the children of the richer classes, by an injurious multiplicity of toys and distractions.

On this point I should be glad to quote some quaint remarks by a teacher of considerable experience, on whose judgment I place great reliance. His illustrations deal mainly with common things, and are set down in a familiar style that may seem to some a little too familiar for publication, and to others occasionally savoring of hyperbole. But, without asking my readers to pin their faith on every one of his opinions, I believe they will generally be found to contain much that is fresh and suggestive. As I shall have frequent occasion to quote him, it may be well to give him, both here and elsewhere, the title of "Preceptor." It will be seen that he is vehement against the evil of distracting young children, and he begins from the very youngest.

"Give," he says, "a baby a ball, and he will begin to study it as Nature dictates. He will look at it, feel it, turn it, squeeze it, suck it, smell it, throw it away, and crawl after it for a second study. All this while he is a Student in the University of the World, and under the supervision of the best of private tutors, Experience. Every faculty is being naturally exercised; through every avenue knowledge is being naturally and pleasurably acquired. Let the student alone, then. You did your part when you gave the child the ball, making yourself the Interpreter between Nature and Nature's student. Now suffer Nature to do her work. You cannot improve upon it.

"But now suppose a couple of kind, well-meaning aunts break in upon the happy and interested child, one shaking a silver rattle in his ear, and the other pushing before him a big white horse or a bleating sheep; and simultaneously let two or three elder cousins or friendly visitors attract his attention by various noises and gestures of endearment. At once the spell of interest is broken. The little creature looks from one to the other, distracted but not attracted, bewildered but not pleased. 'How happy could I be with either!' he would say if he were old enough. But not being old enough, he must endure the consequences of the misplaced kindness of his friends—consequences not quite so transient as they seem! His first voyage of discovery has been rudely interrupted, and the poor little adventurer returns laden with a cargo of nothing. Nay, rather say a cargo of something worse than nothing. For instead of helping the child to implant in his own little heart the first germs of that most precious habit of attention, his too officious friends have done their best to sow the seeds of mental dissipation and inattention."

What is the moral of all this? It is that we must be careful from the first, while giving children enough, not to give them more than enough—that is to say, more than their minds can easily take in. Do not obtrude interesting objects on a child who is wholesomely interested already. To break the natural sequence of a child's thoughts is mentally as mischievous as it is physically to wake a child suddenly out of a refreshing sleep. As it is the mark of a great artist to know when to omit, so it is the mark of a good trainer to recognize the danger of interfering with Nature, and the usefulness of leaving children sometimes to themselves.

5. OBSERVATION.

The faculty of observation is secondary to, and in some degree inconsistent with, the faculty of attention; when attending, *i. e.* given up to the study of one thing, the child cannot always be free to observe other things going on around him.

The varied sights of Nature out of doors are the best stimulus to observation, and the best preservative against the rare danger of excessive concentration; and not having these (however great may be the artificial distractions of town life) town children are somewhat at a disadvantage as compared with country children in the training of the faculty of observing.

A powerful incentive to observation is found in the habit of making distinctions. Until a boy has been taught the different kinds of clouds he will be content to stare vaguely at them; but when he has learned to distinguish between "hair clouds," "heap clouds," "level clouds" —for of course we shall not inflict on him the technical terms for these objects—he looks at them with a new interest and quickened power of observation. And so of trees: to learn the characteristics of an oak or an elm separately is rather dull work; but to note the differences between them is more interesting and appeals more readily to the memory. At a very early age children may be led to take pleasure in collecting and classifying the leaves of plants and trees; and this method of training the observation is within the power even of those bred in towns. Much may be done or undone in a walk with children. "It was my fortune," writes Preceptor, "as a child to be taken for walks by a friend who encouraged me to converse on some subject of literature or history, or to cap verses, or the like, the consequence of which (and in part perhaps of other causes) has been to develop in me a considerable power of attention and abstraction, but a singular inability to observe."

Walking in town may seem a necessarily dull and barren occupation, so far as the observation of natural objects is concerned; yet even in the suburbs and parks of London, the clouds, trees, wind, smoke, weathercocks, shadows, points of the compass, sun and moon, afford objects to which the observation of a little companion may be directed, and topics on which a conversation may be hereafter started.

Indoors something may also be done by making a child shut his eyes and tell you what is on the mantelpiece? what on my side of the room? what on yours? Or sometimes, after showing him a picture, you may examine him in the same way. It will be a good plan first, however, to shut your eyes and present yourself for examination, allowing the child to correct your mistakes and supply your omissions.

Later on, observation may be stimulated by teaching a child to take an intelligent interest in things by learning the How and Why. Drawing is of course a powerful developer of this faculty; but drawing, at the present stage, is out of the question. Let it only be added that for observation, as well as for attention and most other good habits, it is indispensable that the child should be physically and mentally healthy and fresh, and that the moral of the last aphorism holds good for observation, no less than for attention, that a child must not be required to observe something new when he is still engaged in observing something old.

To sum up, there are three dangers to be avoided: (1) vacant staring; (2) excited distraction; (3) excessive concentration. Of these the first is perhaps most to be avoided for country children; the second for those in towns; the third is rare, and in the coming generation likely to be rarer.

6. MEMORY.

The memory will have been developed, first, by the habit of attention; secondly, by the habit of classification and observation; but it may also be stimulated by encouraging a child to give an account of what he has seen or heard, under the guidance of questions so regulated as to help the child to *divide*, and thus bring out an orderly narrative.

Thus, if a child has been to the Zoological Gardens, instead of asking him for "a description of the Zoological Gardens," or "Tell me now, what did you see in the Gardens?"—questions to the indefiniteness of which the poor boy is likely to succumb in silent bewilderment, or else to make confused and chaotic answers—you must help him thus, "So you have been to the Gardens? Well now, I want to hear how the beasts are getting on. First, the savage beasts that eat flesh. Did you see the lions fed?" etc., etc. Then you may proceed to the birds, beginning with the eagles, and so rapidly go through the whole. At the end, if you like, and if the child is in the humor to listen, you may give him a kind of summary of what you have elicited from him, so that he may find himself unconsciously committed to a methodical narrative.

To take once more the ancient Romans for our example, the motto that they used for ruling, "*Divide* and rule," we may utilize for remembering. Associations are of great importance in the cultivation of the memory; and we shall have more to say on this point when we treat of the memory as applied to repetition lessons; but even without intelligent associations, the mere process of *division* is of great help.

"Among other debts," writes Preceptor, "which we owe to Shakespeare, is the invention, or popularization of the word *Honorificabilitudinitatibus;* it affords such excellent practice for teachers and pupils. 'What a word!' says the poor bewildered pupil on first hearing it, 'I shall never remember it.' 'Wait a bit,' you reply. 'Any one can say honŏr.'¹ *Pupil.* 'Yes, honŏr.' *Teacher.* 'Now say, hŏnŏr-ĭfĭcā.' *Pupil.* 'Hŏnŏr-ĭfĭcā.' *Teacher.* 'Say it again; now again; once more; that will do. Now for bĭlĭ; that's easy enough; it's a boy's name. Say it. Now bĭlĭtū. Good; now say, dĭnĭtā. Right. And now, bĭlĭtū-dĭnĭtā. Again; again. Now, you see, there's a rhyme:

Hŏnŏr-ĭfĭcā
Bĭlĭtū-dĭnĭtā.

Say it. Sing it, if you like. Good. Now again. Once more. Now you've done it. We've only to add *tibus* at the end.

"I well remember," he adds, "being taught this very word in some such fashion by my father, and teaching it similarly to my children; and I think that every boy in England ought to be taught to pronounce it, and till he pronounced it easily and rapidly, ought not to be considered to have *passed* in pronunciation."

7. EXACTNESS.

"Writing," as we all know, "maketh an exact man"; but as the child, now under consideration, is supposed not yet able to write, some substitute for writing is needed in the attempt to make him exact; and the best will be oral description by the child of something that he has seen. Some skill is here required to induce children to give anything like a continuous description, without feeling that they are being persecuted or forced to "make an exhibition," than which nothing is more detestable to the young. Under the head of "Observation," above, are set down a few hints as to devices by which this may be effected, and among other means was mentioned the use of pictures. On this point I will once more insert some remarks by Preceptor.

"I was in the habit," he says, "of getting a very good lesson in exactness for a youngster out of a picture-book of animals, containing striking and highly-colored, yet accurate, representations of the *locale* of the several creatures. After a picture had been carefully examined, and the particular animal noted in detail (his shape, color, tail, tusks, mane, etc.), and after comparison or contrast had been drawn between

---

¹ Stress should be laid on the *or* here.

this and others known to the child, attention was next directed to the scenery, hill or plain, rocks, rivers, trees, or other vegetation.

"We used then to shut up the book, and set out upon a hunting expedition to chase the beast, I being the hunter, and my boy the dog. Arrived at the country, the hunter questions the dog as to the nature of the scene, and obtains convincing proof that he has reached the habitat, say of the hippopotamus. At last we spy a creature which the dog is again called on to describe. It is found to be of a greyish blue, with a huge smooth body, short, thick legs, small tusks, small ears, very small tail and eyes, and is either wallowing in some stream or trampling a rice-field. All these particulars having been elicited in rapid dialogue, the animal is chased, slain, and (if possible) eaten; and I used to think that he never perished without having afforded a good mental, as well as physical, exercise to the dog."

Arithmetic of course affords a far better training than this in exactness; but our pupil is not supposed to be at present capable of arithmetic, and such an imaginary hunting scene may supply a hint to parents and tutors as to the kind of means by which exactness may be encouraged simultaneously with observation and imagination.

8. IMAGINATION.

When our minds are dissatisfied with the objects presented to them, we find in ourselves a faculty, called imagination, of creating an image of something better. In order, therefore, that the mind may imagine, two things are generally necessary. First, it must have previously received striking and memorable impressions (for no mind can construct images save out of the mental material already accumulated); secondly, the person must not, at the moment, be able to perceive objects like those which he is imagining. "What a man seeth," says St. Paul, "why doth he yet hope for?" and the same applies to the imagination, which is a kind of strain of the mind attempting to realize things beyond the experience of the senses. If a child is *always* completely satisfied with what he sees and hears, he will be under no stimulus to imagine.

It is for this reason that elaborate toys are detrimental to the exercise of the imagination. They are so complete in themselves that they leave nothing to be supplied by the child's mind.

Fairy stories encourage the imaginative faculty, because they present things old, in combinations so new, as to take the child altogether out of the range of things which he sees, and stimulate him by pleasurable associations to realize visions utterly unlike his own experiences.

Several of Æsop's fables may be dramatized by children and for children; and such dramas, like the hunting exercise mentioned in the last section, besides stimulating other faculties, develop the imagination also.

9. ORDER.

A child will learn habits of order in part by seeing order in every part of the household around him.

Yet if he is allowed too long to enjoy the results of order without himself contributing to them, he is in danger of assuming that order can be maintained without effort, and of ignoring the disadvantages of disorder because he has never experienced them.

He must, therefore, begin at a very early age to put away his own toys, and occasionally to feel the inconvenience of not having put them away. If he leaves things about, so that they are mislaid, he must search for them, and so gradually learn that disorder means inconvenience and annoyance.

10. DUTY.

Duty seems naturally to connect itself with rights and possessions. Even toys are felt by a child to have a kind of claim upon him to be preserved from misuse and destruction; and the task of taking care of them and keeping them in order introduces to him a rudimentary form of responsibility.

But with much more force does the possession of pet animals enforce the sense of duty. That birds and rabbits are to be regularly fed is intelligible to very young children indeed; and though a child's office be merely to see that a kitten has its milk, or to throw out crumbs to the birds after breakfast, some little perception of duty is thereby instilled.

It is well to begin very early to apportion to young children little duties and offices in the household, the more real and useful the better; but almost any are better than none, unless they are so palpably superfluous that even a child perceives their uselessness.

11. THE APPETITES.

Healthy and active children are not in much danger of becoming greedy or epicurean, unless the example of their elders leads them wrong. Where they are not extremely delicate, and averse to food, it is best to assume that they will eat whatever is set before them, and to allow them occasionally to try a little of the Spartan sauce, "hunger," rather than to give way to their whims and fancies about food.

"Where there is a tendency to greediness it may be well," suggests Preceptor, "to try to rule the appetite for food by the appetite for play, making some game or amusement follow immediately after the meal; or during dessert a bird-cage may be placed on the table (as Froebel suggests), or a microscope may be called into use."

Fastidiousness is probably more difficult to cure than greediness; and it is not always easy to distinguish natural and constitutional aversion to certain kinds of food (*e. g.* fat, rice, milk) from an unnatural craving for strong and agreeable flavors. Preceptor is doubtless right in thinking that the appetite for luxurious food may be sometimes driven out by the appetite for play. But medical advice ought to be taken before parents compel a child to eat whatever they may put on his plate. Even where a child is exempted from the necessity of eating certain kinds of food, the habit can often be broken by insisting that a very small portion shall be eaten, and gradually increasing the amount. The parents, having once determined what the child can, and what he cannot, be expected to eat, must carefully avoid giving him anything that he cannot eat, and must rigidly insist that nothing shall be "left."

The disgust manifested by parents at any symptoms of greediness, and their displeasure at fastidiousness, will go some way to cure these faults; and wherever dining is enlivened by cheerful conversation, intelligible to children, there is an additional preservative. But by far the greatest safeguard is abundance of exercise, and such an arrangement of meals that the child shall not be called to eat till he is hungry.

Under the head of "appetites" there come other desires, natural and harmless when not carried to excess, such as love of sport, love of bed (in the morning), love of the fireside, as to which only one general rule can be laid down, viz., that a child should be very speedily imbued with the notion that the law and order of the household are superior to his own desires, and that he must be prepared continually to conform himself to regulations. Occasionally, as children grow older and more capable of appreciating reasons, it may be well to point out to them how the full indulgence of this or that desire may interfere with the comfort of others; but it is best at first to dispense with arguments of this or any sort, and to take one's stand on Law, assuming and inculcating that Law is to be obeyed, and that "no child must expect to do what he likes."

12. THE WILL.

The same training that breeds the habit of attention tends to strengthen the will; and those distractions which were said above (§ 4) to be unfavorable to the former are no less unfavorable to the latter.

For the development of the will two opposite kinds of exercises are useful.

1. Sometimes we must set easy tasks, so as to generate a habit of reasonable self-reliance, and prevent the pupil from becoming dispirited by continuous failures.

2. Sometimes we must set more difficult tasks, such as involve some wholesome strain of the powers, so as to lead the child up to a higher standard of exertion, and to prevent him from becoming too easily contented with himself.

The judicious interchange of hard and easy exercises is a part of moral as well as of intellectual training; and the parental instinct or intuition is never better employed than in discerning between those temptations which the childish will may reasonably resist, and be the stronger for resisting, and those, on the other hand, which are likely to prove too strong for resistance, and to which, consequently, a child ought not to be exposed.

Never make it your aim to break a child's will.

Of course, where a child is stubbornly disobedient, disobedience must be punished and obedience enforced; but you must all the while remember that you do not want to destroy the child's will, but to turn it in the right direction. There is more than a mere difference of words in this distinction. There are many punishments of a humiliating and degrading nature which will be adopted by those who desire to "break the will," and which are very efficacious for that purpose; but by those who do not want to "break," but to "bend," such punishments will be suspected, as destroying the very thing we desire to preserve and improve.

13. OBEDIENCE.

Children would be generally obedient if they were ruled unselfishly, uncapriciously, and intelligently.

If a child is engaged in some interesting and harmless occupation, and the nurse abruptly calls him away to show him something pretty which he does not care for, he will go back to his amusement with a feeling of resentment, less disposed to trust the wisdom of commands, and less willing to obey next time. Again, if children are sent suddenly off to bed, in the midst of some absorbing play, without a word of warning or a little tact in sobering down the excitement of the game, so as to prepare for the end, there is very likely to be a tendency to murmur.

By "warning" and "tact" it is not meant that the hour of bedtime should be delayed. On the contrary, it should be adhered to unalterably; or, if it is ever deferred on very rare and special occasions, this should be done from the parents' own will, and *never on account of the child's request.* But it is very easy for a sensible nurse or mother (provided she has leisure to supervise the children) so to arrange matters that a story or game may just come to an end at the right time.

Requests to "stop up a little longer" should be not only never granted, but even prohibited. But, on their side, the parents would do well to consider, when they find children habitually lying awake, and habitually unwilling to go to bed, whether they may not have fixed the hour of bedtime unreasonably early. In such cases it would be well to make it later. If the mother—for whom in this matter no nurse can possibly be an adequate substitute—is in the habit of "hearing prayers" before the little one retires for the night, she will find that the sobering influence of this preparation is one of the best antidotes against bad temper and childish rebellion. But then the prayers must not be a mere form, not hurried through, and not entirely above the child's comprehension. A brief petition for father and mother, sisters and brothers, and that the little one may be "made a good boy," together with the familiar verse addressed to "Gentle Jesus, meek and mild," make up the best possible prayer for a little child. More than this is likely to be less intelligible, and possibly tedious.

But much will depend on the circumstances of the prayer. "I was present once," writes Preceptor, "in a Yorkshire cottage-inn, while the mother was hearing a little child say its prayers for the night; and I remember that the performance included not only the repetition of the Apostles' Creed, but also answers to two or three Biblical questions, such as, 'How many Persons are there in the Trinity?' 'Who was the first man?' 'Who was the first woman?' Yet I felt that the little infant service, if I may so call it, was of the sort that goes upward. And why? Because the mother's questions were imbued with so deep a reverence, and because the family and guests preserved such a reverent silence, that the little one itself seemed to feel that there was reverence in the air. I don't believe the child understood anything, but he seemed to me to *feel* much."

There appears to be in these remarks a force which applies to every household prayer. The mother must be a kind of help to her child to enter a higher atmosphere. The little one must not only learn from her lips, but catch something from her spirit. If this be borne in mind, it will be unnecessary to dwell on such details as that the child must not begin to speak directly he is on his knees, must not gabbe, must not get up directly he has finished, and so on. Minute regulations of this kind are only of importance in so far as they are signs of a mother's reverence, which may almost be said to form the most important part of a child's prayer.

This mention of reverence as an agent in making children obey leads us to lay down a general rule that the love, trust, and reverence felt by children for their parents are the most powerful and legitimate causes of obedience; and for the very young, before they have yet learned to understand the full force of words, the mere countenance of the father or the mother often sufficiently warns them whether they are doing well or ill.

In the next place, among the means for securing obedience comes the judicious utilization of the natural desire of most children to be "useful." It is usual to say that children delight in destroying; but they delight more in doing what their elders do, and especially something that is "of use." In a multitude of little ways a nurse or mother can give a child this most pleasurable of childish pleasures, and at the same time instil the obedient habit: "Do you think you are strong enough to hold this for me?" "Can you manage to do that?" "Are you clever enough to find this?" "Are you old enough to do that!"

Thus, by a very legitimate guile, the young may be taught to put on the yoke in their earliest days.

Reward, direct reward, for obedience, must never be given. Indirectly, children will, of course, feel the pleasure of obedience in the sense of helpfulness, and in the approbation of their elders; and sometimes they may be allowed to see distinctly that, by obeying, they have gained some pleasure which disobedience would have forfeited. But under no circumstances must obedience be *bought.*

Nor must obedience be courted or besought. "I have heard," says Preceptor, "some parents petition for obedience in tones or words which constituted a sensible provocation to a refractory child, stimulating rebellion: 'Now, I know, you will be a good child, and do this'; 'Really, my darling, I must have you do that'; 'Wont you be a good boy, and come here?' All this is as bad as it can be. The parents must be careful before committing themselves to a command; but, once committed, they must issue it as a command, in perfect faith that it will be obeyed, and there must be no retraction, hesitation, coaxing, or even arguing."

Of course, sooner or later, occasions must arise when the child's will comes into conflict with the will of his rulers, and has to give way. And it is to prepare for this crisis that the habit of unquestioning obedience must be early formed. It ought never to be necessary (unless the child has some unusually strong and mischievous propensities) to resort to force in order to secure obedience; yet force must be used rather than failure endured.

For minor faults, minor punishments may sometimes be needed. As far as possible, they should be made to spring naturally out of the fault, unpunctuality being punished by the loss of some pleasure for which the offender arrives too late, and so on. But this cannot always be managed. In most cases the child must take for granted (from his general trust in his parents) that rules are made for his good, and that it is just that the breaking of rules should be punished. For further details on this point, see below (§ 18).

In conclusion, parents and tutors must bear in mind that, if they cannot secure obedience without constantly punishing, either the circumstances in which they have to rule must be very unfavorable, or (much more probably) they themselves are on a wrong track, and some blame rests with them. Too often, inexperienced trainers of children wish to govern them by suppressing nature, instead of directing nature. The former task is as impossible as to suppress a stream; the latter is (comparatively speaking) as easy as to direct a stream. "How often," writes Preceptor, "do I hear of teachers giving boys impositions for 'talking in class'! That always seems to me extremely *young.* During my twenty years of experience in teaching, I don't think I ever gave a boy any kind of punishment for 'talking in class.' 'How on earth do you manage,' young teachers sometimes say to me.

By teaching in such a way that the boys don't want to 'talk in class,' and by letting them talk when not 'in class.'"

These words of Preceptor appear to me to apply to training of all kinds, as well as to class-teaching. A tutor who is always punishing should ask himself from time to time, "Is not the fault partly with me? Do I understand my pupil? Am I trying to dam up, instead of directing and utilizing his natural energies? One of us certainly is wrong, but am I certain that it is the taught, and not the teacher?"

14. KINDNESS AND HELPFULNESS.

It is natural for children to infer from their early habits of dependence and helplessness, that it is their part not to help but to be helped; and unless the natural corrective of younger brothers and sisters is introduced, a child may grow up obedient, orderly, and truthful, but without the kindly instinct of helping others. "I remember," writes Preceptor, "an amusing instance of the natural selfishness of children, when a boy of some three years old for the first time found his customary romp with his father interfered with by the claims of a little sister, aged one. In answer to the boy's expostulations when the father replied that 'he must play with baby sometimes,' there was a touch of pathos in the boy's very natural reply, 'You didn't use to, once.' It is to be feared that too often children without brothers and sisters grow up undisturbed in this natural selfishness till a period long after childhood."

All the more needful is it to find for solitary children such substitutes as can be procured for the salutary influences of companionship. Kindness to animals, besides being a habit to be taught for its own sake, is no small help towards teaching kindness to human beings. The habit of helping parents, touched on above (§ 13), is also of use. If the parents are in the habit of themselves being helpful to others—not always an easy habit to acquire in our unneighborly metropolis—the children will perhaps be more influenced by their example than by their precepts. It is also well for children to associate with worship the regular custom of making some small contribution for "the poor people" out of their pocket-money.

Books and lectures on the duty of kindness may be of some use if they are joined with practice of some kind; otherwise, they are worse than nothing.

15. TRUTHFULNESS.

An imaginative child, while very young, will sometimes invent fictions where he ought to state facts; and this, not through fear of punishment or hope of reward, but from the delight of indulging the imagination. But this habit, which ought to be carefully distinguished from self-interested falsehood, is soon checked by pointing out the mischief of it, and by showing how good and useful is such a custom of exact truthfulness in a child as will enable his parents and friends to trust implicitly every word he utters. Still more powerful will be the effect upon the child's mind of a constant adherence to exact truth on the part of elders, even at the cost of inconvenience.

Truthfulness must also be encouraged (1) by avoiding excessive punishments, which drive a child to falsehood through intense fear; (2) by invariably treating untruthfulness as a grave moral offence, even where no great inconvenience results from it. Flogged children and spoiled children compose the main body of the army of liars.

Untruthfulness is often engendered by the failure of those in authority to distinguish between grave faults and inconvenient faults. Playing with fire, for example, is a very inconvenient fault in children; and, if it has been expressly forbidden, it may become a very grave moral fault in those who are old enough to understand the force of the prohibition; but, at the worst, it is not so grave a fault as stealing, or lying, or as the use of vicious language. Now it is to inconvenient faults of this former kind that children are mainly liable. Their restlessness, their curiosity, their ignorance of natural laws, their weakness of body, and inexpertness of motion render them peculiarly likely to break, to disarrange, and generally to destroy; and it is sometimes a hard trial for the mother to see these childish characteristics produce before her eyes the destruction of some cherished ornament, and yet to keep her temper.

Yet she ought to reflect how very much more influence will be exerted upon her children by the expressions of her countenance and the hasty utterances of passion than by the formal exhortations of more sober and conventional moments. None are so ready as children to detect the discrepancies between the natural and the artificial utterances of their elders; and there is a two-fold mischief when a child is led not only to discern something like hypocrisy in his parents, but also to adopt their natural, rather than their artificial standard of morality, and to esteem falsehood as a venial offence, in comparison with the breaking of a piece of china through an act, not of disobedience, but of mere thoughtlessness.

With young children, even when well trained, and still more when they have fallen into habits of inexactness and petty approximations to untruthfulness, very great care should be taken not to drive them into a definite falsehood by too abrupt and sudden questions. Many a child will tell you the truth if you give him time, but may slip into a falsehood if you are too hasty with him, in the instinctive desire to put the best color on his actions and cut a creditable figure; and the danger is the greater, if he be impulsive, sanguine, and unusually sensitive to praise and blame.

Nowhere, therefore, is the tact of a teacher better exercised than in such cases as these, giving the pupil breathing-space for reflection, and so wording the question as not to terrify, but to induce confession, yet without leading him to gloss or extenuate his fault.

Of course, where a habit of truthfulness is established, a straightforward question is best, as being most respectful to the child questioned, and most bracing to the robust nature; but for a waverer no tact can be too great, provided it does not display want of faith. Instead of the direct question, "Did you do this?"—which may probably frighten the child into a "No" before he is aware, you say, "Now I shall certainly be vexed if you have done this, but I shall not be nearly so vexed as if you were to say what was not true. How did it happen? Tell me all about it." Sometimes it may be well to state definitely the punishment that will be inflicted. Suppose, for example, a child has broken some very valuable piece of furniture, and is trembling for fear of some quite terrible punishment proportioned to the mischief he has caused. You may say, "Well, of course you did not intend this, but I must give you some punishment for your carelessness"; and then mention what it will be, finally asking the child to "tell you how it happened."

16. SIMPLICITY.

The habit of simplicity is valuable, partly and principally because it is allied and favorable to truthfulness, partly because it helps to develop originality.

A word on the latter of these two points. Much of the quaint simplicity and apparent originality of a child arises from his endeavor to adapt his limited experience and vocabulary to the continually enlarging circle of his life. "Hence," says Preceptor, "when new things present themselves to a child, he tries to describe them by combinations of old words, calling a tarpaulin 'a big black blanket,' or cork soles 'foot-prints,' and the like. And hence also, being entirely unconventional, ignorant of metaphor, and necessarily familiar with daily change, he is sometimes amusingly consistent and thorough in his adoption of new thoughts and literal interpretations; like the boy of seven years old who, having been told that his first day's hunting was to 'make a man of him,' was overheard on the evening of that day praying (in defiance of all rhyme and custom) that 'Gentle Jesus, meek and mild,' would 'listen to a little *man*.'"

Children should be allowed as long as possible to follow out their thoughts and adapt their old to their new experiences in this unconventional way; for this unbiased, fresh, and consistent manner of looking at things tends to the encouragement of the reasoning faculty. Therefore, even when no strangers are present, parents will do well not to derive too much open amusement from the quaint sayings and doings of their children. Not, of course, that they are to suppress a smile when they hear of the "big black blanket" or the "red foot-prints"; but they are not to "chaff" the child on these linguistic coinages, not to bring them up in joke against him time after time. "Well, it is something like a blanket, but we generally call it a tarpaulin," is the best way of dealing with the child's invention. Thus you put the child on your own level; and while you help him to enlarge his vocabulary, you encourage him to confide to you similar childlike linguistic experiments hereafter.

But if, on the contrary, you impress upon the child that he has said or done something extremely amusing (whereas he has only been doing or saying something that is to him quite natural), and if you induce him to say or do the funny thing over and over again, and to make himself a clown for your delectation, then you must not be surprised to hear him afterwards repeating the exhibition, and making himself a clown for the delectation of the servants and others, and gradually falling into the habit of saying and doing things, not because they are natural, but because they seem to him likely to be clever or funny.

Still worse is the result when children's oddities are paraded before strangers. Many parents, sensible enough in the ordinary affairs of life, appear quite insensible to the mischief they do children in "showing them off." Covertly or openly attempted, such exhibitions are readily detected by a child, who is singularly keen to perceive from the slightest tone or expression of his elders that he is being "drawn out"; and he either resents it by retiring into the inmost recesses of shyness, or else he acquiesces and exhibits himself as an actor. The latter alternative is, perhaps, the worse of the two; but either is bad. If he rebels, he may become rude, shy, and disobedient; if he complies, he is in danger of becoming pert, affected, and insincere. In either case he loses that fresh simplicity which is the greatest charm of childhood, and learns to suspect his very parents of something approaching to insincerity.

One reason, perhaps, why the children of great men hardly ever do anything worthy of their parents is because, much being expected from them, they are, from their earliest years, watched and noticed to excess. A most necessary part of a child's training is that he should be often left alone; only thus is there any hope of developing original power.

Some may object that if you continually correct a child's droll originalities you make him prematurely sensible, and cut short nature's period of childhood. It is not so. The effect is precisely opposite. By correcting him, without laughing at him, you prevent him from being laughed at, you save him from becoming affected or shy, and although this or that particular childish *word* may be lost, you encourage him to retain the childish *method;* but by laughing at him and not correcting him you gain the repetition of a childish phrase at the complete sacrifice of the childish disposition.

Hence, even for those who like children mainly for the amusement they afford, and who use them as little better than playthings, it is a great mistake to harp upon, or exhibit, a particular specimen of their simplicity. "The big black blanket" will never be repeated a second time with the original naturalness, or enjoyed with the original zest:

if you procure its repetition, you destroy the simplicity which might have given rise to other sayings as good or better.

17. REVERENCE.

It is hardly possible for a child to feel reverence at all unless he feels it for his father and mother; and in the modern and (in the main) wise attempt to make children obey parents from love and not from fear, care must be taken that, in the absence of fear, reverence is not also banished. If, therefore, parents join sometimes in the sports of their children, a marked line should be drawn between play and earnest. Let the former be a republic; but the latter must always be a monarchy.

Reverence is naturally felt by a child for one who is stronger, wiser, and better than himself; and at first a child, in favorable circumstances, imagines his parents to be perfect in these points. As the child becomes inevitably disabused, it is important that he should feel reverence for strength, wisdom, and goodness in others besides his parents. For this purpose society, history, and poetry may be in due course utilized; but the child whom we are now considering is far too young to be impressed by history and poetry, or, in any important degree, by society. Long, however, before these influences can be felt, the child is susceptible to the feeling of awe for One above, whom he sees approached by his parents in an attitude of reverence, and whom he is taught to approach in the same spirit.

As to the influence exerted on children by the attitude of the parents towards the Father of all, the little that is to be said falls more fitly under the head of Religious Instruction, which will be found briefly discussed at the end of this book. But it may be worth while to say emphatically here that conventionality and insincerity, most dangerous to children wherever witnessed, are most dangerous of all, if witnessed in the religious acts of their parents.

Take such a simple action as "saying grace." This custom, presenting itself to children before they have been made acquainted with the common worship of the congregation in church or chapel, is perhaps more impressive to them than is generally supposed, if without any parade or affectation a few simple words are uttered, as a natural expression of thanksgiving and acknowledgment. But if the parents repeat the words as a mere form, or hurry over it, or omit it in the presence of strangers, or repeat it in their presence, but in an apologetic manner as if ashamed of it,—in any of these cases it would be very much better, so far as children are concerned, that it should not be repeated at all.

"Most people," writes Preceptor, "would laugh at the assertion that grace was sometimes said in such a manner, or in such circumstances of religious training, that a child hardly knew whether the prayer was addressed to a Being above or to the creature below; yet I well remember a child once taking note of the omission of the customary grace, and reminding his father that 'he had not *said his prayers to the chuckies.*'"

Perhaps we shall not be over-subtle in saying that there is some little danger to the reverence of the rising generation when there is too wide and too early a taste for parody. It is natural that a child should love incident, stirring, startling incident; even narrations of the kind called "blood and thunder" are not (for boys, at all events) very objectionable. But although it is well that they should not be indifferent to humor, it is a bad sign when the young are attracted by mere verbal witticisms or by that kind of purposed purposelessness which is best suited to afford mere amusement, than by the impossible marvels and hairbreadth escapes of fairy stories and tales of adventure. Few stories have the art of blending plot and incident with intense humor like Thackeray's inimitable *Rose and the Ring.* "For the most part," says Preceptor, "even the cleverest of parodies should be locked away from children till they are past their teens. It augurs ill when a boy of nine or ten prefers *Alice in Wonderland* to the *Seven Champions of Christendom,*—ill for the promise of imagination and originality, but also, to some extent, ill for the development of still higher qualities."

18. PUNISHMENTS.

In the reaction against arbitrary or unapt punishments, some people have been led to the conclusion that, as an invariable rule, all punishment should be natural, that is, should follow naturally as the result of the offence. If, for example, a child tells a lie, he is to be punished (so it is maintained) by the distrust which naturally awaits his future statements till he has regained a character for truthfulness.

But it seems clear that this rule cannot be always adopted, either with physical or moral errors. If a child plays with fire, a natural and convenient punishment would no doubt be that he should burn his fingers in moderation. But Nature in such cases is not moderate, and may punish the child once for all by leaving no child to punish a second time, or by grievous and permanent crippling or disfigurement. In the same way with moral offences, if a boy who has told a lie is to be treated for a length of time as a liar, his self-respect may be permanently lowered or destroyed, and so he may become a moral cripple.

The best rule seems to be that parents or teachers, in punishing, should avoid all appearance of vindictive punishing, not because *they* are injured or inconvenienced, but because a wrong has been done, and right demands correction and amendment. Provided the child feels that the punisher has no pleasure in punishing, it will not always be necessary that he should recognize exactly that the punishment springs by a natural sequence out of the offence.

Yet in minor offences it is desirable that the connection between cause and effect should be retained as far as possible. Unpunctuality, for example, may be punished by the consequent missing of some pleasure; carelessness by having to search for something or put something away at an unpleasant time; thoughtlessness by not being entrusted with some acceptable privilege requiring thought, and so on.

But moral offences should be punished, if possible, morally; and the best moral punishment for a young child is the moral shock and pain felt by the parents and communicated from them to him.

Indeed, in one sense, this is the punishment most "natural." In the world, lying may be punishable by the rough methods of the world, such as lasting disgrace, disbelief, and physical pain or inconvenience; but what is natural in the world is not natural from a father or mother. In most cases the child's sense of the grief he has caused to those whom he respects, his feeling of their disapproval, and the consequent cessation, even though it be but for a day, of the fun and free delights of his ordinary life, will suffice, without any severe and prolonged punishment. If that does not suffice, there should be a resort to "the last resources of a parent," physical punishment. Flogging does not spring naturally out of lying; but in spite of any philosophic dicta to the contrary, there is more hope of curing a boy of lying by flogging him, than by distrusting him, for days together, as a liar.

It is a common saying that "you must not punish when you are in a passion." But what is meant by being "in a passion"? If it is meant that you are not, at the moment of punishing, to retain any sense of personal vindictiveness, that is undoubtedly true, but inadequate. The feeling of vindictiveness ought not to need banishing; it ought never to have been present. If, on the other hand, it is meant that you are to wait till your repugnance to dishonesty, or to deceit, or to cruelty has died away, the answer is that this feeling—which may be called resentment, as distinguished from vindictiveness—ought never to die away. Resentment is the salt of punishment, which otherwise degenerates into the mere infliction of pain for the prevention of inconvenience.

Further, let it be remembered that punishment, if fit, is effective in proportion as it is certain and speedy. It ought not, therefore, to be delayed by one who is conscious of being wholly free from personal irritation any longer than is necessary to investigate the truth of the charge and select the fittest penalty.

II. MENTAL TRAINING.

19. REGULARITY.

Parents must not attempt to teach their children as a mere pastime for themselves, or as an occasional and irregular occupation.

Irregularity causes children not only to forget or drop the thread of a subject, but also to anticipate the possibility that "the lesson may not be heard"; and a very small amount of such anticipation discourages a studious child from putting forth his best efforts, and encourages a lazy one to neglect work on the chance that he may not be detected.

A certain amount of regular irregularity, however, will do no harm. I have heard of a very successful school for young boys where it is the regular custom to have short hours for work on fine days and longer hours in wet weather; and under judicious supervision and a firm control it is possible that such a system may work well. Certainly, for the very young, books should be put away almost entirely during the out-of-door time of the year, not to be opened till the shortening days once more suggest in-door pursuits.

But such irregularity as this is hardly to be called irregularity; it is part of a system, and probably a better, though less simple system than that which would prescribe uniform hours for work all through the year.

The irregularity that is to be avoided is that which springs from the engagements, distractions, or caprices of parents. This is an unmixed evil, so far as the child is concerned; for he soon perceives that there is no sort of system in the cessations of his work, and that they spring from causes out of his sphere of vision, which may at any time recur; and the feeling that at any time, and for no apparent reason, his studies may be stopped, unsettles, and, if I may so say, unsteadies a young mind.

Second-rate regular teaching is better for the very young than first-rate teaching, if the latter be very irregular. Parents whose occupations do not allow them to give regular instruction may with advantage test their children's progress from time to time; and they may in some cases throw light on special difficulties in their children's work; but, if they cannot teach regularly, they should not assume the sole responsibility of teaching them.

20. EXACTNESS.

The general fault of home training is that it encourages inexactness and slovenliness. Being in close sympathy with the children, both parents and private tutors are apt to "understand what they mean," and to give them credit for meaning what is right, when what they have actually said or written is wrong. Never let a parent or private tutor give a child "the benefit of the doubt" in matters intellectual.

It also frequently happens that, having formed a somewhat too high conception of their pupil's mental ability, they do not like to make him go through the drudgery which is sometimes necessary to produce exactness. "Personally," writes Preceptor, "I believe I owe my inaccuracy as a mathematician (besides a general inexactness of mind in matters of detail) to the too kind indulgence of a private tutor who taught me Arithmetic. Not only did he yield to my importunities when I told him that I was sure I could never find out where my Long Division sum was wrong, but even when he had pointed out my error, he would never insist on my doing the sum again. I liked him very much at the time; but I bitterly dislike the results of his kindness now."

In a school, boys are more likely to be cured of little inexactnesses and eccentricities, because their work is constantly inspected along with that of other boys, and judged impartially by the same standard; but in a household this standard is absent, and must be supplied by the parents or tutors unaided. Let it be, therefore, taken as a motto for home training that the teacher is to be "careful about small things." Parents, even more than class-teachers, must set their faces against the common excuse of careless children, "It was only a slip, I knew better."

21. ADAPTATION AND VARIATION.

Yet regularity and exactness in home teaching are not inconsistent with some variation of lessons, adapting them to the special needs and stages of the pupil's development. Lessons cannot be thus flexibly adapted in class-teaching, because what may suit one pupil may not suit another. In a school it is necessary for a class-teacher to consult the interests of the greatest number, slightly sacrificing the very dull, and still more the very clever, for the sake of the commonplace majority, and endeavoring to compensate the two extremes by a little extra attention out of class. But it is one of the greatest advantages of home teaching that both the clever and the dull, and the different stages of progress in the clever and the dull can be specially considered, and the teaching correspondingly adjusted.

1. Sometimes when a child is approaching a critical point in a study, manifesting a great interest in it, and making rapid progress, it is well to take advantage of this tide and to increase considerably the amount of time given to that study, at the expense of others, so as to float the child over the obstacle which but for this effort might else have kept him for some time stranded and stationary.

2. When a child is growing dispirited and discouraged with the feeling that he is making no way in some study, and is perhaps falling into the habit of doing his work in an inferior manner, it is well to drop that study altogether for a time, returning to it after he has had time to forget his discouragement and to break himself from his bad habits.

But in such a case the teacher must take great care that the child shall not feel that he is desisting because of failure. With a little tact, this can easily be arranged. The child's last lesson can be made so easy or can be so carefully explained, that it shall be in some sense a success, at least as compared with previous lessons; and after he has been praised, so far as he honestly can be, for at last overcoming his difficulties, the teacher may announce his intention of putting by the book for a time.

3. When the child returns to the subject, the teacher must use all possible art to make the first few lessons completely successful. By dividing the subject into very small parts, by careful and constant revisions, by conversations familiarly eliciting the child's difficulties and preparing the way for overcoming future difficulties, the teacher may, and indeed must, *force* the child to know his first lesson, so that he may make a fresh and more hopeful start.

4. Here a caution may be useful. *The teacher must never make any, even the slightest variation of lessons in answer to a pupil's request.* To do this would be to shake the child's confidence in his teachers, making him uneasy, unsettled, self-introspective, and conceited. Should the child, therefore, make any such request, he must be refused with some abruptness, and be taught not to repeat it. None the less, the teacher should make mental note of the pupil's state of mind, and accept it as a proof that things are not going satisfactorily, and that some change must be soon made.

But if a child who has been long under our training expresses a desire for a change, we ourselves must be somewhat in fault. For we ought to have ascertained the pupil's flagging interest from its natural signs, without waiting till it was expressed in definite words. Out of school hours, too, while talking to the child, not as master, but as friend, a tutor may easily find out the childish likes and dislikes, troubles, difficulties, and successes. And of course these opportunities are still more accessible to parents.

5. As the child should occasionally have easier tasks, to inspire him with hopefulness and self-reliance, so should he occasionally have more difficult tasks, to test and invigorate his powers, and to put him on his mettle.

22. THE TRANSITION FROM PLAY TO WORK.

Almost all children learn for some time, not as a work, but as a pleasure. It must be left to the teacher's discretion to decide when he should first mention the words "work" and "lessons," and how long he should continue to treat learning as an amusement to his pupils.

Much will depend upon their age and temperament. If they are old, and not very docile, "work" will have to be brought to the front, and clearly distinguished from play, that they may no longer delay to form habits of obedient and regular industry, and may learn to bend before they grow too stiff. It is not well with such natures to defer long the awkward and critical transition which takes place when the pupil has to be told plainly that the occupation which he has been hitherto pursuing as an optional amusement, he must now pursue as a compulsory task.

On the other hand, for young, docile, and lively pupils, the gain is great if learning remains, as long as possible, a pleasure and a privilege. Progress is thus far more rapid, and the child acquires one of the most valuable of habits—the love of knowledge.

This transition may be smoothed by a little preparatory conversation in which the dignity of "school" is held out as a prospect for the boy when he grows a little older; some children may also be influenced by being told that, if they work, they will be able to help their parents, and to be of use to their brothers and sisters; and the power derived from certain kinds of knowledge may be illustrated by stories which may afford a useful stimulus. But, in most cases, the knowledge that his parents and elders have to work, and that work of some kind is expected from every grown-up person worthy of respect, will be sufficient, when combined with the love of approbation, to make any child tolerate patiently, or even accept with some degree of pride the necessary irksomeness of work.

For let this be distinctly understood by the teacher, and let him, when the time comes, not fail to make his pupils also understand, that work must be at times irksome. Mental, like bodily labor, must sometimes task and strain the powers, though it should never overstrain them. The intellect is like the body in requiring the alternation between wholesome strain and wholesome relaxation, if it is to become healthy and robust.

23. INTRODUCTION AND GUIDANCE.

Before beginning to teach any subject, the teacher should endeavor to excite the pupil's interest by conversations and stories illustrating the utility of it. Reading is, nowadays, so obvious a necessity that stimulus in this study is less needed than in others. Otherwise it would be easy to multiply stories about savages who have so marveled at a "speaking paper" that they have worshiped it as a god; or about boys and men who, in modern times, have been helped by ability, or harmed by inability, to read.

Similarly, as a preparation for Arithmetic, stories may be found, such as the well-known one in *Sandford and Merton*, about the horse-dealer who offered to take for his horse (since the rich gentleman objected to the price) one farthing for the first nail in the horse's shoe, two farthings for the second, four for the third, eight for the fourth, and so on, doubling the number every time, there being only twenty-four nails in all; and how the gentleman willingly assented to this arrangement, till he found that he had pledged himself to pay more than seventeen thousand four hundred and seventy pounds. Under the heads of the different studies, hints will be hereafter given as to the best means of giving preliminary stimulus.

When the pupil has begun a new subject, he must not, at first, be left to himself. It is not with book-tasks as it is with nature-tasks. Books do not supply (as Nature often does) the means of experimenting, of varying the aspect of the subject, and of obtaining new materials to reason about. Consequently, if a child cannot make out a book-task, he either gives it up as hopeless, or becomes fretful, dispirited, and listless; or else he dashes at some wrong conclusion, and contracts the habit of "plunging." At first, therefore, everything in a new subject must be done by the child under the supervision of the teacher.

Not that the child is to be *told* everything. This would be fatal to his self-reliance and progress. Nor that he is to be permitted to make no mistakes. This would be going against Nature's method of teaching by correction. But the tutor's business will be in the course of each lesson to secure the observance of that Golden Rule of teaching which interchanges easy tasks with difficult ones, at once encouraging self-reliance and discouraging conceit, sustaining interest and developing the understanding.

Although the teacher must be prepared to give much time and trouble in the introductory lesson, or lessons, of each subject, he must nevertheless not lecture, he must converse. But the guidance of the dialogue will require almost as much preparatory thought as a lecture. Not a word must be retracted (unless deliberately, see § 80) and, above all, no confused impressions must be given. It would be better that the pupil should receive a clear erroneous impression—which can afterwards be clearly proved to be false, and removed—than two or three impressions, each more or less true, and each inconsistent with the others.

N.B.—If the teacher cannot spare the necessary time for this preparation, he must not attempt to eke out the deficiency by giving his pupils tasks out of a book to prepare without supervision. Let them play. They will be far better employed in playing than by learning slovenly habits of thought or practice under the appearance of working.

24. READING.

Reading may be conveniently begun in the late autumn and continued till the early spring, when it may be dropped, or at all events lightened, to be taken up again and perfected in the following winter. The advantage of this course is, that during the long evenings, when the child cannot be playing in the open air, the reading-task finds him at greater leisure and (for want of other things to do) he is likely to welcome the study as a variety of occupation.

If children are in the country and can find plenty to do, reading may perhaps be deferred till six; otherwise it may be begun at five, or four; and there have been not a few cases where it has even been begun at three, without apparent disadvantage. But so early a commencement requires watchful care on the part of the teacher, that the lesson may be given up when it appears to cause the slightest uneasiness or strain to the child.

It is now a recognized principle among teachers that children *must not be taught or allowed to spell before they read*. Reading must be taught first, spelling afterwards.

In teaching reading, the right plan is to begin, not with letters, but with syllables, such as *cat, can, cap, sit, fit, pit*, and the like, which the child must be taught to pronounce and remember, as syllables, without any regard (*at first*) to the letters *c, a, t, n, p*, etc., composing them. The system has this obvious advantage, that it is freed from the contradictions attending the alphabet or spelling-system. When a boy is told that *a* is called *ai* (as in *pain*), and yet that *c, a, t* spells *cat*—not *cait*—he is plunged at once into difficulties that should be deferred as long as possible, I mean, the anomalies of English pronunciation. "All the bad readers whom I have ever had to do with," says Preceptor, "have learned reading on this bad system; and whenever I hear a big fellow of ten or eleven stumbling over hard words, I always put my ear close to him and catch him spelling." The new system, which is sometimes called the Look and Say system, avoids the stumbling-block of the alphabet.

A great number of good reading-books are now in existence based upon the Look and Say, or (as it might perhaps be better called) the Syllable principle; but the use of them requires some discretion in the teacher, for the following reason. Some of the more modern books on this system, being adapted for teaching children in large classes, are very properly intended to suit the dullest of the dull; and they consequently introduce a vast amount of drill by repeating variations of syllables, whether they have, or have not, any existence in our language, e. g. *badge, cadge, fadge, madge, dadge, sadge*, etc. Now all this, though it may be necessary, and not perhaps very tedious for a slow, steady, but somewhat dull boy, may be unnecessary, tedious, and even irritating for a quick and lively one. Again, other reading-books, of a somewhat earlier date, good in other respects, may be a little deficient in syllable-drill.

The best plan for the teacher at home will be to use one of the more rapidly progressive reading-books, yet not to trust entirely to it, but to reinforce it by *writing (of course in printed characters) in the margin of the reading-book, little supplements, from time to time introducing the child to new syllables*. However excellent and stimulating the book may be, the child will generally be more stimulated by these additions than by the original text; and though he may not be called on for some time to write or print on his own account, he is unconsciously being prepared for learning how to do so by watching his tutor print.

It is absolutely necessary that the child should be taught to pronounce words apart from their context as well as to read them in their context. Otherwise he will read by rote, trusting to his memory, and will make little progress in distinguishing syllables. "It is surprising," says Preceptor, "to what extent the powerful memory of the young will impose upon a teacher, and still more upon an inexperienced Examiner, in this matter of reading. I remember that in a certain Elementary school—this was in the old days when books were 'set' for examination, and there was no reading at sight—a boy passed with flying colors, although he could not read at all, or (to put the same fact in the shape in which the teacher expressed it to me) he could read just as well with the book upside down as in the ordinary position."

After a few lessons in reading supplemented thus by the teacher, the child may be taught the sounds of the consonants, pronouncing them, however, not in the ordinary way with vowels, *ess, tee, eff*, etc., but as the mere beginnings of sounds, *s* being a mere hiss, and *f* a sound of the teeth against the lips, *s—, f—*. Those consonants which sound differently before different vowels should not be taught by themselves; for example, *c* must be taught at first, not by itself, but as part of *can, cat, cane, car, care*, and then in *cot, con, cone, cod*, and in *cud, cut, cub*. Not till he is familiar with these words, and on the point of passing to words of two syllables, should he be introduced to *cell, cent, cit, cite*, and be told to distinguish between the soft sound of *ce* or *ci* on the one side, and the hard sound of *ca, co, cu* on the other. The same of course applies to *g*.

Most unfortunately, reading (which is almost necessarily the first subject in which a child receives special lessons) cannot proceed far without bringing the pupil into contact with the anomalies of English pronunciation, which constitute a sad stumbling-block in the way of definite and logical teaching. The reading-book should certainly avoid these for the first few lessons; and the teacher should freely alter any words in the text-book, however simple in themselves, which seem to introduce such anomalies too soon (*e. g.* the word *put*, which is anomalous for a child hitherto accustomed only to the sound of *u* in *up, sup, cut*, etc.).

"I am not sure," writes Preceptor, "whether the plan of thus altering the book and substituting a new word—'because this word is pronounced *pût*, and you are not yet accustomed to that sound'—is not as stimulative a way as any to induce a child to remember the exceptional word; for many children (of the quicker sort, at all events) are exceptionally stirred to remember, and to prove that they can remember, facts that are said to be 'too difficult' for them. If also a list is printed by the tutor for the child containing anomalous words thus 'put aside for the present,' they will be the more easily recollected; and in due course no difficulty at all will be found in them when the pupil meets with them in a context which hleps to make them intelligible."

The transition will be easy from words of one syllable to words of two. *Cannot* presents very little more difficulty than *can-not*. The few abnormal final syllables, such as *-ble* and *-tion*, will be soon mastered, not by themselves, but by being repeated in such words as *sta-ble, a-ble, ca-ble, fa-ble;* and then all will go smoothly.

The home-teacher will do well to beware of "books written in words of one syllable." *Sandford and Merton* and *Robinson Crusoe*, tortured into monosyllables, are sure to contain passages in a tedious or inexact style; and to turn good English into bad is neither justifiable nor necessary in order to teach beginners how to read.

A great deal more may be done than is customary in the way of teaching children to read with modulation and distinctness. No doubt some have naturally a better voice and a keener sense of rhythm than others; but all can be kept from drawling and droning if they hear people about them read and speak well, and *if they are accustomed from the first to read as they speak.* No boy drawls or drones in the playground or the nursery.

Drawling, like all other unnatural reading, is caused by reading aloud what one does not understand or enjoy, or by hearing others drawl. The remedy against it is, first, to see that the child can understand and enjoy his earliest reading lessons; second, to prevent the child from ever hearing bad reading.

In order to produce a habit of natural reading there should be interspersed several short questions and answers in the early reading exercises, because in familiar dialogues it is more easy for a child to read naturally, that is to say, as he speaks, *e. g.* "Can Tom see me now? Yes, Tom can see me, and I can see Tom." The teacher should for some time to come read every passage aloud before the pupil reads it. Grant that the pupil may sometimes be hereby led to trust to his ears, recalling what the teacher has read, rather than to his eyes, examining the syllables before him; yet this danger is slight compared with that of falling into an artificial monotone, by stumbling over the passage unassisted, pronouncing it without intelligent appreciation.

It is one of the greatest advantages of home-training over class-training for young children that reading can be taught much more easily at home than at school.* In a class, bad readers must necessarily sometimes be "put on," and their bad reading drags down the rest of the pupils. For as in stammering, so in reading, children are wonderfully and unconsciously imitative. At home the child need never (it is to be hoped) hear any but good reading, and may thus, by unconscious imitation, acquire a good style. At school to read with any taste or feeling is often so rare, that the boy who is guilty of it is voted a "prig" by his schoolfellows, where the standard of reading does not happen to be unusually high. It cannot be too often repeated that no child (in whom the organs of speech are duly developed) will read badly if he is well taught and does not hear bad reading. But it should be added that children are more prone to imitate bad reading than good, and that the hearing of a very little bad reading goes a long way to prevent the formation of the habit of reading well.[1]

Defects of utterance require special treatment. Very little attention can be paid to them at schools; but by parents and tutors a great deal could be done by practicing a child regularly in the sounds in which he is deficient. For example, if he does not pronounce the dentals distinctly he may be exercised daily in repeating a list of words, such as *tender, delicate, splendid, dutiful, dusty, tattered and torn*, etc., having first pronounced the initial sounds—*t* and *d*—several times; and so of other sounds.

25. QUESTIONING ON READING.

In order to accustom the pupil to remember what he has read, a few simple questions should be asked, bearing upon each reading lesson, even upon the first.

The questions should be varied in two ways. Thus, supposing the reading lesson says, "The cat is on my bed," the question may be put first as an *ellipse* (to use the term employed by Stow). "The cat is on —?" and the pupil fills up what is wanting—"my bed"; secondly, it may be put as a question for information. "Where is the cat?" "On my bed."

Later on, pupils will find in their reading lessons expressions that require explanation; and then the teacher will need a knowledge of the art of explaining. The best explanation is that in which the teacher tells the least and elicits the most. For this purpose he must avoid lecturing and keep close to dialogue, putting before his pupils some facts which they know, that he may lead them to understand some fact which they do not know. What we know, as children, is, for the most part, what we can see; and therefore this process of teaching is called by Stow "picturing out," because, by it, the teacher and pupils together depict or represent things unseen by things seen.

Although Stow spoke of this system as new, it is in reality the basis of all teaching by parables. The Parable of the Sower, for example,

---

[1] If it had not been a principle of this book that it should contain as little as possible that the Author had not tested by experiment, another method of teaching reading would have been described at some length.

This method would *begin with sounds, and then proceed to syllables*. Thus, the teacher would make the child pronounce the initial *p—, b—, f—*, (not with vowels, but merely as initial sounds,) and then set down on the black-board the printed symbols. Next he would make the child pronounce *at, it, et*, and afterwards set down these symbols. He would then make the child pronounce *p, b, f* before the *at, it, et*, and when the child had done it he would set down *pat, pit, pet; bat, bit, bet*, etc., in each case beginning first with the child's experiences and needs before proceeding to satisfy the needs.

This, which may be called the Oral or Extempore system, could very soon be replaced by a book; "but," says Preceptor, "I feel sure it would be found a far more stimulative introduction to reading than could be supplied by any text-book." He adds, however, that he himself has never seen it tried except in the process of teaching the deaf and (so called) dumb to read aloud.

"pictures out" the unseen operations of good and bad visible influences. "Picturing out" is indeed the basis of all metaphor, and of a large part of all language. When we speak of a thought, for example, as impressive, we "picture out" the operation of the thought by saying that, as a seal impresses itself on wax and leaves a mark behind, so a certain thought imprints itself on our mind, and leaves behind a copy of it which we cannot see with our eyes, but can none the less remember.

Recondite though these considerations may appear, the principle and practice of "picturing out" must be thoroughly mastered by every teacher before he can consider himself qualified to explain even the simplest difficulties of language to the young. Without this key all explanations are sure to be unsystematic, vague, and pointless, and are likely to be either unintelligible or inadequate. With it, any metaphor can be explained, provided the child is familiar, or can be made familiar with the visible facts on which the metaphor is based.

26. WRITING.

Before learning to write many children may with advantage be allowed to print. Any slight disadvantage arising from the danger of falling into a style incompatible with flowing handwriting, may be obviated by careful attention subsequently, when the child begins to learn the latter; and the stimulus may be useful, not only because it shows the child at once the use of his new acquirement, but also because it teaches him to spell.

In order to teach the child to write well, he should not be allowed to write "small hand" till he has gone through a sufficient course of "large hand"—sufficient to teach him the proper shaping of the letters. In "large hand" defects are much more easily detected than in small. Children naturally prefer the latter as being easier and "more advanced"; but if they are to write well their wish must not be gratified till a good style of "large hand" has been formed.

"Copies," in which the letters are printed in red or brown ink, over which the pupil has to write, are to be used for a longer or shorter time, according to the pupil's progress. The assistance is to be lessened gradually; but care must be taken that the pupil does not dispense with assistance too soon. The teacher may sometimes advantageously supplement the printed copies by tracing the letters himself to be covered by the pupil.

It is most important in writing that the child should not *repeat errors*. When looking at a boy's copy-book, you will frequently find a mistake scarcely perceptible in the first line, slight in the second line, more marked in the third, and grossly wrong in the fourth and following lines. To obviate this, the teacher should be on the watch to mark with a red pencil any error; and the pupil should not be allowed to write more than one new line until the teacher is satisfied that the error is not repeated.

It is not now thought necessary to inculcate minute directions for holding the pen; but stooping, putting the tongue out and the head on one side, and other constrained and unnatural attitudes should be noted and forbidden at once.

If the teacher requires written exercises in grammar, dictation, etc., at a time when the pupils are in the early stage of writing, he must give up the hope of their acquiring a rapid, legible, flowing hand of the best kind. It is, therefore, sometimes a question whether the handwriting must be to some extent sacrificed to the general progress of the pupil, or the progress to the handwriting; and circumstances must determine how that question must be answered. But, in any case, neatness may be ensured.

In all writing lessons, the light should enter from the left, so that the shadow of the writer's hand may not darken the paper on which he is writing.

27. DRILLING, SINGING, DRAWING.

It does not fall within the province of this work to do more than mention these subjects. For the methods of teaching them the reader is referred to the works of specialists. But they are mentioned here because, when we are beginning to train the mind and understanding systematically, it seems well to take in hand also the systematic training of the body and the senses, so that the whole nature may be systematically developed.

Drilling, more especially, is useful as a counterpoise to the sedentary studies of reading and writing. But drilling cannot be taught at home except under great disadvantages, as the simultaneous movements of large numbers contribute greatly to the spirit, liveliness, and efficiency of drill. In a town it is better to combine the children of two or three families for drill, or to send a child to a drilling class.

In cases where a child is becoming precociously fond of books and given to sedentary pursuits, it is well—especially where there are no brothers and sisters—to send him to a Kindergarten for the sake of the drill, singing, and sense-training, and to forbid all home work.

28. SPELLING.

The child who has learned to read in the right way, that is by syllables, will be generally found utterly unable to spell when he is for the first time asked to write down the simplest word. He will at first confuse *pin* and *nip*, *ten* and *net*, *nap* and *pan*. On a moment's reflection the reason is obvious. He has from the beginning learned syllables, not separate letters; and even though he may have picked up the names of the letters, still he has never needed to arrange the letters of a syllable in their proper order.

This inability may at first disappoint a young teacher, but there is no cause for disappointment. The pupil will rapidly learn the art of spelling as soon as he learns the art of writing; and until he learns how to write he has no need to learn how to spell.

Some teachers lay great stress on the oral teaching of spelling, but the anomalies of our English pronunciation make it a preferable course to trust for spelling rather to the eye than to the ear. The best means for teaching spelling are (1) not to let the pupil write much at first from dictation; (2) to encourage the child to read for himself (for it is familiarity with the sight of words that is the main help here); (3) to make him copy passages from manuscript or print; (4) to enlarge his spelling vocabulary from time to time by writing down on the black-board a new word, and by bidding him write three or four sentences immediately of his own composition, introducing this word; (5) whenever the teacher is intending to dictate a passage, he should first write down on the board any words that may be reasonably expected to be unfamiliar to the pupil, rubbing them out before the dictation commences.

The object of all these rules is the same, it is *to prevent the child from ever spelling a word wrongly*. Once let a child spell "beleeve," and you will have thrice as much trouble in teaching him how to spell "believe" as you would have had if you had never let him spell it at all till he could spell it correctly. A child is, if possible, *never to have had two impressions of the spelling of a word*, because two impressions will result in one blurred impression. He is never to *think* about spelling. If he needs to pause at all, he must write the word down, and see how it *looks*.

A little oral teaching may be useful at first while the child is learning for the first time to distinguish letters from syllables; *p, i, n*, pronounced aloud, will be more readily distinguished from *n, i, p*. And it may be useful to make him spell aloud (1) a certain number of the more anomalous words, in order to show him the similarity of the sounds represented by the same letters, *fought, sought, bought;* (2) a certain number of words of the same sound with different meanings, *due, dew, sea, see*, each of which should be immediately introduced into a sentence composed and written by the pupil.

Rules in spelling are of very little use. The only one of much value to beginners is that, where the sound "eeve" is preceded by *c* it is spelt *ceive;* but this still leaves the beginner open to mis-spell *leave, believe, sleeve*.

"For older pupils," says Preceptor, "who know something of the history of English, it is sometimes useful to be reminded that the anomalies of (1) *exceed, proceed, succeed*, (2) *precede, recede, concede*, are to be explained by the fact that the former words entered our language through the French (the French *é* being altered into *ee*, as in '*agreeable*') whereas the latter, coming to us directly from the Latin, retained the Latin spelling." But such a rule would be only useful for those who have a considerable acquaintance with the English language and literature; and in English spelling the only really useful rule is that "there are no rules."

29. PUNCTUATION.

Correct reading is, of course, almost necessary as a preparation for correct punctuation; for punctuation implies pauses, and if a child makes no pauses in reading, he is only consistent in making no punctuation in writing. As soon, therefore, as a child begins to read, he should be taught the use of stops; and the best stop to begin with is the note of interrogation, because it necessitates a marked difference in the modulation of the voice.

The pupil should then be shown, by instances, how much the meaning may be altered by the omission of stops and capital letters. Abundant examples may easily be constructed, one or two of which will suffice.

(1) "At what time will you come to-morrow?" is entirely different in meaning from "At what time will you come? To-morrow?"

(2) The use of the full stop and comma may be illustrated by the difference between "We dined at six o'clock. Half-an-hour before, most of our guests had arrived," and "We dined at six o'clock, half-an-hour before most of our guests had arrived."

Occasionally the teacher may give his pupils unpunctuated and ambiguous sentences of this kind, which they are to punctuate in more than one way, if possible, so as to produce different meanings. But these exercises should be sparingly used, partly lest they should bewilder a child who may not be able to make satisfactory sense out of the unpunctuated passage, partly lest they should habituate him to the absence of punctuation. More will be gained by insisting on punctuation whenever a passage is copied from a book or manuscript, and afterwards taken down from dictation. And here let the teacher watch the child while writing, and see that he does not write the whole passage first and *put in the stops afterwards.* This slovenly habit is fatal to true appreciation of punctuation; but children constantly fall into it because they do not like to interrupt their writing by stopping to punctuate. But they must be taught that it is impermissible thus to write down mere words, without sense, or with the wrong sense. They are to write down sentences, not words; and sentences require punctuation.

For want of early training in this simple subject children grow up to youth, and youths to manhood without a knowledge of it; and there are many fairly educated people who use commas scantily, and inverted commas never, with what occasionally disastrous consequences may be readily imagined.

30. NUMBERS.

Elementary arithmetic may be taught very early, say at four or five years old.

It should be taught experimentally, first by means of the fingers, then with an abacus, chess-board, marbles, tin soldiers, counters, or other devices for representing numbers by concrete objects.

These helps, however, should not be retained too long; and it is important that, from an early stage, the child should be familiarized with more than one kind of these concrete representations. It is not well that a child should be able to tell that 5 and 3 are 8 on his abacus, but not with marbles or counters. By discovering that 5 and 3 are 8, whether on fingers, or abacus, or on chess-board, or in marbles, he is more easily prepared to see that 5 and 3 are 8 universally, and thus to dispense with concrete assistances.

Before passing beyond the first ten digits, he should learn addition and subtraction within those limits, discovering that 5 and 3, or 3 and 5, make 8; 3 from 8, 5: 5 from 8, 3, etc. He may even be introduced to the rudiments of multiplication by discovering that 4 and 4 make 8, and that this is the same thing as saying that 2 fours make 8; that 3 twos make 6, 4 twos make 8, 5 twos 10.

When the child begins to learn the numbers above ten on the abacus, he ought to be made at once to understand the *Law of Recurrence*.

The numbers after ten may be described to him, at first, as "one and ten," "two and ten," "three and ten," "four and ten," etc. Afterwards those may be shortened into "one-teen," "two-teen," "three-teen," "four-teen," "five-teen," and he may be left for a few days with these names, till he is casually told by his teacher that "one-teen" is commonly called "eleven," "two-teen" "twelve," and "three-teen" "thirteen." Not the least inconvenience will have been experienced from the little piece of un-learning; and the child will have had impressed on him the law of recurrence in a manner most likely to bring it home to him.

Similarly, as regards numbers after "nine-teen," he should be told that the number following nineteen ought to be called "twice-ten"; but to distinguish it better from "two and ten," "ten" is changed into "ty," and it is called "twice-ty," "twain-ty," or "twenty"; and in the same way "thrice-ten" is called "three-ty," or "thirty," and so of the rest. The child will probably soon forget these disused names; but some result of them will remain in the sense of law, and in the feeling that "there is a reason for things"—a very valuable acquisition for a young arithmetician.

For the purpose of illustrating the recurrence in the names of the numbers, the abacus is preferable to any other device, because it can easily be made to exhibit them in rows of tens, one row below the other. Looking at these rows, the child can see at a glance how the facts correspond to the names; and he may be taught not only to count horizontally, 1, 2, 3, 4, 5, etc., but also vertically, thus, four, four and ten, four and twenty, four and thirty, etc.; one, one and ten (or eleven), one and twenty, one and thirty, etc.

31. FIGURES.

Symbols should now be introduced, in order that the child may begin to construct his own tables. Having written down naught and the first 9 digits, you say, "Now we have no more signs to use. How then can we write the larger numbers, such as two and ten, three and ten, four and ten? We must repeat the old signs. For example, to write three and ten, or thirteen, we can set down 3 for the three, and 1 *on the left hand side of the* 3, *to represent a single ten* (13). Similarly to represent two and ten (or twelve) set down 2 for the two, and 1 *on the left-hand side of the* 2, *to represent a single ten* (12); and to represent one and ten (or eleven) set down 1 for the one, and 1, *on the left-hand side of the one, to represent a single ten* (11).

"How do we know, in the number 11, which of the two 1's represents a ten? By remembering that the figure on the right hand always stands for *ones*, and the figure on the left of it for *tens*.

"But now how shall we represent ten itself? If we put down 1 by itself and say 'that shall stand for ten,' we shall not be able to remember when we see it afterwards whether it means one or one-ten. How then can we distinguish between them? Thus, by calling it 'naught and ten,' and writing down (just as we did 'one and ten,' 'two and ten'), 0 on the right hand for naught, or nothing, and 1 on the left hand for the ten."

The explanation of 10 will be the only point that need present any difficulty; the subsequent explanations of 23, "as meaning three and two tens," 34 "as meaning four and three tens," etc., will be found comparatively easy.

As for the hundreds, the pupil will not find it hard to see that we must "begin again" a second time when we reach ten tens, writing down 0 for the ones, and 10 *on the left-hand of the* 0, *for the tens* (100). He may then be taught to write down "ten tens and one" (101), ten tens and two (102), etc., and finally be told that ten tens are called one hundred; so that 100, instead of being described as "no ones and ten tens," may be described as "no ones, no tens, one hundred."

The child must now be practiced in reading numbers of three figures forwards and backwards, thus: 234, two hundreds, three tens, four ones (or units), or four ones, three tens, two hundreds. And, in the following lessons, this exercise of reading small and large numbers forwards and backwards must be constantly recapitulated.

32. TABLES.

Hitherto the child must not have been allowed to write figures for himself, but must watch the teacher make them at the pupil's dictation, and the teacher must take great pains to write them in precisely the way in which he would like the pupil to write them. For the purpose of uniformity in figure writing, the paper should be divided into equal squares of a good size; for it is no less important for good figures than for good writing that a child should begin with "large hand." At this stage the child may be permitted to write down a few figures for himself, under close supervision, that he may construct his own "Tables."

He should begin with Tables of Addition of numbers under 10; and Tables of Subtraction should be constructed at the same time, thus:

7 and 6, 13; 6 from 13, 7; 7 from 13, 6.

The teacher should note what parts of these Tables appear to be most difficult for the pupil to recollect, and should practice him specially in these, making him impress them upon himself by repetition and writing, so that he may learn them by heart. He ought not to be allowed to go far in Arithmetic till he can add *without pausing to think*, and of course he must not now be allowed to use fingers, or the assistance of the abacus. The latter may still be allowed in experimenting and making discoveries with numbers, but not for the ordinary purposes of calculation. In order that finger-counting may be discouraged, the pupil should for some time calculate aloud, *and in the presence of the teacher*. And just as in reading the pupil was not allowed to spell to himself, so neither must he count to himself; he must calculate, as he reads, on the "look and say" principle; and in answer to the question, "8 and 7?" he must reply at once, without either counting or thinking, "15."

Having committed to memory the statement that 8 and 7 make 15, the pupil must be asked, What do 18 and 7 make? From the abacus he ascertains, and writes down 25. What do 28 and 7 make? From the same source he writes down 35. What 38 and 7? 45. What 48 and 7? 55. The teacher must continue these questions till he *forces* the pupil to discover for himself that his formula, "8 and 7 make 15" will always help him to determine the *unit* figure of the result when two figures are added together of which one ends in 8, the other in 7. The same process must be repeated with 7 and 6, 17 and 6, 27 and 6, 6 and 7, 16 and 7, 26 and 7, etc. Thus the pupil will learn to add with rapidity numbers under 100 to numbers under 10.

He is now in a position to construct for himself Tables of Multiplication. But first he should receive a little stimulus to urge him to undertake his new labor with zeal. Tell him to make ten heaps of marbles, 7 in each heap. And how many do they make altogether? "I must count." "Well, count, then; but I will write down the number on a piece of paper, which I will fold up and give to you; and see whether I am not right." It makes 70. "Yes, you are right. Then ten heaps of 7 marbles make——?" Seventy. "Seventy what?" Seventy marbles. "And ten heaps of 7 nuts would make——?" Seventy. "Seventy what?" Nuts. "And ten heaps of 7 ones, or units, make——?" Seventy units. "Then we will say that ten sevens always make——?" Seventy. Having repeated the process with ten heaps of 8, of 9, of 6, of 5, etc., you force the pupil at last to discover the law, which he would express in his own way by saying that "ten times a number make that number with —ty at the end."

This short cut is so charming to a child that it is well to leave him to enjoy it for a time without further observation; but in the next lesson, asking him what 70 means, and receiving the answer, 70 units or 7 tens, you thereby show him that the new rule tells us that ten sevens are the same as seven tens; and this he may verify at once for himself by his marbles. In the same lesson you may teach him "eleven times" in the same way, by experiment. The advantage of thus beginning with "10 times and 11 times" is that you at once show a boy the manifest utility of his new knowledge, and at the same time give him *something to learn which he cannot fail to remember*.

After this stimulating foretaste you must now proceed methodically to show him how to construct tables of Multiplication by means of Addition. And here the main business is that the pupil may not be discouraged by the prospect of the burden of committing so great a mass to memory. For this purpose it is expedient not to form the whole of the Tables at once. And before he begins to learn any portion by heart, very often a few remarks of the teacher may help to lighten the labor. For example, in learning "twice," you may show him that he is only repeating in a new form what he has said before in his Addition Tables; for "twice 9 are 18" is the same thing as saying that "9 and 9 make 18." Again, when he comes to learn the more advanced Tables, *e. g.:* "7 times," the child may be shown that he has already learned 7 times 2, 7 times 3, etc., up to 7 times 6, in the previous Tables, so that a good deal of the apparently new work is really repetition of old work.

But when all is done that is possible in the way of help, the task of committing the whole to memory has to be faced; and the truest kindness is to see that the child learns the whole at last, without trusting in any kind of external aid, such as *Memoria Technica*, or anything else. There is no reason, however, why the teacher should not resort to any devices that may facilitate the process without impairing the result. "Children," says Preceptor, "are so constructed that they (and perhaps their elders as well) more easily remember what they take in indirectly with unconscious interest, than what they try to remember with a conscious strain. Very often a child will remember 8 times or 9 times better if he is allowed to write it out or print it in large colored figures; or should he find a difficulty in remembering some particular formula, *e. g.* 8×9 = 72, very often you may stamp it on his memory by some irrational jingle, such as:

"'This rhyme is mine, and strictly true,
That 8 times 9 are 72.'"

But our object is that the child should repeat the Tables without stopping to think about rhymes—especially when, as in this instance, the rhyme will mislead, if one number, *e. g.* 7, be substituted for another, *e. g.* 8. As a rule, the pupil must depend upon practice and repetition, oral and on paper, for the mastery of the Tables. But Preceptor's hint about writing out and embellishing those Tables which present most difficulty, may very likely be found useful.

As soon as the pupil is pretty familiar with the Multiplication Table he should be taught to repeat the corresponding Division Tables, *e. g.* five times six is thirty; fives into thirty, six; sixes into thirty, five.

But it may be well not to teach the Division Tables at first, lest they should break the "swing" of the Multiplication table, and increase the difficulty of learning it.

33. THE FIRST FOUR RULES APPLIED TO NUMBERS ABOVE A HUNDRED.

Before proceeding to apply the "four rules" to numbers above a hundred, the pupil must be practiced still more in reading symbols into units, tens, and hundreds, or hundreds, tens, and units (as above, p. 42), and he must now be introduced to thousands.

Coming now to the "first four Rules" applied to large numbers, we have to speak of the reasons for those Rules, or rather of the methods by which the pupil can be led to the Rules, as the result of his own experience. In every case, if possible, the pupil should be helped to discover a Rule for himself; but great care is necessary to avoid confusing him by proceeding too fast; or by using terms or phrases that he does not understand; or by assuming, as axiomatic, truths which he is not at present prepared to accept. If we can succeed in leading him to the Rules for Addition, Subtraction, and Multiplication, we may perhaps dispense with the process in Division, merely indicating it to him in the case of small numbers, and leaving him to take the rest on trust.

(i.) *Addition.*—The first lesson may be somewhat after this fashion:

"If we have two heaps of fruit, the first containing 5 currants, 4 strawberries, 3 plums, and 2 pears; and the second containing 4 currants, 3 strawberries, 2 plums, and 1 pear; and if we wish to add them together, so as to make the two heaps into one, tell me, what must we say the one large heap will contain? You cannot at once answer. Write down, then, in a line what the first heap contains, putting the fruits in order of size, the smallest fruit to the right, and the largest to the left. Write down what the second heap contains in another line exactly under the first line. Now draw a straight line below these, and below this straight line write down what the large heap will contain, beginning from the small fruit on the right."

2 pears,	3 plums,	4 strawberries,	5 currants.
1 pear,	2 plums,	3 strawberries,	4 currants.
3 pears,	5 plums,	7 strawberries,	9 currants.

"Now suppose we wish to add together the numbers 2345 and 1234. Read out the first number, beginning with the ones"? 5 ones, 4 tens, 3 hundreds, 2 thousands. "Now the second": 4 ones, 3 tens, 2 hundreds, 1 thousand. "Write them in two lines, in the same way in which you wrote down the heaps of fruit, putting the ones to the right, and add them together, beginning from the ones."

2 thousands, 3 hundreds, 4 tens, 5 ones.
1 thousand, 2 hundreds, 3 tens, 4 ones.
———————————————————————————
3 thousands, 5 hundreds, 7 tens, 9 ones.

"Now read out the result you have written down, beginning from the right": 9 ones, 7 tens, 5 hundreds, 3 thousands. "Now read it out, beginning from the left": 3 thousands, 5 hundreds, 7 tens, 9 ones. "Write it down in the ordinary way": 3579.

Having had a little practice in sums of this kind, *in which the totals of tens, hundreds, etc., do not exceed nine*, the pupil must now be told to add two numbers in which the totals exceed nine, *e. g.* 237 and 958.

2 hundreds, 3 tens, 7 ones.
9 hundreds, 5 tens, 8 ones.
———————————————————
11 hundreds, 8 tens, 15 ones.

"Read out the result, beginning from the right": 15 ones, 8 tens, 11 hundreds. "But 15 ones are the same as 5 ones and—how many tens?" One ten. "Then we can set down 5 in the column of ones, and carry the one ten to the column of tens, thus making 9 tens instead of 8 tens. Again the 11 hundreds are the same as 1 hundred and——?" 1 thousand. "We can therefore set down 1 hundred in the column of hundreds, and carry the thousand to the thousand column. Thus the result, beginning from the right, is——?" 5 ones, 9 tens, 1 hundred, 1 thousand. "Read it out from the left": 1 thousand, 1 hundred, 9 tens, 5 ones. "Write it down." 1195. The working may now be repeated more briefly thus, after writing "thousand," "hundred," "ten," over the different columns:

Thousand.	Hundred.	Ten.	One.
	2	3	7
	9	5	8
1	1	9	5

"8 ones and 7 ones are 15 ones; set down 5 ones and carry 1 ten; 1 ten and 5 tens are 6 tens; 6 tens and 3 tens are 9 tens; set down 9 tens; 9 hundreds and 2 hundreds are 11 hundreds; set down 1 hundred and carry 1 thousand."

After a little practice in sums of this kind, with the headings of the columns thus set down, the headings may be dispensed with. But for some time it will be useful for the pupil to work sums aloud, the teacher setting down the figures, so that the pupil may unconsciously learn a neat way of writing, and the teacher may detect any habits of inaccuracy, slovenliness, or failure to comprehend the arithmetical process.

(ii.) *Subtraction.*—In subtraction it is (or was) a common error to speak of "borrowing," *e. g.* in subtracting 19 from 41—9 from 1, you cannot: *borrow* 10; 9 from 11, 2; now *pay back* 1 to the 1 in the lower line; 2 from 4 is 2. This is obviously an incorrect method of reasoning. For if you *borrow* 10 from 19, you make it 9, and when you *pay back* the 10 to the 9, it becomes 19 again, not 29. The correct explanation of the process depends upon the truth that, *in subtracting one number from another the result is not altered if the same number be added to both.* This, therefore, must first be shown to the pupil as follows: "Subtract 5 from 9, what is the result?" 4. "Now add 1 to 5 and also to 9, and subtract 5 and 1 (*i. e.* 6) from 9 and 1 (*i. e.* from 10), what is the result?" 4. "Yes, the same as before. Again, if instead of adding 1 to each, you add 2, and then subtract 5 and 2 (*i. e.* 7) from 9 and 2 (*i. e.* 11), what is the result?" 4. "The same as before." After this, you add successively to the two numbers 3, 4, 5, 6, etc., and elicit from the pupil that in each case the result of the subtraction is 4, *the same as before.*

41
19
--
22

"Then it seems that when I am subtracting one number from another, if I add the same number to both, the result of the subtraction is still——?" The same as before. "Repeat the whole sentence." When I am subtracting, etc. "Try it for yourself, subtracting 5 from 8. Repeat the rule again."

"We have now to subtract 19 from 41, and you will see the use of the rule you have just learned. Can you subtract 9 from 1?" No. "Then we will add 10 ones to the unit column of 41, and afterwards we will add 1 ten to the ten-column of 19; and the result of the subtraction will be the same as before. 9 ones from 11 ones leave——?" 2 ones. "Now add 1 ten to the ten-column of 19; what will that make?" 2 tens. "And subtracting 2 tens from 4 tens, we shall have——?" 2 tens. "The result then is twenty-two."[1]

tens	ones	
4	11	41
2	9	19
2	2	22

Briefly, the process can now be gone through thus: "9 from 1, you cannot; add 10 above; 9 from 11 is 2; add a 10 below; 2 from 4 is 2."

Of course in larger numbers the principle is the same; but the teacher had better not risk confusing the child by entering into further explanations. It may be quietly assumed that the same process is to be continued of adding 10 to the top line where needed, and then

---

[1] Another process consists in *shifting a ten* in the larger number, thus: 9 from 1, you cannot; shift a ten in 41 from the ten's place to the unit's place, making 3 tens and 11 units: 9 from 11, 2; 1 from 3, 2. This depends upon the truth that *a number (e. g.* 41) *is not altered by shifting its parts* (*e. g.* 4 tens and 1 unit; 3 tens and 11 units).

adding 1 to the next figure of the bottom line, by way of compensation.

But if a more than usually quick and intelligent child detects that in larger numbers you are not adding tens, but hundreds and thousands, you may explain the matter further to him thus, by an example, subtracting 9999 from 11111: "9 ones from 1 one, you cannot; add 10 ones to the one 1; 9 ones from 11 ones leave 2 ones.

```
11111
 9999
 ----
 1112
```

"But since we added 10 ones to the top ones, we must now add the same (*i.e.* 1 ten) to the bottom tens; 9 tens and 1 ten make 10 tens; 10 tens from 1 ten you cannot; add 10 tens to the 1 ten; 10 tens from 11 tens leave 1 ten.

"But since we added 10 tens to the top tens, we must now add the same (*i.e.* 1 hundred) to the bottom hundreds; 9 hundreds and 1 hundred make 10 hundreds; 10 hundreds from 1 hundred, you cannot; add 10 hundreds to the 1 hundred; 10 hundreds from 11 hundreds leave 1 hundred.

"But since we added 10 hundreds to the top hundreds, we must now add the same (*i.e.* 1 thousand) to the bottom thousands; 9 thousands and 1 thousand make 10 thousands; 10 thousands from 1 thousand you cannot; add 10 thousands to the 1 thousand; 10 thousands from 11 thousands leave 1 thousand.

"But since we added 10 thousands to the top thousands, we must now add 1 ten thousand to the bottom ten thousands; no ten thousands and 1 ten thousands make 1 ten thousands; 1 ten thousand from 1 ten thousand leaves no ten thousands."

If children could thus be practiced in working sums of subtraction aloud, they would be greatly strengthened in the power of realizing the meaning of figures and of reading them into words.

(iii.) *Multiplication.*—Let the pupil multiply 6 by 4, and note the result (24). Then let him divide 6 into any two parts (1 and 5, 2 and 4, 3 and 3); let him multiply each of the two parts separately by 4 and add the two products (4 and 20, 8 and 16, 12 and 12); and let him thus discover:

Rule I.—*When a number has to be multiplied, it makes no difference whether you multiply the whole, or multiply the parts and add the products.*

When the child has been led to the discovery of this law by experiments with small numbers, and has learned it by heart, we shall tacitly assume that it holds good for all numbers, and shall proceed to apply it to the multiplication of numbers above 10.[1]

But first we must practice the child in multiplying tens together.

---

[1] Before beginning, we remind the pupil that twice 6 is the same as six times two; 7 times 4 the same as 4 times 7, and so on; so that, when two numbers are multiplied together, it matters not which is the multiplier and which the multiplied.

"Suppose I have to multiply twice a number by three times the same number. Twice 4 multiplied by three times 4 is——?" 8 multiplied by 12, *i.e.* 96. "Now alter the order of multiplying, and multiply twice 3 by 4 times 4; the result is——?" 6 multiplied by 16; I do not know this. "Using the rule just given, you can divide 16 into two parts, 10 and 6, and after multiplying them separately, you can add the results." 6 times 10 is 60, 6 times 6 is 36; 60 and 36 are 96. "The same result as before; so that we see that if we have to multiply twice a number by three times a number, it makes no difference if we first multiply two by three, and then the number by the number, and then multiply the two results.

"Now let 10 be the number, and suppose I have to multiply twice 10 by 4 times 10; then the result will be the same, whether I multiply twice 10 by 4 times 10, or twice 4 by——?" 10 times 10. "That is by——?" 100. "And what is twice 4 multiplied by 10 times 10?" It is 8 multiplied by 100 (*i.e.* 800).

"In the same way twice 10 multiplied by 3 times 10 is the same as twice 3 multiplied by 10 times 10, *i.e.*——?" 6 multiplied by 100, or 600. "Hence you see we get a very useful rule."

Rule II.—*If you have to multiply a number of tens by another number of tens, we can multiply the two numbers together as though they were ones, and then put hundred after the result.*

For example, "3 tens multiplied by 4 tens are 12 hundreds, or 1200; 4 tens multiplied by 5 tens give——?" 20 hundreds (*i.e.* 2000).

Required to multiply 13 by 24.

Here, by Rule I, instead of multiplying 13 by 24, we may multiply 13 first by 4 and then by 20, and, if we add the products, the result will be the same. Again, instead of multiplying 13 by 4, we may first multiply 3 by 4, and then multiply 10 by 4, and the results will be the same.

We proceed, therefore to multiply 13 by 4 and by 20, and we begin with 4: 13 multiplied by 4 is (by Rule I) the same as 3 and 10 multiplied by 4; 3 multiplied by 4 is 12 (*i.e.* 2 units and 1 ten);

```
 13
 24
 ---
 52
260
---
312
```

set down 2 units, and "carry" the 1 ten; 1 ten multiplied by 4 is 4 tens, which, with the 1 ten "carried," makes 5 tens. Having multiplied 13 by 4, we have now to multiply 13 by 20 (*i.e.* 2 tens); 13 multiplied by 2 tens is (by Rule I) the same as 3 and 10 multiplied by 2 tens; 3 multiplied by 2 tens is the same as 2 tens multiplied by 3, or 6 tens; set down 0 for the units, and 6 for the tens; 1 ten multiplied by 2 tens is (by Rule II) 2 hundreds; set down 2 hundreds.

Having now multiplied 13 first by 4 and then by 20, we add the results, 312; and this (by Rule I) is the same as the result of multiplying 13 by 24.

Before passing to any other sums, it will be good practice to multiply in the same way 24 by 13, and to show that the result is the same;

and to multiply 24 by 6 and 7, or by 8 and 5; or to multiply 13 by 12 and 12, or by 10 and 14; and to show that in each case the result is the same.

After all this preliminary training, the teacher may now work the sum above written, briefly thus; "4 ones multiplied by 3 ones is 12 ones; set down 2 ones and carry 1 ten; 4 ones multiplied by 1 ten is 4 tens; set down 5 tens; 2 tens multiplied by 3 ones is 6 tens; set down 6 tens;[1] 2 tens multiplied by 1 ten is 2 hundreds; set down 2 hundreds. Now add."

These and many other sums should be worked by the pupil aloud, the teacher setting down the figures at the dictation of the pupil, who must be trained gradually to increase the rapidity of the process.

But when the pupil is allowed for the first time to set down a sum for himself, great care must be taken not to hurry him, nor to allow him to begin a habit of writing the figures out of the exact vertical columns; and, if possible, the sum should be so simple that he may succeed in his first essay.

The teacher must use some discretion in teaching the above reasoning to children: 1st, he must be perfectly familiar with it himself; 2d, he must be on the alert to detect signs of bewilderment in his pupils; 3d, he must give it up soon, if he finds he does not carry them with him.

Yet even if he does not succeed in making his pupils comprehend the whole of the demonstration, he should *keep the form of the demonstration in mind when working a sum aloud for them.* For example, after multiplying 13 by 4, he will say, "We have now multiplied 13 by the 4 ones; it remains to multiply 13 by 20, or 2 tens," etc. Thus he will gradually instil into their minds some apprehension of the reasons for the process.

(iv.) *Division.*—The teacher must be prepared to find the explanation of division more difficult than that of multiplication and subtraction; and none but very easy examples should be given to illustrate it. Perhaps, in the case of a child who is not very quick, it may be better to dispense altogether with the explanation, simply dictating the steps, and trusting partly to the analogy of multiplying, and partly to the inherent proof contained in each example, in the hope that the pupil may gradually be led to an apprehension of the reasons of the process.

Before beginning the division of large numbers the pupil should be taught to divide, accurately and rapidly, small numbers in which the divisor is not exactly contained, *e. g.* 73 divided by 9 is—8, and 1 over.

Let the pupil divide 12 by 2, and note the result (6); then let him divide 12 into its parts (taking care that the numbers are even) (*a*) 10

---

[1] The 0 (to signify that 6 stands for 6 tens, or 60) had better be inserted for some time.

and 2; (*b*) 8 and 4; (*c*) 6 and 6; (*d*) 4 and 4 and 4; (*e*) 2 and 6 and 4; and let him divide the parts by 2 and add the quotients, (*a*) 5 and 1; (*b*) 4 and 2; (*c*) 3 and 3; (*d*) 2 and 2 and 2; (*e*) 1 and 3 and 2. Thus let him discover that in all these cases the quotient is the same as when the whole number was divided, so that he may be led to:

Rule.—*When a number has to be divided it makes no difference whether you divide the whole or divide the parts and add the quotients.*

The pupil must now be reminded of what he has probably already learned on a small scale, when doing little sums that illustrate the division of small numbers, viz., that 6 apples divided by 3 give 2 apples; 6 marbles divided by 3, 2 marbles; 6 tens divided by 3, 2 tens; 6 hundreds divided by 3, 2 hundreds; 6 thousands divided by 3, 2 thousands.

Required, to divide 435 by 3:

3)435
 100
 40
 5
 145

By our Rule, 435 divided by 3 is the same as 400 div^d by 3, and 30 div^d by 3, and 5 div^d by 3; or, if we please, it is the same as 300 div^d by 3, and 120 div^d by 3, and 15 div^d by 3; or we may divide 435 into any other parts we please, and divide them separately, adding the quotients.

Begin with the hundreds. Threes into 4 hundreds? Not exactly divisible. But 3 hundreds are divisible by 3. We will therefore take away 1 hundred from the hundreds, so as to leave 3 hundreds, and "carry" the 1 hundred (in the shape of ten tens) to the 3 tens, making up 13 tens. Threes into 3 hundred? 1 hundred; set down 1 hundred.

Threes into 13 tens? Not exactly divisible. But 12 tens are exactly divisible by 3. We will therefore take away 1 ten from the tens, so as to leave 12 tens, and carry the 1 ten (in the shape of ten units) to the 5 ones, making up 15 ones. Threes into 12 tens? 4 tens; set down 4 tens.

Threes into 15 ones? 5 ones; set down 5 ones:

3)4734
 1000
 500
 70
 8
 1578

More briefly we may now dictate a sum of this kind thus: threes into 4 thousand? 1 thousand and 1 thousand over; set down 1000; threes into 17 hundred? 5 hundred and 2 hundred over; set down 5 hundred; threes into 23 tens? 7 tens and 2 tens over; set down 7 tens; threes into 24 ones? 8 ones; set down 8 ones.

More briefly still, the next step will dispense with the rows of naughts, by showing that, if we take care to write the thousands and hundreds in the places of the thousands and hundreds, the naughts are unnecessary.

34. THE TRANSITION TO FRACTIONS.

Before proceeding to Fractions, and indeed before proceeding to Long Division (the explanation for which must be taken upon trust by children, as it is far too lengthy to be imparted without confusing them) a good store of easy problems should be worked involving "the first four rules" applied to small numbers and to small sums of money.

In the course of these, they must be taught, with care and iteration, the different meanings of an answer in division.

Supposing 12 oranges are to be equally divided: the question may be (1) how many oranges are to be given to each of 4 boys, and in that case I divide the number of oranges (12) by the number of boys (4), and the answer (3) represents the number of *oranges*. But the question may be (2) how many boys can be sharers, if each is to receive 3 oranges, and in that case I divide the whole number of oranges (12) by the number of oranges in a single share (3), and the result (4) tells you the number of *times* 3 oranges are contained in 12 oranges; and hence we can infer how many heaps or shares of 3 can be made, and how many boys can share.

Hence our pupils will obtain a useful rule, that:

When a number of things is divided by a number of the same things (e.g. a number of oranges by a number of oranges, of pence by pence, of boys by boys) *the answer is a number of* TIMES; *but when a number of one kind of things is divided by a number of another kind of things (e.g.* a number of oranges by a number of boys, a number of soldiers by a number of regiments, a number of sailors by a number of ships) *the answer represents some number of the first kind of things* (oranges, soldiers, sailors).

At this stage the Definitions of Multiplication and of Division should be taught and committed to memory, as well as the terms Multiplicand, Dividend, Multiplier, Divisor, Product, Quotient, etc.

The Arithmetical Problems should be varied in every possible way (the numbers being kept small) so as to familiarize the pupil with the different practical applications of Arithmetic. For example, in a certain number of yards how many telegraph posts can be set up? How many revolutions of a wheel can take place? How many sentinels must be posted? How many desks can be placed? How many boys can stand with arms folded? How many with arms outstretched? All these are simply so many changes rung on one simple method of utilizing division.

In order to increase the number of these problems, and to take advantage of the strength of the memory while it is strongest, it is desirable that children should learn the ordinary Tables of "Weights and Measures" (rejecting those which are of no use) before proceeding to fractions.

At this stage it will be useful to teach the pupil to substitute for "added to," diminished by," "multiplied by," "divided by," the signs , $+$, $-$, $\times$, $\div$, care being taken that these signs are, from the first, shaped exactly; and in order that the $+$ may be distinguished from the $\times$, let the $+$ slope a little, if anything to the left. He may also be allowed to use the sign $=$ to denote "is equal to."

At first it well be well that the pupil, though using these signs for convenience in writing, should orally interpret them by the old terms, "added to," "diminished by," etc., not being introduced to the terms *plus* and *minus* till a lesson or two have familiarized him with the written use of these symbols.

The careless use of the sign = must be strictly prohibited. Some boys use it merely as a link to connect together different parts of a problem, thus: "If 12 be multiplied by 3 and then by 4, and the product be divided by 2, what is the quotient?" "$12 \times 3 = 36 = 36 \times 4 = 144 = 144 \div 2 = 72$ Ans. Such slovenly statements must be at once branded as "not true." And any pupil who thus abuses the use of the sign = must be condemned to return to the tedious "is equal to" for a week, at least.

35. FRACTIONS.

There are many ingenious methods of showing children the meaning and laws of fractions. Whatever methods may be adopted, the teacher will always bear in mind the principle that the pupil is to be led to the unknown from the known; and that, as far as possible, he is to discover truths for himself.

Break a thin stick into three parts as nearly equal as you can manage. Each of these *fragments*, you tell him, is a third part, or a "third" of the whole. In Arithmetic, when one whole is thus divided into equal parts, each part is called, not a fragment, but a *fraction;* but the meaning is the same, viz., "a breaking." How are we to express in writing such a fragment or fraction in Arithmetical writing? We might write it $1 \div 3$; but we prefer to write it $\frac{1}{3}$, which means 1 divided by 3, or 1 divided into three parts.

Let the child then break a stick into 2, 3, 4, 5, 6, etc., parts, and write down neatly the Arithmetical signs by which he must express these parts, viz., $\frac{1}{2}$, $\frac{1}{3}$, $\frac{1}{4}$, $\frac{1}{5}$, $\frac{1}{6}$, etc.

Now what does the lower figure in each case tell us? It tells us the number of equal parts into which one, or unity, is divided. By what names shall we call these equal parts? We will call them a half, a third part, a fourth part (or quarter), a fifth part, a sixth, etc.

Hence we see that the lower number of a fraction always tells us the *name* of the parts into which unity is divided. Therefore, the lower figure in a fraction may be called the *Namer*.

Before proceeding further, let the child write down several fractions for himself, *e.g.* $\frac{1}{20}$, $\frac{1}{55}$, $\frac{1}{240}$, and read them aloud; and let him, after a while, be allowed to drop the word "part" (it being explained to him that this is allowed for the sake of brevity), so that he may now speak of "one twentieth," "one fifty-fifth," "one two-hundred and fortieth," etc.

Let the pupil for some time call the lower figure of the fraction the Namer, without being allowed to puzzle himself with the less intelligible term (which merely expresses the same thing in a longer word) Denominator.

Next point out that, in breaking a stick or anything else into equal parts; you may take a number of them together. For example, if the stick has been divided into six parts, each of which is called a sixth, you may take 2, 3, 4, or 5 of these together, thus making two sixths, three sixths, four sixths, five sixths, according to the number of parts taken together.

How shall we write down these fractions, say, for example, five sixths? Since we are taking five sixths instead of one sixth, we must write 5 where we wrote 1 before, above the line, to represent the number of the parts, $\frac{5}{6}$; and similarly for the rest, $\frac{2}{6}$, $\frac{3}{6}$, $\frac{4}{6}$.

Since the upper figure represents the number of the parts taken together, it may be called the *Numberer*.

This name should be allowed for some time without permitting the pupil to use the term Numerator, which merely expresses the same thing in a longer word.

36. FRACTIONAL EXPERIMENTS.

Let the pupil take a sheet of note paper, folded in the ordinary way, and having unfolded it, and then refolded it, let him be told to observe that when it is refolded it is folded into *half* of the whole size.

Now let him fold it a second time into a *quarter*, then into an *eighth*, and lastly into a *sixteenth* of the whole size. Lastly, let him unfold it to the full size, and observe the creases dividing the paper into halves, quarters, eighth parts, sixteenth parts; and let him write down *in words* how many of the smaller parts are contained by each of the larger parts.

He will find that a half contains two quarters, or four eighths, or eight sixteenths; also that a quarter contains two eighths, or four sixteenths; and that an eighth contains two sixteenths.

Pointing out to him that he may use the term "is equal to" instead of "contains," and that he may use the symbol = to denote it, you will now bid him write down his discoveries, thus:

$$\frac{1}{2} = \frac{2}{4} = \frac{4}{8} = \frac{8}{16}$$
$$\frac{1}{4} = \frac{2}{8} = \frac{4}{16}$$
$$\frac{1}{8} = \frac{2}{16}$$

Let him then be asked to find out from his note-paper, and to write down how many eighths there are in three quarters? How many sixteenths there are in three eighths? How many in five eighths?

$$\frac{3}{4} = \frac{6}{8}$$
$$\frac{3}{8} = \frac{6}{16}$$
$$\frac{5}{8} = \frac{10}{16}$$

Now with the aid of a foot-rule, measure off on a stick, or (better) show your pupil how to measure, a foot divided into inches and half-inches. *Carefully avoid using the terms "feet" or "inches,"* but speak of it as a piece of wood divided into 12 parts, each part again being divided into 2 smaller parts, so that the whole stick is divided into 24 parts. And bid him write down how many of the twelfth parts are contained in half the stick? How many in a quarter? He will find that:

$$\tfrac{1}{2} = \tfrac{6}{12}; \quad \tfrac{1}{4} = \tfrac{3}{12}.$$

How many of the twenty-fourth parts are contained in half the stick? How many in a quarter?

$$\tfrac{1}{2} = \tfrac{12}{24}; \quad \tfrac{1}{4} = \tfrac{6}{24}.$$

"Let us now run over our results again. We find that $\tfrac{1}{2} = \tfrac{2}{4}$; how many times is the numberer 2 greater than the Numberer 1?" Twice. "And how many times the Namer 4 greater than the Namer 2?" Twice. "Again $\tfrac{1}{2} = \tfrac{4}{8}$; how many times is the Numberer 4 greater than the Numberer 1?" Four times. "And how many is the Namer 8 greater than the Namer 2?" Four times. "In the stick also we find that $\tfrac{1}{2} = \tfrac{6}{12}$; how many times is the Numberer 6 greater than the Numberer 1?" Six times. "And how many times the Namer 12 greater than the Namer 2?" Six times. "Then we find that, whenever two fractions are equal, if the second Numberer is a certain number of times greater than the first Numberer, the second Namer is also—?" The same number of times greater than the first Namer. Write down this:

1. Rule.—*Whenever two fractions are equal, if the second Numberer is a certain number of times greater than the first Numberer, the second Namer is the same number of times greater than the first Namer.*

Then ask the pupil whether $\tfrac{1}{2}$ is increased when the Namer and Numberer are both multiplied by 2, by 4, by 6, by 8, by 12. And having shown him, by reference to the above results which he has written down, that $\tfrac{1}{2}$ is not altered, lead him to the—

2. Rule.—*A fraction is not altered when the Numberer and Namer are multiplied by the same number.*

Let us now find out what we have been doing in multiplying the Numberer and the Namer by the same number, and in saying that the fraction is not altered. "What does the Namer name?" The parts into which unity is divided. "Then in multiplying or increasing the number of the Namer, I have increased the—?" Parts into which unity is divided. "I should not say 'increased the *parts*,' but 'increased the *number of parts*.' If the fraction is $\tfrac{2}{3}$, and if I multiply the Namer by 2, I should not say *I increase the part, a third, to the part, a sixth;* for a sixth is smaller than a third; but I should rather say I increase the *number of parts* into which unity is divided from 3 to 6. In reality I *diminish* the *parts* (from a third to a sixth), but I *increase* the *number of the parts* (from 3 to 6). Here let me stop to remind you that, when you speak of the *number of parts* in connection with the Namer, you must always distinguish it from the Numberer. The Namer names the number of *parts into which Unity is divided;* the Numberer tells you how many of these parts are *taken together.*

"Now I resume. In multiplying the Namer 3, I have been increasing a certain number of times—what?" The number of parts into which Unity is divided. "And in multiplying the Numberer by the same number of times—what?" The number of those parts taken together. "Then our rule tells us that, when I increase the number of parts into which unity is divided, and increase by the same number of times the number of those parts taken together, the fraction remains—?" The same. "Apply this rule, beginning with a half, doubling the number of parts several times: one half equals two quarters, equals—?" Four eighths, equals eight sixteenths, equals sixteen thirty-seconds, etc.

Since a fraction is not altered by multiplying the Namer and Numberer by the same number, it follows that—

3. Rule.—*A fraction is not altered by dividing the Namer and Numberer by the same number.*

This may be proved to the child by showing (as above) that if you diminish the Namer you increase the size of the parts of unity, and if you diminish the Numberer, *i.e.* the number of those parts of unity, the same number of times, the fraction must remain unaltered.

But it would probably be sufficient and more intelligible to illustrate this truth by examples, thus: We have seen that $\frac{1}{2} = \frac{2}{4} = \frac{4}{8} = \frac{8}{16}$, where the Numberer and Namer have been multiplied by 2, by 4, by 8. Reversing these, we see that $\frac{8}{16} = \frac{4}{8} = \frac{2}{4} = \frac{1}{2}$. Here the Numberer and Namer have been divided by 2, by 4, and by 8, and yet the fraction has remained unaltered in value.

37. ADDITION OF FRACTIONS.[1]

"Add together a halfpenny and a farthing; what is the result?" Three farthings. "Exactly; and in order to get this result, what did you do to the halfpenny?" I turned it into farthings. "Now add a half and a quarter; what is the result?" Three quarters. "And in order to get this result, what did you do?" I turned the half into quarters.

"Now when you add pence and farthings, or pounds and shillings, or tons and hundredweights, or, generally, a number of things of one name or denomination to a number of things of another name or denomination, you reduce them to the same—?" Denomination. "Exactly; and you have to do the same thing with fractions; but as the name or denomination of a Fraction depends on its Namer, or

---

[1] By this time the pupil should be introduced to the terms Denominator (for Namer) and Numerator (for Numberer).

Denominator, we generally speak of reducing Fractions so that they may have the same Denominator.

"If, therefore, I wish to add $\frac{1}{2}$ to $\frac{1}{8}$, what must I do to the $\frac{1}{2}$?" Turn it into eighths. "What must I do to the $\frac{1}{2}$ in order to turn it into eighths?" Multiply it by 4. "No, for 4 times $\frac{1}{2}$ would be—?" Two. "If, therefore, you multiplied the fraction $\frac{1}{2}$ by 4, you would alter its value, and not reduce it to the same Denominator as $\frac{1}{8}$; you wish to leave its value unaltered, and yet to turn the Denominator into 8."

If the pupil cannot, upon consideration, tell you what is to be done, you must remind him of Rule 2, that *a fraction is not altered by multiplying the Numerator and Denominator by the same number*. Then you ask, "By what number must I multiply the Denominator of $\frac{1}{2}$ in order to make the new Denominator 8?" By 4. "And by what number must I multiply the Numerator in order not to alter the value of the fraction?" By 4. "And what does $\frac{1}{2}$ then become?" $\frac{4}{8}$. "And we obtained this result by multiplying the smaller Denominator by such a number as to make it equal to the larger Denominator, and by multiplying the Numerator by the same number."

After several instances of this kind, in which one fraction is added to another by reducing the former to a fraction with the *same Denominator as the latter*, we proceed to instances where *both* fractions are altered by being reduced to fractions with the same Denominator. "Add a pound to a florin." Twenty-two shillings. "In order to get this answer, what did you do to the pound and the florin?" I turned them into shillings. "Yes, in order to add money of different denominations you turned them both into money of the—?" Same denomination. "And so, in order to add two fractions of different denominations, you must often turn them *both* into fractions with the same denominator."

Required, to add together $\frac{1}{3}$ and $\frac{1}{4}$.

"Take your stick, which is divided into twelve equal parts, or twelfths; suppose I have to add $\frac{1}{3}$ and $\frac{1}{4}$ of the stick. I see that $\frac{1}{3}$ of the stick contains a certain number of these twelfths. How many twelfths?" 4 twelfths. "Write down in arithmetical signs, that one third is equal to four twelfths." $\frac{1}{3} = \frac{4}{12}$.

"Here you have multiplied the Numerator and Denominator of the first fraction by 4, have you not?" Yes. "Well, note that 4 is the Denominator of the second fraction. And now look at the stick, and tell me how many twelfths there are in $\frac{1}{4}$. Write down the result in arithmetical signs." $\frac{1}{4} = \frac{3}{12}$.

"Here you have multiplied the Numerator and Denominator of the second fraction by—?" 3. "Yes, and note that 3 is the Denominator of the first fraction.

"Now, therefore, knowing that one third is equal to four twelfths, and that one fourth is equal to three twelfths, we know that one fourth added to one third is equal to—how many twelfths?" Seven twelfths. "Write down this result in arithmetical signs, viz., that a third added to a quarter is equal to four twelfths added to three twelfths, and that this is equal to seven twelfths."

$$\tfrac{1}{3}+\tfrac{1}{4} = \tfrac{4}{12}+\tfrac{3}{12} = \tfrac{7}{12}.$$

"Now, in order to add any two fractions in this way, we want a rule to guide us. Let us see what we have been doing. In order to alter the shapes of the two fractions above, so that, without having their values altered, they should have a *Denominator common to both*, we multiplied the Numerator and Denominator of the first by 4, which was the Denominator of the second. "And we multiplied the Numerator and Denominator of the second by—?" 3. "Which is the—?" Denominator of the first.

Try the same method with $\tfrac{1}{2}$ and $\tfrac{1}{4}$. "What does the first become when its Numerator and Denominator are multiplied by the Denominator of the first?" $\tfrac{2}{8}$. "Add the results." $\tfrac{2}{8}+\tfrac{2}{8}=\tfrac{5}{8}$. "Verify these results on the stick. Are they true?" Yes. "Then now repeat the—

4. Rule.—*In order to add two fractions, multiply the Numerator and Denominator of the first by the Denominator of the second, and the Numerator and Denominator of the second by the Denominator of the first. Then add the two Numerators, retaining the Common Denominator.*[1]

88. THE VALUE OF A FRACTION.

"What is the meaning of $\tfrac{3}{4}$ of an orange?" That one orange is divided into 4 parts, and 3 of these are taken together. "True; but I shall now show you that $\tfrac{3}{4}$ has another meaning. Suppose I take 3 oranges at once and divide them among 4 people, what will each receive? You cannot at once answer. How many quarters will there be in 3 oranges?" 12. "And twelve quarters divided amongst 4 people give to each —?" 3 quarters. "Then you see that $\tfrac{3}{4}$ of an orange is the same as 3 oranges divided by 4." Yes. "And, similarly, $\tfrac{3}{4}$ of a hundred is the same as 3 hundreds divided by 4." Yes. "And therefore $\tfrac{3}{4}$ of a unit (*i.e.* $\tfrac{3}{4}$) is the same as 3 units divided by 4 (*i.e.* $3 \div 4$)?" Yes.

Now let us see whether this rule holds true in other cases, viz., that a Fraction is the same as the Numerator divided by the Denominator. "According to this rule, what would be the value of $\tfrac{48}{4}$?" 12. "How many quarters are there in 12 things?" 48. "Then is it true that $\tfrac{48}{4} = 12$?" Yes. "Again $\tfrac{8}{2}$ are—?" 4. "$\tfrac{16}{4}$ are—?" 4. Then from all these cases we see that—

---

[1] As for the Rule of Least Common Multiple, it can be advantageously deferred. When the pupil has to add three fractions, let him (at first) add two together, and add the result to the third. He will thus all the more appreciate the rule of the L. C. M. when he reaches it, as shortening a lengthy process.

5. Rule.—*The value of a Fraction is the same as that of the Numerator divided by the Denominator.*

Hence when we speak of five sixths we mean either (1) that one thing is divided into 6 parts, five of which are taken together, or (2) that five things are divided by 6.

39. MULTIPLICATION AND DIVISION OF FRACTIONS.

(i.) *To Multiply a Fraction by a Whole Number.*[1]

"What is 7 times 5 oranges?" 35 oranges. "7 times 5 ounces?" 35 ounces. "7 times 5 millions?" 35 millions. "7 times 5 quarters of an orange? 35 quarters of an orange. "7 times 5 halves? 35 halves. "7 times 5 sixths?" 35 sixths. "Write down in arithmetical signs that 7 times 5 sixths (*i.e.* 7 multiplied by 5 sixths) is 35 sixths."

$$7 \times \tfrac{5}{6} = \tfrac{35}{6}.$$

"What is 5 times 7 eighths?" 35 eighths. "Write this down."

$$5 \times \tfrac{7}{8} = \tfrac{35}{8}.$$

"Hence, in order to multiply a fraction by a number, what must we do to the Numerator?" Multiply it by the number. "And what to the Denominator?" Nothing.

Then write down the—

6. Rule.—*In order to multiply a Fraction by a Whole Number multiply the Numerator by it, and leave the Denominator unchanged.*

(ii.) *To Divide a Fraction by a Whole Number.*

"Suppose I have three separate quarters of an orange, and I wish to give half of my three quarters to a companion, I can cut each quarter into two eighths, can I not, and keep three of the eighths, while I give him the other three?" Yes. "What, therefore, is $\tfrac{3}{4}$ when divided into two equal parts, or, in other words, when divided by 2?" Three eighths. "Write down in arithmetical signs that three quarters divided by 2 is equal to three eighths."

$$\tfrac{3}{4} \div 2 = \tfrac{3}{8}.$$

"In the same way, suppose there is a stick of chocolate twelve inches long, cut into separate twelfth parts (or inches), of which I have received five; and suppose I wish to share my five twelfths (or inches) equally with a companion, or, in other words, to divide it by 2., I can divide each of my inches into half, can I not, and give him five half inches, while I retain five half inches myself?" Yes. "In other words, five inches, when divided by 2, is five half inches?" Yes. "Now an inch is a twelfth part of a foot; what part of a foot is half an inch? If you cannot tell at once, count how many half-inches

---

[1] Here it may be explained that a number that is not a fraction is sometimes called a *whole number*, in order to distinguish it from a fraction, or broken number.

there are on the foot rule." 24. "Then a half-inch is what part of a foot?" A twenty-fourth. "Therefore, in saying that five inches, when divided by 2, are equal to five half-inches, we really say that five *twelfths* divided by 2 are equal to—?" Five twenty-fourths. "Write down in arithmetical signs that five twelfths divided by 2 are equal to five twenty-fourths."

$$\tfrac{5}{12} \div 2 = \tfrac{5}{24}.$$

"Now here we have been dividing first $\tfrac{3}{4}$ by 2, and then $\tfrac{5}{12}$ by 2. Have we in either case altered the Numerator?" No. "Have we altered the Denominator?" Yes. "What have we done to it?" Multiplied it by 2. "But 2 is the Whole Number by which we are to divide, is it not?" Yes. "Then, in order to divide a Fraction by any Whole Number, what must you do?" Multiply the Denominator by the Whole Number. "Write that down."

7. Rule.[1]—*In order to divide a Fraction by a Whole Number, multiply the Denominator by it, and leave the Numerator unchanged.*

(iii.) *To multiply one Fraction by another.*

Required to Multiply $\tfrac{11}{12}$ by $\tfrac{3}{4}$.

"If I multiplied $\tfrac{11}{12}$ by 3, the result (by Rule 6) would be $\tfrac{33}{12}$."

"But this would be too much; for I have multiplied by 3 instead of by $\tfrac{3}{4}$, *i.e.* (Rule 5) $3 \div 4$. The multiplier has therefore been 4 times too great; what must I do to diminish the result?" Divide by 4. "And $\tfrac{33}{12} \div 4$ is (by Rule 7) what?" $\tfrac{33}{48}$.

Hence

$$\tfrac{11}{12} \times \tfrac{3}{4} = \tfrac{33}{48}.$$

"How have we obtained our new Numerator?" By multiplying the two old Numerators together. "And how the new Denominator?" By multiplying the two old Denominators together. "Then now you can write down the following:

8. Rule.— *In order to multiply two Fractions together, multiply the two Numerators to obtain the new Numerator, and the two Denominators to obtain the new Denominator.*

(iv.) *To divide by a Fraction.*

"How many halves are there in 1?" 2. "Then 1 divided by $\tfrac{1}{2}$ is—:" 2. "How many quarters are there in 1?" 4. "Then 1 divided by $\tfrac{1}{4}$ is—?" 4. "What is $1 \div \tfrac{3}{4}$?" You cannot tell at once. How many quarters are there in 1?" 4. "Then $1 \div \tfrac{3}{4}$ is the same as 4 quarters divided by 3 quarters, is it not?" Yes. "And this is $\tfrac{4}{3}$?"[2] Yes. "Write down your results."

$$1 \div \tfrac{1}{2} = 2.$$
$$1 \div \tfrac{1}{4} = 4.$$
$$1 \div \tfrac{3}{4} = \tfrac{4}{3}.$$

Hence we obtain a—

---

[1] Rules 6 and 7 may afterwards be amplified by showing that multiplying the Denominator produces the same result as dividing the Numerator, and that dividing the Numerator produces the same result as multiplying the Denominator.

[2] Not 4-3 quarters (see Rule, Par. 34), but 4-3 times, or units.

9. Rule.—*In order to divide by a Fraction, invert the Fraction and multiply.*

Another Method.

The following method is not experimental; but it is brief, and has the advantage of applying to the division of a Fraction, as well as of a Whole Number, by a Fraction.

(1) Required to divide 12 by $\frac{3}{4}$.

If I divide by 3, instead of by $\frac{3}{4}$, the answer would be $\frac{12}{3}$; but as I have divided by a divisor 4 times too large, the result is 4 times too small, and must be multiplied by 4; it is therefore

$$\frac{4 \times 12}{3}$$

Here we have inverted the Fraction and multiplied. The pupil will readily see that (by Rule 5) the result is 16, and can verify the result on a foot rule by ascertaining that there are 16 three quarters of an inch in 12 inches.

(2) Required to divide $\frac{3}{4}$ by $\frac{5}{7}$.

If $\frac{3}{4}$ be divided by 5 instead of by $\frac{5}{7}$, the result is (Rule 7) $\frac{3}{4 \times 5}$

i.e. $\frac{3}{20}$; but, as the divisor is 7 times too large, the quotient is 7 times too small, and requires to be multiplied by 7; this is $\frac{3 \times 7}{20}$ or $\frac{21}{20}$.

From both these instances we obtain the Rule given above.

40. THE MODERN RULE OF THREE, OR METHOD OF UNITY.

The "Rule of Three," as it used to be taught with the old-fashioned method of "stating," affords little, if any, opportunity of appealing to the reason; but when it is taught according to what is called the Method of Unity, presupposing a knowledge of Fractions, it is a most valuable mental exercise.

Thus, suppose the question to be, "If 5 apples cost $2\frac{1}{2}d.$, what will 21 apples cost?"

The price of 5 apples is $2\frac{1}{2}d.$, or $\frac{5}{2}d.$

Therefore the price of 1 apple is $\frac{1}{5}$ of $\frac{5d.}{2}$ or $\frac{5d.}{2 \times 5}$

Therefore the price of 21 apples is 21 times $\frac{5d.}{2 \times 5}$ or $\frac{5 \times 21d.}{2 \times 5}$ or $\frac{21d.}{2}$ or $10\frac{1}{2}d.$[1]

1. In time, *but not at first*, the pupil may substitute ∴ for "therefore," = for "is," and × for "of" and for "times." He may also be allowed, instead of repeating the same words three times, to indicate them by " " " .

---

[1] The process of *cancelling* factors common to the Numerator and Denominator follows at once from Rule 3, Page 56.

2. But he must never be allowed to carry his desire for abbreviation so far as to write (which he will probably do if not checked) "5 apples = $2\tfrac{1}{2}d$." or "5 apples cost $2\tfrac{1}{2}$ (omitting the d which denotes pence).¹

3. Before beginning any sum of this kind, the pupil should be asked to give a rough answer to the problem by common sense. Thus, in the question about the price of 21 apples, he should be asked, "Will the price demanded be more or less than $2\tfrac{1}{2}d.$?" More. "How much more?" As much more as 21 apples are more than 5 apples. "And how many times 5 is 21, roughly?" Four times. "Then roughly the new price will be how many times more than $2\tfrac{1}{2}d.$?" About four times. "And 4 times $2\tfrac{1}{2}d.$ amount to —?" $10d$. This will enable the pupil at once to detect any gross inaccuracy in the answer.

4. In spite of this and other precautions, most children, after "doing" the Method of Unity for a few days, will probably—from natural aversion to thinking—fall into a mechanical way of writing their sums.

When the teacher sees signs of this, he should set the pupil a sum on the same principle, but in a different shape, thus:

"If 5 men do a piece of work in $2\tfrac{1}{2}$ days, how long will it take 23 men?"

The average pupil will *do* this sum very rapidly, thus:

$$5 \text{ men do it in } 2\tfrac{1}{2} \text{ days or } \tfrac{5}{2} \text{ days.}$$

$$\therefore 1 \text{ man } \text{"} \text{ "} \frac{5}{2 \times 5} \text{ days.}$$

$$\therefore 23 \text{ men } \text{"} \text{ "} \frac{5 \times 23}{2 \times 5} \text{ days.}$$

$$\text{Ans.} = \tfrac{23}{2} = 11\tfrac{1}{2} \text{ days.}$$

It would be a most valuable antidote to thoughtlessness and to the slight conceit that is sometimes bred by a confidence in mechanical methods, to point out the extreme absurdity of this answer, and to convince the boy thereby of the utility (1) of the preliminary question, "Will the time demanded be more or less than the time given?" (2) *of the necessity of reasoning, as well as writing figures.*

If the pupil had reasoned before he began to write, he would have seen at once that 23 men will take less, not more, time than 5 men to

---

¹ The Author has been for many years in the habit of setting almost every week a sum of this kind in an entrance examination: If 216 lbs. of soap cost £5 8s., what will 800 lbs. of soap cost? And a very large number (a fourth or fifth, at least, of those who have attempted it) have stated it thus, omitting not only the sign lbs., but also the signs £. s.:

$$216 : 800 :: 5_{\,\prime\prime}8 : x.$$

Then, having taken for granted that $5_{\,\prime\prime}8$ means 5s. 8d., they proceed to show that 800 lbs. of soap cost about £1. 5s. less than a quarter of the price of 216 lbs.

do the same piece of work, and might further have seen that the answer would be about the fifth part of $2\frac{1}{4}$ days.

41. DECIMAL FRACTIONS.

Only one or two hints on this subject will be given. It presents very little difficulty, if ordinary fractions have been thoroughly mastered, and if at first the pupil is constantly reminded of the unexpressed Denominator.

(1) The Rule for the multiplication of Decimals may be illustrated experimentally by small numbers; thus: To multiply .2 by .2. This is the same as $\frac{2}{10} \times \frac{2}{10}$, or $\frac{4}{100}$, which is expressed by .04. Similarly, .12 multiplied by $.12 = \frac{12}{100} \times \frac{12}{100} = \frac{144}{10000} = .0144$. In these two instances we see the general Rule.

Multiply as in whole numbers, and point off decimal places in the product equal to the sum of the decimal places in the multiplier and multiplicand, adding naughts to the left if necessary to complete the number.

(2) For the Division of Decimals it is a good rule, at all events for beginners, to multiply the Divisor and Dividend by such a power of 10 as to convert *both* into whole numbers.

Thus
$$\frac{.00543}{103.75} = \frac{543}{10375000}.$$

(3) The process of expressing a circulating Decimal as an ordinary Fraction is commonly taught by a mechanical rule which in no way exercises the reasoning powers. But no rule at all should be given. The logical process itself can be easily understood, and is very little longer than the ordinary mechanical one. It should therefore be not only understood, but *regularly employed by the pupil*, as follows:

Express 13.34567 as an ordinary fraction.

The fraction may be represented by F.

Then $F = 13.34567567$, etc., (1).

Multiply both sides of (1) by 100.

$F \times 100 = 1334.567567567$, etc., (2).

Multiply both sides of (2) by 1,000.

$F \times 100 \times 1000 = 1334567.567567$, etc., (3).

Subtract the second line from the third.

$F \times (100,000 - 110) = 1334567 - 1334.$

$$F = \frac{1334567 - 1334}{99900}.$$

Whence in time the pupil may discover for himself the general rule that:

The Numerator of the new Fraction is formed by subtracting the non-repeating part of the decimal from the whole decimal, including the whole number, and the Denominator by writing down as many nines as there are repeaters, and as many naughts as there are non-repeaters.

42. GENERAL CAUTIONS.

1. Children should not be allowed (as they are in many schools) to have the answers to their sums.

The possession of the answers encourages them to scamper over the working of a sum without thought about the reasonableness of the method, knowing that "the answer will tell them" whether their method has been correct.

2. As to the correction of errors, it is well that error of miscalculation (as well as method) should be corrected, as far as possible, by the pupil himself. A child should not be allowed to say, or fall into the way of thinking, that a sum "won't come out right." On the contrary, he ought to be made to believe that a sum "*must* come out right"; and if a sum, right in principle, has resulted in an erroneous answer, owing to some miscalculation, the sum should be returned to him, that he may work it over again and detect his error. "But may not a child weary himself thus endlessly, by repeating some error into which he may have fallen by a temporary lapse of memory, fancying, for example, that $8 \times 9 = 73$, or that 28 cwt. $= 1$ ton? A mistake of this kind cannot be detected by the child himself, though he may labor for twenty-four hours."

True; and, therefore, after a child has made one attempt to correct an error, the teacher may come to his assistance in one of two ways: (1) either he may tell the pupil to refresh his memory as to "8 times" in the Multiplication Table, or to study the Table of Weights and Measures, and then to try again; or else, (2) the pupil may work the sum aloud before the teacher, and have his error or errors pointed out; but, in either case, the teacher should not be satisfied till the pupil has worked through the whole sum by himself correctly.

(3) Children should be taught to be slow, and to think, in the reasoning part of arithmetic, but to be quick, and not to think, in the mechanical part.

If a child is slow in calculation, he is likely to be inaccurate; for his slowness increases the chance that he will not be able to keep up the strain of attention for the necessary time to finish the process of calculation.

Working in competition with others, working against time, and constant repetition of Tables, whenever an error in any Table has been made—these are the best means for securing rapidity in the mechanical processes of Arithmetic.

ENGLISH COMPOSITION AND GRAMMAR.

43. A NATURAL STYLE.

In teaching children English Composition, the teacher must be on his guard against destroying the naturalness of their style. A child must not be expected to use the ample vocabulary or flexible phraseology of his elders; and if his rudimentary attempts at composition are corrected by the standard of a mature composer, he is likely to be discouraged by the multiplicity of the corrections, and also to fall into a premature and affected employment of language that has for him but little meaning. Of all dangers, artificiality in composition is the most to be avoided. It is difficult, and, indeed, hardly possible, to recover the power of writing naturally when once lost; and an unnatural style is an obstacle to thinking clearly, as well as to writing forcibly. Therefore:

Let children write, as they speak and as they think, after the manner of children.

But of course we are not to leave children at a stand, to be children always in thought and language. We must endeavor both to improve their style and to develop their faculty of thought, taking care that the former may keep pace with, but not outrun, the latter. Even a child can understand, besides grammatical errors, (1) the mischief of ambiguity, (2) the utility of brevity, and (3) to some extent, the superiority of pointed, forcible, and picturesque expressions over those which are flat, dull, and colorless. Later on, he may also be made to understand (4) the advantages of order. On the whole, we may say, as a general rule:

Let the teacher insert no correction of which the pupil cannot see the advantage.

44. THE USE OF CONVERSATION FOR THE PURPOSE OF COMPOSITION.

It is obvious that if we are to improve a child's power of writing, and yet to encourage him to write as he speaks, we must not allow him to speak in a slovenly way.

Care will be required here, on the one hand, not to pass over so many inexact or uncouth expressions as to confirm the child in bad habits of expression, and, on the other hand, not to correct him so constantly, especially before strangers, as to make the very act of speaking a burden to him. It must be remembered, also, that in conversation, as in everything else, the child will imitate those around him, and will be fluent or hesitating, exact or inexact, weak or forcible, very much after the pattern of those with whom he has to do.

45. THE USE OF LETTERS IN COMPOSITION.

The best exercises for young children are letters; because in letters they may most easily acquire the art of writing naturally, that is, the art of writing as one would speak.

If possible, the letters should be *bona fide*, *i.e.*, letters written to some one who is, or may be supposed to be, interested in reading them. They may be corrected by pointing out, (1) how nouns or pronouns have been unnecessarily repeated; (2) how facts have been inexactly or ambiguously expressed; (3) how incidents, or features in incidents likely to be interesting to the intended reader, have been omitted by the child. Corrections of the kinds (1) and (2) will increase ease, neatness, and exactness; corrections of the kind (3) will increase picturesqueness of style.

Without any direct praise of the style, the teacher may sometimes apply a useful stimulus by finding occasion to say of a better letter than usual, "I think —— will be interested in reading this letter."

"In correcting letters," says Preceptor, "the teacher must carefully distinguish between differences of thought and differences of expression, and must very seldom correct the former. For example, a brother and sister having seen a hare in the field, may describe the sight in two totally different manners. I remember that a boy of a statistical and matter-of-fact turn of mind, actually described such a sight thus: 'Yesterday, while we were driving along the road to ——, a hare started in a field about twenty yards to the right of us, and ran some sixty yards in a northwest direction, after which, it turned into a wood on the left, and disappeared.' But his sister, seeing precisely the same thing, might describe it thus: 'As we were out on a drive, we saw such a pretty brown hare, quite close to us; and as soon as it saw us, it rushed away over the grass, and hid itself in a thick wood.'"

Here our teacher will probably agree with Preceptor that it would be equally unwise to try to make the boy's style more picturesque, and the girl's more statistical. Each must write what is in his own mind. All that the teacher can do with advantage will be to make an occasional comment on the boy's style, to the effect that "——will not be much interested in this letter;" or, on the girl's, that "—— will not be able to understand from this letter when, or where, this or that took place, or how it happened."

46. THE USE OF TALES IN COMPOSITION.

Letters cannot be regularly used as exercises; for it cannot regularly happen that a child will have matter for a letter; and more harm than good will be done by compelling him to write letters when he really has nothing to say.

Another method of teaching English Composition is to tell children interesting stories, and (some time afterwards) to require them to set down one of these stories in writing.

"History," writes Preceptor, "unless treated from its romantic and picturesque side, is by no means adapted for these exercises. Until a child is old enough to understand the relative importance of historical events—a narrative of wars, rebellions, intrigues, treaties, and negotiations is mostly unintelligible, and entirely dull. Biography is not much better for very young children. In the life of a great statesman or general, neither the obstacles to success, nor the successes, nor the failures are upon the level of a child's experience and understanding, and the following brief 'Life of the Earl of Essex'—which was actually sent up to me—represents, without exaggeration, the marvellous instinct with which the boyish mind relieves itself of indigestible encumbrances, and selects those few attractive incidents which it can retain without injury: 'The Earl of Essex was a great man. He lived in the reign of Queen Elizabeth, who gave him a ring and a box on the ear. He was executed in that reign.'"

For older children, some of the stories of ancient history (such as the death of Leonidas at Thermopylæ) can be made intelligible and attractive; but, for the younger, it will be more profitable to employ fiction, and the ordinary fairy tales will be found the best and simplest. If the teacher can tell stories of his own, and if his own stories interest children more than the far better tales which he remembers from Grimm and Hans Andersen, the inferior are, for the purpose in hand, superior. In any case, spoken stories are much better than stories read from a book.

The favorite stories should be repeated several times before the child is asked to write them down. Thus, besides stimulating his imagination, you will have insensibly enlarged his vocabulary and his store of idioms; and if you do not too much "speak down to" the child, he will gradually shake off the first stiffness of a child's style, and acquire flexibility and variety.

Teaching by stories has two great advantages over teaching by letters. First, you can criticise the boy's narrative, when dull and tedious, by reminding him that he has left out this or that point of interest; secondly, you can criticise faults of arrangement by pointing out how the disarrangement confused the story. This cannot be done so well with a letter, which the pupil may naturally regard as a narrative of his own, which he tells as it occurred to him; but the story is yours, and the pupil more readily acquiesces in your right to dictate how it should be told, and appreciate the superiority of your version over his.

47. TYPICAL SENTENCES.

At this stage the pupil may now, without danger of corrupting or, if I may use such a word, artificializing his style, be taught the use of a few forms of sentences.

He ought to have begun, before this time, to learn English Grammar; but, whether he has begun or not, he can be drilled in the use of conjunctions and participles by turning two sentences into a third, thus:

(1) "Dinner was now ready. (2) We all sat down."
(3) "As dinner was now ready, we all sat down."

Or, again, having given the child two short and simple sentences, such as, "John laughed. Thomas cried," you may drill him in the exercise of combining these two sentences, by means of some "joining word," thereby producing many different senses, thus: "John laughed because, since, as, while, when, though, Thomas cried."

You may then show the pupil how, without altering the sense, these "joining words" may be put first in the sentence: "If, because, since, as, while, when, though, Thomas cried, John laughed."

The following exercise may be useful as a pattern, with the aid of which it will be easy for the teacher to construct others of the same kind:

"Once the weather was very dry. A thirsty crow searched everywhere for water. She could not find a drop. She was croaking for sorrow. She spied a jug. Down she flew at once. She eagerly pushed in her bill. It was of no use. There was plenty of water in the jug. She could not reach it. The neck of the vessel was so narrow. She had tried in vain for half an hour to reach the water. She attempted to tip the jug over. It was too heavy for her. She could not stir it. She was on the point of giving up in despair. A new thought struck her. Said she, 'I will drop some stones in the jug. The water will rise higher. In time it will rise up to my bill.' She was nearly fainting with thirst. She bravely set to work. Each stone fell. The water rose. Half an hour had passed. The clever crow had drunk every drop in the jug."[1]

48. ENGLISH GRAMMAR.

If rightly taught, this subject may be made (even for young children of six or seven) a most interesting and rational study; but, as generally taught, it is the most mechanical, the most meaningless, and the most stupefying of all studies.

The reason for this deplorable failure is that the subject is over-

---

[1] "It is probable," writes Preceptor (but the Author has no experience to warrant more than a conjecture), "that much more may be done than is usually supposed possible, to improve the style of older students, by the use of typical sentences. Take, as an example, Denham's description of the Thames:

'Though deep yet clear, though gentle yet not dull,
Strong without rage, without o'erflowing full,'

on which many changes might be agreeably rung. 'Learned without pedantry, and witty without malice; though brief he was never obscure, and though forcible never coarse.' 'Though generous yet just, though rapid yet never rash, he was firm without obstinacy, and discreet without a trace of fear.'"

loaded with superfluous technicalities and confused mis-statements borrowed from Latin grammar. For example, in such a sentence as "The tall tree is in the field," a child is even now occasionally taught to "parse" the word "tree" as "a *common* noun, *neuter gender, third person.*"

Now as there are no inflections of gender at all in English adjectives, it is impossible, from the structure of a modern English sentence, to tell whether "tree" is neuter (as in Greek), or feminine (as in Latin), or masculine (as in French). All that can be said with truth (*in English*) is, that the word "tree" represents an object that is inanimate, which some people irrationally call "neuter."

Is this worth saying? Is it worth while compelling a boy, every time he parses a "Noun," to write down that it represents an animate or inanimate object. Why may he not, with equal advantage, write down that it represents a fluid or solid substance?

Again, the epithet "common," in "Common Noun," is intended to indicate that the Noun is not a *proper* name denoting a single object, like "Thomas"; nor does it denote something of an abstract nature, like "walking," "blindness," but it is a name "common" to the whole class of trees. But of what possible advantage is it to overload a child's memory (we cannot say his mind) with distinctions so subtle as these?

Lastly, why should the pupil be taught to repeat that "tree," in the above sentence, is "in the Third Person"? This merely means that the verb "is," agreeing with the Subject or Nominative "tree," is in the "Third Person"; and (seeing that *every Noun* may be said to be "in the Third Person" when it is the subject of a Verb) why not be content to confine this statement to the Verb, instead of extending it to the Noun? If the pupil is told that the Verb has different forms, according as its subject is the First, Second, or Third Person, and that *every Noun subject* requires the Verb to be "in the Third Person," that is intelligible; but to force a boy to write down, after every Noun, that it is "in the Third Person" is a cruel waste of time for a dull boy, and an impudent attempt to impose upon a quick boy. Naturally, the vast majority of boys, the dull and ordinary, not being able to apprehend the slightest reason for all these reiterated technicalities, give up the subject as unintelligible, and, trusting entirely to memory, dispense altogether with the understanding.

The consequence is that while many children who have learned English Grammar for several months or years can repeat with great promptness long, difficult, and sometimes erroneous and inadequate definitions of the Parts of Speech, and are fluent in such valuable pieces of grammatical information as that "cow" is the feminine of "bull," and "ram" the masculine of "sheep," they are very often unable to tell the Parts of Speech in the easiest sentence with any degree of certainty or accuracy. In no other subject are children so frequently in the habit of answering wildly, and in a tone of interrogation, displaying that promptness to substitute new answers for the old answers, which is an invariable proof of total ignorance.

Discontent with the results of the parsing system has led many to substitute for it "Analysis of Sentences." But even the teaching of this subject has been unnecessarily complicated and confused by a want of common sense and of constant reference to first principles. For example, one of the most popular treatises on Analysis confuses together (or till recently confused) the two quite distinct uses of the Relative Pronoun in the two sentences, (1) " The man that is passionately fond of music gains much pleasure," and (2) "The concert had great attractions for my brother, who is passionately fond of music."

In (1) the words, "that is passionately fond of music" are equivalent to an Adjective, viz., "music-loving"; in (2) the words " who is passionately fond of music," are equivalent to " for he is passionately fond of music," and constitute a new *sentence conveying the reason* for a previous statement. But, in the Treatise just mentioned, one uniform rule having been mechanically laid down for the use of the Relative Pronoun in analysis, this manifest distinction was ignored; and certified masters of considerable standing and of more than ordinary ability were taught, and taught others, to perpetuate this indiscriminating error, and to say that in both cases "the Relative Pronoun introduces an Attribute."

The remedy seems to be in teaching English Grammar and Analysis, 1st, and most important of all, *not to teach anything that the teacher does not himself understand and perceive to be true;* 2d, not to teach anything that does not develop the mind of the pupil or facilitate the comprehension of language; 3d, to avoid technicalities as far as possible, and, where they are necessary, to use such terms as explain themselves; 4th, although it may be necessary *in a written Grammar*, which aims at completeness, to deal with a great number of grammatical distinctions and to use a good many technical terms, the teacher will do well to pass over some, or altogether omit them, in order to dwell more on others which are of greater importance.

One of the best mental exercises in Grammar for young children is the "Parsing," or distinguishing the Parts of Speech. Mechanically taught, this is useless, or worse than useless; but if children can be taught to classify words rationally, as they would classify leaves, or stones, or figures, the hrocess combines something of the interest of botany with something of the interest of logic. The following are the principles on which a child should be taught how to tell the Parts of Speech:

1. The pupil must be taught by experiment, *i.e.*, experimenting with words.

2. As the specimens with which a boy is taught botany must be such as he himself can see, handle, and dissect, so the words with which a boy is to be taught grammar must be such as he himself can

use with ease and accuracy, because he thoroughly comprehends their meaning.

3. Starting from his own words the pupil must be led to answer the question, what his words *do*, or what they *tell* him. For example, in "Thomas runs," "runs" tells you what Thomas *does*, Thomas tells you the *name* of the person who runs; or, again, in "the black dog runs quickly," "black" tells you what kind of a dog it is; "quickly" tells you *how* he runs.

4. Having made separate columns for these different classes of words, the boy may collect specimens (extracted from sentences of his own) of the words that tell him (1) the *names* of persons and things; (2) the *kinds* of things; (3) what any thing *does;* and (4) *how, when,* or *where* anything is done.

5. After this, you may teach the pupil (by experiments) how inconvenient it sometimes is to repeat a name, or noun, every time we want to speak of a person or thing; and thus you may lead him to see the use of "he," etc., etc., and other (5) words that stand *for nouns*. (6) By showing him how to *join two sentences* by the insertion of a word between them, you lead him to classify "words that join sentences," which for a time he may be allowed to call *Joiners*.

6. The ordinary definition of a Preposition, which introduces the word "relation," is totally unfit for children. But you may point out how, in answer to the question *where? whither?* or *whence?—i.e.,* in answer to questions about *place*—we find ourselves unable sometimes to reply in one word, and are obliged to use two or three words, as "*in* the room," "*to* the room," "*from* the room." Words thus *placed before* names are called *Prepositions* (i.e., "*placed before*"). When a list has been made of them by experiment, they may be committed to memory.

7. Not till the child is familiar with the classification of the *functions of words*, i.e., readily able to tell you what words *do*, should he be introduced to the names of the classes of words based upon this classification.

8. Some teachers wrongly suppose that there is little difference between this system (which may be called the *inferential*) and the ordinary system (which may be called *explanatory*); and they fancy that equally satisfactory results can be obtained by allowing the pupil to start with the definitions of the terms Verb, Adverb, etc., provided that, after he has assigned any word to its class, he is compelled to tell you *why* the word is a Verb, Adverb, or whatever else.

But a little experience and the laws of human nature should prevent us from confusing two systems radically distinct.

9. When a boy has once said that a word is a verb, he will easily find a reason for it somehow. Our object is to keep the mind of the pupil *free from prejudice;* but having committed himself to a theory, he is no longer impartial. And the duller sort of boys are so fond of

such technicalities as may seem to dispense with the use of the understanding that they will naturally flee to the technical term *first*, and put off thinking about the reason till afterwards, that is to say, forever.

Let none, therefore, suppose that the system of *giving reasons* for Parts of Speech is the same as that of *inferring the Parts of Speech from the functions of the word in the sentence*.

A thorough drill in "stating functions" should be practiced before the names of any Parts of Speech are communicated to the pupil.

10. A great deal of time is often wasted and hand-writing spoiled by doing too many grammatical exercises on paper, especially where grammatical abbreviations are not allowed. Answers that can be given orally in a very short time occupy much space, and involve much weary and unprofitable repetition.

The written exercises should therefore be few, in comparison with the oral; and before a written exercise is allowed, the teacher should write out several model exercises, showing how to arrange the answers, how to economize space, and how to save needless repetitions.

11. In Elementary Grammar, although the book may call attention to anomalies early, for the sake of completeness and logical order, the teacher should omit them at first, recurring to them afterwards. For example, in introducing the pupil to Adjectives, the teacher should at first speak only of the class of words that tell us *the kind of thing*. Afterwards he may mention other Adjectives, such as Numeral, Demonstrative, etc.

12. In order to impress upon the pupil that the Part of Speech always depends upon the Function of the word, *i.e.*, upon what the word *does*, it will be useful to show him by instances that the same word may often belong to different Parts of Speech in different sentences. In illustration of this rule, the pupil should be taught to parse sentences containing "before" and "after," used now as Prepositions, now as Adverbs, now as Conjunctions.

13. In the higher Grammar, special attention should be given to sentences containing Relative Pronouns. In such a sentence as "The cat that killed my canary was black and white," a boy will naturally think the verb "killed" more important than the verb "was"; and so undoubtedly it is, so far as the canary and its owner are concerned. Hence, when the boy applies the familiar rule, "To find the Subject of a Verb, ask the question, Who? or What? before the Verb," he will naturally say, What killed my canary? The cat. Therefore "cat" is the subject of "killed."

To guard him against this error (which is extremely common) he must be warned that:

Rule.—*Whenever there is a Relative Pronoun in a sentence, two verbs should be parsed before the Subject of either is written down.*

He will then ask not only, "Who killed?" but also, "What was black and white?" The cat. Therefore "cat" is the subject of "was." Hence he will be led to rectify his error, and to see that the subject of "killed" is the Relative Pronoun "that."

The omission of the Relative must also be noted on such sentences as, "Where is the book I lent you?"

14. The distinctions between the Participle and the Verbal Noun should be carefully taught (1) "*Walking* on the ice, I fell," and (2) "I like *walking*."

15. The distinctions between different kinds of Infinitives, *e.g.* (1) "I like *to walk;*" (2) "I have come to Switzerland *to walk;*" (3) "The physician advised me *to walk;*" "The general ordered him *to be put to death;*" "She taught me *to sing*."

16. One negative caution may be given. In teaching Grammar, it ought not to be the teacher's object to enable the pupil to *speak* English, but to *understand* it.

To speak English, he will best learn by speaking and reading it, not by committing to memory lists of irregular words, mostly of foreign origin, such as "cherub," "cherubim," "appendix," "appendices," "locus," "loci," etc.

Such words as these, boys will either never use, or they will learn to use them by hearing others use them; and those who use them intelligently (by whom alone they should be used) for the most part use them correctly.

On the other hand, the confusion of the parts of the two verbs, *lie* and *lay*, is very common in some classes of boys; and the misuse of the Past Indicative and the Passive Participle of *sing*, *drink*, etc., is not much less common.[1] Attention to real existing grammatical errors of this kind is by no means misplaced.

17. As to the Analysis of Sentences, the best and most obvious kind is that which shows how every sentence that is complete in itself can (however complicated) be reduced to three or four parts: (1) a Verb; (2) a Subject, with an adjective or adjectives; (3) one or more Adverbs; (4) an Object, with one or more adjectives. Thus:

The horses	Subject.
that had been caught by our soldiers	Adjective.
being (i.e., *since they were*) *unable to find pasture,*	Adverb (Cause).[2]
were slain,	Verb.
by orders of the general,	{ Adverb (of Cause or Circumstance).
in order to supply food to the starving citizens:	Adverb (of Purpose).[2]

---

[1] "In a certain part of England," writes Preceptor, "not far from the center of the national life, it is very common, at public dinners, to hear a speaker thank the guests for having so very cordially *drank* his health; and, in the same region, not only hens, but boys, and even men, are in the habit of *laying* upon the grass."

[2] As it is often difficult to determine whether an Adverbial phrase represents circumstance, cause, instrumentality, agency, or purpose, it will probably be best to let the pupil omit distinctions of Adverbs.

49. THE IRREGULARITIES OF ENGLISH IDIOM.

(For advanced pupils.)

Into this subject the pupil would not enter until he had reached at least his twelfth or thirteenth year; and some may think that for those intending to learn Latin or Greek attention to the irregularities of the English Language may be unnecessary.

But there is one respect in which a pupil's native language far exceeds others in the mental training it affords through the elucidation of idiomatic difficulties. Every irregularity arises by deviation from some regularity. Having at command the regular construction from which the deviation has arisen, a native possesses some at least of the *data* for determining the causes of the irregularity. In Latin and Greek a boy may be unable to analyze an irregular idiom for want of this knowledge; in English, for an English boy, this obstacle will, at all events, be absent.

The following are the principles upon which the pupil should be taught to analyze idiomatic difficulties. Ascertain the regularity from which the irregularity is derived, whether it be:

(1) Desire of brevity.
(2) Confusion of two constructions.
(3) Desire to avoid harshness of sound or construction.

(1) "He loved her *as* his own daughter," *i.e.*, "as (he would have loved) his own daughter" (Brevity).

(2) "All of us remonstrated." This is illogical. You can say "some, many, none, few, ten, one, *of*, i.e., *out of* or *from* us, remonstrated," but you cannot logically say " all *of* us "; you ought to say " all we," as in the Bible, " all we like sheep have gone astray."

But the much more common idiom with "of," as in " one, two, three, four, etc., *of* us " has been *confused* with " all *we*," and the result of the confusion is " *all of us*."

"Confusion" is the most common cause of irregularities of construction in the English Language, as in many others, and it may be illustrated by the common tendency to confuse together any names or titles that have any similarity. Thus, suppose there are two Dictionaries, one by "Liddell and Scott," the other by "Lewis and Short "; if a boy speaks, by a slip, of "Liddell and Short," or "Lewis and Scott," it is an error of *confusion;* and how very common such errors are we all know. But it is this same confusion applied to syntax which has produced most of the irregularities of language.

(3) "It is you that say so."

Here the regular construction would be "It that says so is you."[1] But first the desire (iii.) to avoid the harsh emphasis laid on "it" causes a transposition " it is you that *says* so."

Secondly, this sentence is (ii.) confused with the straightforward

---

[1] Compare "Thou art *it that* hath cut Rahab."

statement, "you *say* so," and the result is the irregular idiom, "It is you that say so."

With these two keys of Syntax, viz., "Brevity" and "Confusion," occasionally adding the use of the key "Euphony," a student may open a multitude of idiomatic mysteries, in English as well as in other languages.

50. MEMORY.

The memory in some children appears to be much stronger than that of men, in others, it seems weaker, and a few seem to have scarcely any power of learning anything by heart.

The words "appears" and "seems" are used deliberately, because in many cases what appears to be a naturally defective memory is really a fair memory spoiled by defective training, and capable (if taken in hand not too late) of regaining some of its original power.

1. Memory may be cultivated by training a child from the first to do one thing at a time, or, in other words, by cultivating in him the habit of *Attention* (see § 4).

2. A memory may also be strengthened by cultivating the faculties of *Imagination* and *Association*, so that the child may readily call up *images* of the things which he hears described, and afterwards may recall thoughts by *associating* them with these mental pictures. For example, if a child is taught to associate the youth of Francis Bacon with the apt reply which he is said to have made to Queen Elizabeth's inquiry about his age, that striking association will readily enable the pupil to remember the date of Bacon's birth.

3. A serviceable memory will obviously be strengthened by *judgment* and the faculty of *selection*, which will enable the child, when reading or hearing about any facts that may be described as "central," to eliminate many details of little importance and to select those circumstances which are essential or important, clustering them round their appropriate centres.

4. Every one knows that memory is strengthened by *repetition*.

5. Memory is probably not much affected by the will in any direct way. It is doubtful whether any one can remember the parts of a Greek or Latin verb by greatly desiring to remember them. All that the will can do seems to be of a preliminary and negative nature. A boy, while learning his Greek verb, can *will* not to listen to the jokes of his companions, or to an organ-grinder in the street; and in some boys the will is entirely, in others only partially, able so to exclude distractions as to let him concentrate all his attention on the matter in hand. The rest must be done by the process of repetition. Attention and repetition enable him so to associate the forms of the verb together that one calls up the other, and in the end *amo* readily suggests twenty or thirty other forms; so that indirectly the will helps the Memory, by fostering and protecting it.

But in a direct way the will appears to do nothing for the Memory;

and the boy who—instead of thinking about the similarities and dissimilarities of am-o,-as,-at,-amus,-atis,-ant,—is simply *willing* to learn his Latin Verb, in order that he may escape punishment or gain reward, is really taking his thoughts off that which should be the object of them, defeating himself, and harming, not helping, Memory. For this reason, teachers must not always treat children that cannot remember as though they did not "wish to remember." Any child, even the laziest, would wish to remember rather than to forget and be punished. The fault lies very often not in the will, but in the interest.

The truth is that we remember best by no means those things which we desire to remember, but those things which (1) present themselves to us from the first in the most interesting or incisive form, or (2) are impressed by constant repetition.

As for the power of repetition, one illustration is sufficient. No one finds any difficulty in repeating the Alphabet forwards, while very few could repeat it backwards. Logically, one order should be as easy as the other; but, in practice, one order is so common and the other so rare, that the former seems to come to us by second nature, while the latter always implies an effort.

But few teachers understand the importance of "the first impression" in matters of Memory. A word that takes the ear and is clearly pronounced, such as "Mesopotamia" will have a much better chance of being remembered than shorter and less euphonious words, inarticulately uttered.

"Above all things," writes Preceptor, "avoid blurred impressions. When Dr. Johnson (a man of singularly wide and retentive memory) heard a person's name for the first time, he would always repeat it, and generally spell it over to himself. If people of less powerful memories adopted the same habit, they would probably find it more easy to remember names. But it is often too late to do this when you have once formed a blurred impression. You hear a person, say, of the name of Robson called 'Mr. Robson,' or 'Mr. Robinson,' you are not certain which, and you do not at once take the trouble to ascertain which; unless some striking inconvenience forces you to remember that it is 'Robson,' and not 'Robinson,' you may go on for years occasionally meeting the man, and not unfrequently talking about him, and yet always in doubt between the two names."

The following suggestions may therefore be useful for helping children in performing memory-tasks.

(1) Let the child learn them when he is at his freshest, and not too tired to be interested and receptive.

(2) Before the task is learned, go through it with him, reading it incisively, and explaining difficulties.

(3) Divide it into parts; and, if possible, point out a connection between the parts.

Even when no connection can be established, the division into parts is a most important preparation for a memory-lesson. How hopelessly the child looks up at the stars, thinking that no one can ever master their relative positions! Yet let the child begin with Charles's Wain, and then draw lines from this to the Pole Star and to others, and he will find that, by dividing the stars into "constellations," he speedily acquires a knowledge which he would have thought impossible. The same rule holds for the memory of other things (§ 6). As the teacher's motto is "Divide and teach," so should the pupil's be, "Divide and remember."

(4) Let there be sometimes an interval of a night between the teacher's explanation and the pupil's learning, so that there may be time for "unconscious cerebration,"—a power which all teachers must recognize.

(5) In some children, what may be called the sound-memory is most powerful, in others, the sight-memory. It is well to utilize both. To be compelled to learn a memory lesson in a schoolroom where silence is enjoined is a severe restriction for children in whom the sound-memory is strong.

6. In learning rules for which it is difficult or impossible to give children intelligible reasons, there seems no reason why recourse should not be allowed to artificial associations, such as rhyming verses. For lists of exceptional genders, such a help appears quite justifiable. The rational faculty, having no province here, cannot be supposed to have its sovereignty weakened by the appeal to mere memory.

7. But in learning dates it is probably best to trust mainly to the reason. The verses or other means sometimes adopted for impressing dates on the memory have these disadvantages: 1st, that they are generally either long or else arbitrary; 2d, that they take up so much attention as to indispose the boy for appealing to his Reason.

Again, the artificial system is not progressive. For if a boy relies on *Memoria Technica*, he requires separate artificial helps for every date in the history of every nation; but if he learns by heart a few important dates, and gradually clusters round these, as centers, a knowledge of groups of less important incidents, he will gradually form a kind of star-map of chronology, which will be of some value to him as a mental training, besides the utility of the information. Should the *Memoria Technica* unfortunately vanish from the brain, every vestige of information vanishes with it; but, even though he may forget the precise date, the boy who has appealed to his reason may remember that Mohammed, for example, began to gain followers at the commencement of the seventh century, that the Saracens invaded Spain early in the eighth century, and that Charlemagne, who drove back the tide of invasion successfully, was crowned emperor at the beginning of the ninth century.

But the use of Reason ought not to prevent the careful learning by heart of some of the more important dates, and these ought to be repeated over and over again till they are indelibly impressed on the memory.

8. In answer, therefore, to the question, What should be learned by heart? the answer will be: Learn (a) things that cannot be recalled by the reason, e.g., lists of genders, tables of weights and measures; (b) things that need to be recalled more quickly than the reason will recall them; (c) things that could not readily be recalled in so exact or so fit a shape by the reason as by the memory, e.g. Euclid's Axioms, the verses of poets, etc.[1]

In other matters, the appeal should be made not to the Memory, but to the Reason; and the pupil should be encouraged to answer questions on History, Algebra, Geometry, Arithmetic, not in the words of the book, but—so far as he can with accuracy and fitness—in his own words.

9. A memory-lesson, if learned at all, should be thoroughly learned. After two or three lessons, the whole should be revised; and constant revision should be practiced till the pupil is quite familiar with it.

10. In order that a child may remember, he should have intervals for reflection. The brain is bewildered and wearied if it is hustled from one subject to other subjects for many hours together, all novel, and all requiring sustained attention. Play gives rest from work, but not time for reflection. For this reason, in day-schools, a daily walk to and from school is of great value for the strengthening of the memory.

51. REPETITION OF POETRY.

The repetition of poetry is important because, besides strengthening the memory, it enriches the vocabulary, enlarges the imagination, and improves the sense of rhythm.

1. *Choice of passages.*—In selecting a passage to be learned, the teacher must remember that it is not the language of poetry, but the *thought*, that for the most part creates difficulties for children. We must not fancy that long words in poetry repel boys that can read fluently. Poetry, by its very nature, is averse to lengthy, technical, and abstract terms, such as create difficulties in prose. But the *subject-matter* of poetry is very often altogether above the heads of children, though expressed in the simplest language. The *In Memoriam* is written mainly in monosyllables; yet there is in it little which a child could thoroughly understand; and for a young boy, ignorant of the meaning of the "loss of friends," and wholly unable (so Nature has decreed it) to realize the meaning of death, it is impossible really to understand (and not desirable that he should be forced to appear to understand) even the following simple stanza:

> "This truth came borne with bier and pall,
> I felt it when I sorrowed most,
> 'Tis better to have loved and lost
> Than never to have loved at all."

---

[1] See Fitch's *Lectures on Teaching*, p. 135.

But give a boy a piece of description, narrative, or stirring incident, and you will find that long words will create little difficulty. Such passages may be found in the well-known *Original Poems*, *The Ancient Mariner*, Howitt's *Birds and Flowers*, Macaulcy's *Lays*, and Scott's Poems; but a careful selection might also extract some passages, intelligible even for the very young, from Milton's description of the *Creation*, Shakespeare's *Julius Cæsar* (and perhaps the *Coriolanus*), the story of Orlando rescuing Oliver in *As You Like It*, some of the Choruses in *Henry the Fifth*, and the description of the hunting of the hare (*Poor Wat*) in the *Venus and Adonis*, to which might be added the larger part of Milton's *Allegro* and *Penseroso*. I lay the more stress on Shakespeare and Milton because early familiarity with them, next to the Bible, has more power than the study of any other author to develop a sense of rhythm.

2. *Preparation.*—Having selected your passage, you must then read it to the pupil in such a way as to interest him. Explain difficulties, ask and answer questions; and (if there is leisure for it) draw out from the pupil, by a series of questions, a narrative containing the substance of the passage to be repeated.

In doing this, be careful to dwell on the "joints" or transitions of the narrative, always connecting each new part with the part before, so that the whole chain may be in the pupil's mind in such a way that each link may suggest the next. Never let the child try to keep in his mind three links together. *Two at a time are enough.*

By voice, action, and suggestion, try to call up before the child pictures corresponding to the language.

3. *The First· Repetition Lesson.*—It is very important that a child should be taught at the very beginning to assume, as a matter of course, that he can repeat poetry; and consequently the teacher must spare no pains to make the first lesson a success. The effects of failure here are so disastrous that it seems worth while to set down in full the somewhat quaint and lengthy description given by Preceptor of a First Repetition Lesson.

"I assume," he says, "that the child may have picked up a few nursery rhymes, but that he has not yet learned a continuous passage: and we are now to begin. I select a piece of Jane Taylor's, called 'The Pond,' describing how a disobedient chicken, attempting to swim in spite of her mother's commands, was drowned. After reading it over, I reject the second and third stanzas for the present, because the author speaks in her own person, and breaks the simple course of events; I also reject the last, because it contains no incident, and a moral expressed in language somewhat too elderly for my young pupil of five or six.

"Having mastered the first stanza so that I am *quite sure I can repeat it myself*, I turn the conversation, one morning at breakfast, on ponds;

and putting my saucer before the child, I say, 'I remember a pretty tale about a pond; it begins like this:

"'There was a round pond, and a pretty pond too,'

Here I draw my finger once or twice round the saucer:

"'About it white daisies and violets grew,'

Here I call up the salt-cellar to represent the 'daisies,' and anything else to represent the 'violets':

"'And dark weeping-willows, that stoop to the ground,
Dipped in their long branches, and shaded it round.'

Here I slope two spoons or forks over the saucer, and bend them over to represent the 'willows.'

"If the child is sufficiently interested, I repeat this pantomime; and there, for that day, the matter ends. Next day the same is repeated, and either then or afterwards, when I feel sure the child has grasped the lines, I say, 'Now, you do it,' and I put the 'pond,' the 'violets,' and the 'willow,' *i.e.*, the saucer, salt-cellar, and spoons, ready for him to manipulate.

"If this stanza is correctly repeated (as it was by my youngster) the battle is won. What follows is an easy task. After the lines have been several times repeated, and are quite mastered, I let drop the remark that the story goes on to describe how a disobedient chicken came to this pond and watched the ducklings swimming in it:

"*How the Chicken comes and watches the Ducklings swimming in the Pond.*

"'One day a young chicken, that lived thereabout,
Stood watching to see the ducks pop in and out,
Now splashing above, and now diving below,
She thought of all things she should like to do so.'

The first two stanzas must now be several times repeated, together with their titles. First, let us have 'The Pond,' now, 'How the chicken comes and watches the ducklings swim in the Pond.' We can then introduce a third title, thus: 'After the chicken watches the ducklings, the story tells us how the chicken determined to try to swim'; and the *second and third* stanzas must be repeated together, the third being as follows:

"*How the Chicken determined to swim.*

"'So the poor silly chick was determined to try;
She thought 'twas as easy to swim as to fly;
Though her mother had told her she must not go near,
She foolishly thought there was nothing to fear.'

We continue, 'After the chicken had determined to disobey her mother,' the story goes on to tell:

"*What the Chicken said in excuse for her disobedience.*

"'"My feet, wings, and feathers, for aught I can see,
As good as the ducks' are for swimming," said she;
"Though my beak is pointed, and their beaks are round,
Is that any reason that I shall be drowned?"'

A revision may now be desirable, and when the above four stanzas have been revised, we shall omit the next stanza, which prolongs the chicken's excuse, and continue, 'After the chicken had excused herself,' the story goes on to tell:

> "*How the ignorant creature flew into the water.*
>
> "'So in this poor ignorant animal flew,
> But soon found her mother's cautions were true;
> She splashed and she dashed, and she turned herself round,
> And heartily wished herself safe on the ground.'

The last stanza is introduced by saying that 'After the chicken had flown into the pond,' the story tells us:

> "*How she was drowned.*
>
> "'But now 'twas too late to begin to repent;
> The harder she struggled the deeper she went;
> And when every effort she vainly had tried,
> She slowly sank down to the bottom and died.'

We shall now revise the last three stanzas, the Excuse, the Leap into the Pond, and the Drowning. Finally, we shall practice the child in repeating a rapid summary of the whole poem, viz., the Pond, Watching the Ducklings, the Determination, the Excuse, the Leap, the Drowning."

Much of this detail will seem to many grotesque or superfluous; but we have given it in full, partly because we understand that it contains the record of a lesson which has actually proved successful, partly because many parents or tutors may be desirous of trying this same exercise themselves as a first lesson in continuous repetition, and partly because Preceptor's experience is certainly based on, and clearly exemplifies, two important principles of memory: first, division; second, what may be called the linking system. First, the poem was *divided* by the teacher into sections; secondly, each section was *linked* with the one following it.

The professional teachers of systems of Memoria Technica are well acquainted with the "link-system"; and a string of nearly a hundred names (but carefully selected by the Professor with a view to the natural association between each pair) can sometimes be repeated by boys who, after once hearing it, observe the precept "never to think of more than two at a time." But the applicability of this system to verse-repetition is not so clearly recognized, and requires to be enforced.

For young children we need poems, or (better) songs, of a livelier kind than the Pond, but rather longer, and perhaps with a little more purpose, than the ordinary nursery rhymes. The songs of Froebel are too German for our children, both in the thoughts and in the allusions; but they are on the right lines, and it is to be regretted that we have at present nothing that can quite fill their place. Such poems should be accompanied by action, and if sung and acted by a large number of children together, they ought to be most usefully stimulative for dull children in whom the power of Association is naturally weak.

Cautions.—Two cautions are needed in the exercise of young memory.

1. The teacher must not expect that the child's memory will always retain its original strength. As the judgment strengthens, the memory weakens; and this is true not only of phenomenal memories (such as are recorded in "calculating boys"), but also of ordinary boys and girls.

Where this is the case, the teacher must be quick to discern it, and make allowance for it. But it is a good plan to cover a good deal of ground while the memory is young and strong, and as soon as the child has attained to the understanding of passages worth permanently remembering, to practice him in constant revision of old lessons. A good deal will inevitably slip away; but much that is of lasting value will thus remain.

2. Possibly copious repetition may be found, in some children, incompatible with *good* repetition; where, by "goodness," is meant, not accuracy, but excellence of elocution. The reason is, that it is difficult to find many passages worth permanently remembering, with which a child can so identify himself as to repeat them naturally and forcibly. A "permanent" passage of poetry will contain thoughts fit for men; and a boy, finding them unfitted for him, naturally repeats them as though they were not his, and falls into a monotone, or, at all events, fails in giving the words their due modulation. For boys, therefore, a permanent passage is generally most easily selected from serious poetry, where no great height or depth of passion is touched, and where an even modulation is not out of place, as in Milton's *Creation*, or the 104th Psalm in prose, or the 107th.

A good deal could be done (it is true) for elocution if you could secure that the child should never hear bad reading or elocution. Still, with some children, anything like acting is a physical impossibility; they shrink from it with a dislike which, being often associated with a just reserve, strength of character, and self-respect, deserves itself to be respected. Therefore, while requiring clearness and encouraging spirit, a teacher ought not to expect all children to show much elocutionary execution. But distinctness, at all events, may be enforced; and for this reason the pupil, when reciting, ought to stand at a considerable distance from the teacher.

52. FRENCH.

1. French should be begun between the age of six and seven, and, in any case, before Latin; partly for the sake of the French, because French can be better taught at home than at school; but partly, also, for the sake of the Latin, because, by beginning with French, a spoken language, the pupil acquires a sense of the utility of linguistic study generally, and is more likely to approach Latin, not as being a mere collection of Vocabularies, Declensions, and Conjugations, but as a language, if not to be spoken, at least to be read and used.

2. The first lessons in French should be oral. If a child begins with book-lessons, he is almost sure to trust for his pronunciation more to the book than to the teacher, and so he begins at once to pronounce badly. But if he learns his first French words *only from his teacher's lips*, he cannot (at least as the result of reading) pronounce the x in "deux," or the s in "nous" before a consonant, or leave them out before a vowel, for he does not know that the x and the s are there. For some time no attempt should be made to appeal to the Reason. Phrases, not separate words, should be taught, and no explanation should be given of grammatical structure. In the course of these sentences, the pupil must be told that among intimate friends in France "thou" is used instead of "you," so that the teacher may freely introduce the forms of Verbs in the second person singular.

3. These early phrases and short sentences should be such as to require a frequent repetition of the more common forms of the verbs "avoir" and "être"; and when the pupil is familiar with a great number of these, he may be called on to construct out of his store the Present Tense of "avoir." Then for the first time he may be told to write down these forms, and to note how greatly the pronunciation, to which he is now accustomed, differs from that which would appear to be pronunciation to an English boy reading French words without guidance; and now for the first time some rules of pronunciation may be given to him.

4. The pronunciation of the French *u* and of some of the nasal sounds will always present difficulties to English boys; but more might be done than is done at present to prevent boys from introducing English accent into French.

"I remember," says Preceptor, "being told, as a child, that I should not be able to read French correctly till I could repeat "le malade imaginaire" without laying the slightest accent on any syllable, as though it were 'le-ma-lad-im-ag-in-aire'; and for practical purposes this precept is very useful, as an antidote against the ordinary pronunciation, 'le mállard, or márlard imáginaire.'"

But when teachers try to put this rule in practice—say in the repetition of a Fable of La Fontaine—they will find it not so easy as it seems. For whereas Englishmen use much accent, but little modulation, Frenchmen compensate for their almost complete absence of accent by an abundant modulation, which would sound to English boys "sing-songy" and absurd. It follows that when English boys read La Fontaine without accent *and without modulation*, the effect is flat in the extreme; and teachers who may succeed in repressing English accent will mostly fail in inculcating, or never try to inculcate, French modulation.

However, what cannot be done in a class, where boys are deterred by the fear of "making themselves ridiculous" before their school-fellows, may be done much more easily with two or three private pupils;

and one reason for the early commencement of French is that a foundation of good pronunciation can be much more easily laid at home than at school.

5. The French names of Past Tenses given in most text-books are inconsistent with the terminology which the pupils will afterwards learn in Latin and English. In English the pupil is told that "I have spoken" is the Complete Present (or Perfect), and that "I spoke" is the Indefinite or Simple Past; but in French "j'ai parlé" is called the "Preterite Indefinite," and "je parlai" the "Preterite Definite."

If the names of the French Tenses are retained, it seems best to make no attempt to explain them; for though they can be explained, the nomenclature proceeds on less intelligible and symmetrical principles than those which regulate the names of the English Tenses.

In settling questions about Tenses it is not always necessary to trouble the pupils with the technical names of the Tenses. For their knowledge of the Tense can often be tested by asking them to "translate into French I have spoken, he will speak, you were speaking," etc.

53. LATIN.

1. *When to begin Latin.*—With a quick boy, Latin may be begun at the age of six-and-a-half or seven; but if a boy is in the country and amid circumstances which give him abundant opportunities for healthy exercise and amusement, it would probably be better to delay the study till ten. In towns, it is difficult to know how to fill a young boy's time without Latin. At seven years of age, he is not old enough to study history with any advantage; geography and chemistry, if imparted to him so young, will not be found to remain in him; and Arithmetic, French, and English are hardly sufficient to occupy his time. If opportunity allows, he might be taught something of botany and music; but where a boy of seven is healthy, lively, and interested in his studies, and is making sufficient progress in French and Arithmetic with two hours of work a day, it seems not premature to let him add a daily half-hour of Latin. After a week or two, a half-hour may be taken from French and given to Latin, so that he may be inspirited in his new study by the sense of rapid progress.

2. *The "Double System."*—Undoubtedly the best way to teach Latin is to enable the pupil, in his very first lesson, to utilize his knowledge so as to turn English into Latin, as well as Latin into English.

"As a boy," says Preceptor, "I had the experience of being trained for a time on what used to be called 'the Hamiltonian system,' and then on the old Grammar system, which taught a great mass of Accidence and Syntax before giving the pupil any opportunity of utilizing his knowledge; and as a teacher I taught Latin (for about ten years) on what is called 'the Crude Form system'; but I am convinced that none of these work so well as the 'Double System,' which makes the pupil 'give out' as fast as he 'takes in.'"

3. *Ambiguous Exercises.*—So far, then, Latin is to be taught like French, but it is also to be taught differently. For whereas the object of learning French is (mainly) to be able to speak and understand the language and literature, the object of learning Latin is (mainly) to strengthen the Reason and Judgment. Hence, whereas we began by teaching French without any appeal to Reason, in Latin the Reason must be called into play from the first.

Few text-books sufficiently recognize the necessity of early exercises which shall compel the pupil *from the beginning to use Reason;* but they can be easily composed by the teacher himself. They may be called " Ambiguous Exercises," and can be employed in the very first lesson. For when the pupil has learned by heart "Insula " or "Dominus," he should be at once required to translate into English, "insulæ," "domino," "insulis," etc., having been forewarned that "wherever Latin words are susceptible of two or more renderings, two or more must be given."

4. *The Cases.*—The force and use of the Cases should be explained as soon as they are introduced to the pupil's notice.

Some of the *names* of the Cases, *e.g.* Accusative, are so inherently absurd that no attempt should be made to explain these. The teacher should simply content himself with explaining their use.

But it may be at once pointed out that the Ablative, "besides always expressing (1) the *instrument* by or with which an action is performed, also sometimes expresses (2) separation, *motion from*, or *ablation*," and this should be illustrated at once by an example: *The woman frees the daughter from blame;* Fēmĭnă filĭam culpā lībĕrat.

By this means the boy is warned from the first that when you say *by* or *with* in connection with the Ablative Case, you do not use *by* in the sense of *near*, nor *with* in the sense of *along with*, and thus he is enabled to avoid much unnecessary confusion and bewilderment caused by the ordinary method of learning the Cases without explanation of their force.

The early introduction of the double meaning of the Ablative enables the teacher to introduce, in the very first week of learning Latin, such an ambiguous sentence as "Nautae dextrā fēmĭnam vĭŏlentĭā lībĕrat," which may be rendered, "The sailor's right hand liberates the woman "—either " by violence "[1] or "from violence," so as to oblige the pupil at an early stage to realize the necessity of pondering and judging before he decides on the meaning.

5. *The Discouragement of Guessing.*—The exercises, and especially those from Latin, into English, should not be so easy as to be construed without thought. It is of the utmost importance in teaching Latin to

---

[1] The question whether " vĭŏlentĭa " (a particularly useful word in early exercises) would be used in Classical Latin to represent "by violence " in precisely such a sentence as this is a refinement that need not trouble us at this stage; yet the teacher will do well, even at the outset, to avoid any glaring violations of the best Latin usage.

force the pupil at the commencement of the study *to distrust any inferences as to the meaning of a Latin sentence derived from the order of the words.*

"For a very long time," writes Preceptor, "(in the course of a weekly entrance examination of a most elementary kind) I have been in the habit of asking those boys who profess to have learned Latin—almost all of whom are over thirteen years of age, and have learned Latin two, three, four, or five years—to construe the sentence, 'Oppida magna boni agricolæ habent,' and not one in five has been able to construe these few simple words correctly. Such a translation as, 'They have the great towns of the good husbandmen,' would have been treated as satisfactory, because logical; but almost all have succumbed to the temptation of regarding 'oppida' as nominative 'because it comes first,' and they have then rushed to the conclusion, in despite of Cases and Grammar, that the meaning must be 'Great towns have good husbandmen.'"

This is the natural consequence of setting boys too easy exercises at first—exercises in which the paucity and order of the words, combined with the simplicity of the idioms, encourage a boy to jump at the meaning without troubling himself to think. The method is intended kindly; the teachers wish not to discourage the boys at the start by too difficult tasks. But it is not real kindness. The kinder plan would be to discourage jumping at once, not only by giving each boy a light and portable ladder, but also by making the wall so high that jumping shall either not be attempted, or shall result in an inevitable and retributary fall.

6. *Reasons for Rules.*—Since Latin is to be taught by an appeal rather to Reason than to Memory, the reasons for all rules should be given, so far as is possible.

Some rules—such as the rule which fordids the use of "neminis" and "nemine," and many of the rules and exceptions relating to genders—cannot be explained, and must be simply learned by heart. But many others can be, and should be, explained; and, in particular, the rule of Sequence of Tenses—which is sorely perplexing to those boys who have failed to grasp the difference between the English and Latin Tenses—can be made so easy and intelligible by a clear exposition of the force of the English "Complete Present," and of the wider use of the Latin so-called Perfect, that it is nothing short of cruelty to withhold the explanation.

7. *Recapitulation.*—The pupil should learn to turn his English Exercises into Latin not only in writing, but also orally and fluently.

A good First Latin Book ought to contain so much that the teacher should be able with advantage to make the pupil repeat the old exercises again and again, each time improving in fluency. It should also have appended a copious store of recapitulatory exercises, to test those too mechanical boys who succeed pretty well when they are "doing" one particular Rule, but fail when they are set to work in broader fields. The object should not be to cover a great deal of ground and to get through the book as soon as possible, but to get a firm grasp of first principles, and to combine accuracy with the habit of thinking. *Non multa, sed multum* should be the motto, and the exercises may very well suffice for two years, and may be continued into the stage when the pupil has begun to construe some author.

8. *Aim at the Future.*—Yet, while accuracy should be rated very high, perfect and machine-like accuracy should not be exacted at the cost of real progress and interest.

The teacher should remember, when he finds a boy, at the age of eleven or twelve, making an occasional mistake about a gender, that this boy will continue Latin, probably, till the age of sixteen, and, in many cases, till nineteen, or longer. Five or seven years of future practice ought, therefore, to be taken into account when the teacher considers the object he wishes to attain and the means of attaining it. We are to work for the future, not for the present. The race is to be a long one; and we are to set our minds not on getting over the first hundred yards as rapidly as possible, but on reaching a goal that lies a long way off, the attainment of which will require sustained interest as well as steady labor. A mistake about gender is not so serious a fault as a mistake of judgment: It concerns not the Reason, but the Memory. If these mistakes do not gradually disappear, we may naturally suspect that the pupil is either singularly deficient in memory, or is not giving his mind to the work; and, in that case, some special drill or animadversion may be needed. But if progress in accuracy is perceptible, we need not be uneasy because it is not instantaneous. A year or two more may perfect "the Genders."

9. *Latin Poetry.*—Latin Elegiac verse is so much simpler in its construction than Latin Prose, that it is probably advisable to introduce children to Ovid as their first Author.

But, if this is to be done, some little preparation is required, to teach them a few of the differences between the thought and language of poetry and prose. The best plan is to construe twenty lines aloud with them, pointing out these differences, as you meet examples of them; showing, for example, the terseness of verse, its aversion to adverbs, to conjunctions, to pronouns, and the means by which it dispenses with these parts of speech, thence proceeding to the picturesqueness of poetry, its use of epithets, and of what are called "figures of speech," its love of inversions and varieties, and the like. How much of this preliminary teaching should be given must depend upon the age and disposition of the pupils.

On this point Preceptor's experiences may be of use. "When I was a boy," he says, "I remember spending more than ten minutes over 'Arma virumque cano,' because I had never found 'cano,' in my experience of prose exercises, used to mean 'sing of,' and my poor dictionary of those days happened not to give this meaning. My teacher, by way of meeting my difficulties, quoted, in a sonorous voice, from Dryden, 'Arms and the man I sing,' and asked me what was the difficulty in this? To which I responded, with all the conceit of boyhood and ignorance, 'It is not English. You can say, "I sing a song," but you cannot say, "I sing arms."' Although my answer was, in point of fact, indefensible, and, in spirit, priggish, it expressed the truth, so far as my experience went. I had never read Dryden's 'Arms and the man I sing,' nor Cowper's 'I sing the sofa'; and I still think that it would have been better for me, if my teacher could have taken me with him, step by step, on my first excursion into poetic realms, thereby saving me much fruitless wandering and many painful experiences of the brambles of metaphor, the quagmires of hyperbole, and the intricacies of poetic diction."

Preceptor is probably right in thinking that an introductory lesson of this kind would be of great benefit to most pupils. No doubt, we must avoid telling boys too much, and leaving them too little to find out for themselves. We are not to keep children always in leading-strings, making them helpless and dependent on the teacher. But this mischief could hardly result from one or two such introductory lessons as have been described above. And they might, in many cases, set a too literal boy on the right lines of thought, releasing him from clouds of perplexity, and enabling him to appreciate and enjoy as beauties many things that ordinary boys are apt to consider as hateful pitfalls spitefully inserted in their works by the great classical authors for the express purpose of bringing English boys to grief.

10. *Cæsar* is a somewhat difficult author; and short extracts from Phaderus, Livy, and even Cicero, may well be used first. But the subject-matter of Cæsar, his freedom from allusions, his pedestrian, matter-of-fact style, the limited compass of his history and range of his thoughts, all combine to make him a better author for young boys (to be studied in an entire book) than Livy or Cicero, or (with deference to those who differ) than Nepos. In any case, when the teacher comes to Cæsar, he may do much that is not done at present to make that author easier. And here, as Cæsar is largely read by beginners, and as the object of this book is to afford practical suggestions to teachers, I shall offer no apology for presenting some rather detailed remarks by Preceptor as to the method by which a book of Cæsar may be made at once more instructive and more easy than it is at present.

"Select," he says, "from the book to be studied, fifteen or twenty of the most difficult of the long sentences, exhibiting most prominently the ordinary complications that perplex boys—abundant conjunctions, the idioms of Oratio Obliqua, sentences subordinate to others which are themselves in turn subordinate, ambiguous pronouns, and the like. Do not show these sentences to your pupils as yet; but take them to pieces, and show them the pieces separately. Then, by degrees, put the pieces together, and make the boys help you in building up the complete sentence. Take, for example, the following complicated passage:

"'Interim legatis tribunisque militum convocatis, et quae ex Voluseno cognosset, et quae fieri vellet, ostendit; monuitque—ut rei militaris ratio, maxime ut maritimae res postularent, ut quae celerem atque instabilem motum haberent—ad nutum et ad tempus omnes res ab iis administrarentur.'

"Beginning with the first part of the sentence, you write down on the blackboard in English, and make the pupils turn into Latin.

A. 1.—This (news) he had ascertained from Volusenus, and these (orders) he wished to be executed.

Haec ex Voluseno cognoverat et haec fieri voluit.

"Then, pointing out that 'et' means 'both,' as well as 'and,' and that the Indicatives in *A.* 1 will be changed into Subjunctives when the sentence is made to depend upon a new Verb, in the construction of a dependent question, you bid them translate:

A. 2.—He showed them both what (news) he had ascertained from Volusenus, and also what (orders) he wished to be executed.

. Et quae ex Voluseno cognosset et quae fieri vellet ostendit.

"To this we wish to prefix the statement that—

A. 3.—Meanwhile he called together the lieutenant-generals and tribunes of the soldiers.

Interim legatos tribunosque militum convocavit.

"This we shall do by turning the Verb in *A.* 3 into an Ablative Absolute, although the English will remain unchanged:

A. 4.—Meanwhile he called together...... *and* showed them both ...... executed.

Interim, legatis tribunisque militum convocatis, et quae...... ostendit.

"Here be careful to point out that the italicized 'and' in English does *not* represent the first 'et' in the Latin; the 'and' represents *the Ablative Absolute;* the word 'both' represents the first 'et.'

"The first part of the sentence being now completed, we proceed to the second part, and bid the pupils turn into Latin:

B. 1.—Every order was obeyed by them as soon as given. ("Here we must tell them that the Latin idiom is 'administrare rem ad nutum et ad tempus,' *i.e.* to perform a service at the nod (of the commander) and at the moment of the command.)

"This is accordingly rendered:

B. 1.—Omnes res ab iis ad nutum et ad tempus administratae sunt.

"Next:

B. 2.—He warned them to obey every order (or that every order should be obeyed by them) as soon as given.

Monuit ut omnes res ab iis ad nutum et ad tempus administrarentur.

"To this we will now add the *reason* for the order, and say that:

B. 3.—Military operations (*lit.* the method of military action) (and) especially operations by sea require this.

Id rei militaris ratio, maxime id maritimae res postulant.

"But to this statement about 'operations by sea' we wish to append our reason why the statement 'specially' applies to them, viz.:

B. 4.—Their movements are quick and uncertain (*lit.* they have a motion quick and uncertain).

Celerem atque instabilem motum habent.

"Appending *B.* 4 to *B.* 3, we might insert the conjunction 'quia,' because; but we prefer the idiomatic 'ut quae,' 'as being such as':

B. 5.—Military operations, especially operations by sea, require this, because their movements are quick and uncertain.

Id rei militaris ratio, maxime id maritimæ res postulant, ut quae celerem atque instabilem motum habeant.

"The next question is, Where shall we insert this 'reason' for the warning to obey orders at once. We might have added it at the end: 'Monuit ut administrarentur—quia id rei militaris—haberent.' But we prefer (1) to insert it in a parenthesis, in order to leave the warning itself to occupy an emphatic place at the end; and (2) we will insert it not as a reason given by *us*, but as a reason given by the *speaker* and *as part of his words*, striking out 'id,' and substituting the conjunction 'ut,' *as* or *since*.

B. 6.—He warned them—as was required by all military operations, and more especially by naval operations, in which the movements were swift and uncertain—that every order must be executed by them at a moment's notice.

Monuit—ut rei militaris ratio, maxime ut res maritimae postularent, ut quae celerem atque instabilem motum haberent—(ut) ad nutum et ad tempus omnes res ab iis administrarentur.

"We merely add that the 'ut' before 'ad nutum,' which should regularly follow 'monuit,' may be somewhat irregularly dropped, the verb 'administrarentur' remaining in the Subjunctive as expressing a command in Oratio Obliqua. Nothing now remains but to connect *A* and *B*, by adding 'que' to 'monuit': 'Interim . . . ostendit, monuitque—administrarentur'; and the sentence is now complete."

If boys were thus practiced in building up sentences by adding (in the different shapes employed by the best Authors) causes, circumstances, obstacles, qualifications, amplifications, and the like, it seems probable that the synthetic process would be a useful supplement to the analytic process now commonly in use, and that our pupils would thus learn to write Latin Prose more easily, as well as to construe more intelligently.

11. *Virgil* is a difficult author even for men, and still more for boys. Yet, on the whole, it is advisable to teach Virgil to boys, because it is so much better worth studying and remembering than the easier poetry of Ovid.

The *Eclogues* are wholly unsuitable for all boys; and the *Georgics* are less interesting to most boys than the *Æneid*. As a preparation for the *Æneid* the pupil should read Dryden's translation or Mr. Church's *Stories from Virgil*, so that he may gain some notion of the plot. The teacher should then take two or three lessons, of not less than twenty lines each, aloud with his pupils, ascertaining their difficulties and meeting them as they arise, and gradually familiarizing them with Virgil's peculiarities of style.

As soon as the boy has mastered the construing of some fifty or sixty lines, he should commit them to memory; and the construing must then be carefully revised. Very soon the pupil will be able to prepare his lesson with little help; but for some time to come it will be well that the teacher, in setting the next lesson, should ask a few questions and give a hint or two bearing upon the difficulties of the morrow.

The repetition by heart should be continued throughout the book; and, if the pupil has a good memory, it will be very useful to make him not only read the whole of Dryden's *Æneid*, but also commit to memory Dryden's version of that particular book which is under study. Thus the pupil's English vocabulary will be amplified, his grasp of English idiom will be strengthened (and there is no better author than Dryden as a corrective for boys, at the age when they are liable to be first infected by the Graecisms, archaisms, and other affectations now prevalent in modern English poetry); and he will not only be able to construe with much more force and spirit, but also to enjoy much more the literary beauty of Virgil.

12. *Repetition.*—As to repetition, it is too much to expect, of course, that a child should learn by heart all the Virgil that he construes; but, if he has a good memory, it will be well that he should learn one book, which should be constantly referred to, and constantly revised for two or three years. Then he may learn another in the same way. About two books of Virgil are perhaps as much as can be expected to be always kept up by a boy of good memory. The Second and the Sixth are, in the Author's judgment, best worthy of this close study and permanent retention.

The same principle should be applied to the learning of other repetition lessons in Latin, and also in other languages. Not much is gained by the repetition of a vast number of new passages which the pupil knows he need not recall, or, at all events, need only recall for some forthcoming examination. But let him understand that, whatever he learns, he will have to repeat years hence, and will enjoy and repeat with pleasure tens of years hence, and he will then insensibly adapt the effort of memory to these requirements.

Boys have a power of carrying a great mass in their memories for a short time, and then shaking it all off, so as to leave no trace of its existence; and, if they learn in this spirit, their power of forgetting is truly marvelous. We must, therefore, without overstraining them, or giving them too much to learn, make them clearly see from the first that this is not the spirit in which they must approach repetition. For this purpose (1) we must choose only the very finest specimens of the literature; (2) we must give abundant time for hearing frequent revisions; (3) we must encourage the repetition of it, not as "lines," but as poetry, with force and grace; (4) we must hold out as a reward for successful industry, that when a certain portion is thoroughly mastered no more will be required during the whole of the term except the revision of what has been learned.

13. *Pronunciation.*—As regards pronunciation, something will depend upon the school for which the pupil is being prepared, and on the versatility of the pupil.

The syllabus issued by the Professors of Latin at the Universities of Cambridge and Oxford at the request of the Head Masters of Schools sets forth a scheme of pronunciation now published in many First Latin Books, and used in the highest forms of a few of the principal Public Schools, as well as in the majority of the High Schools for girls. But in the lower forms of Public Schools this pronunciation is not yet used, or only in a very few instances.

The teacher must therefore choose between the advantage of a method of pronunciation which is recommended by the best authorities as at least approximately correct, and which rapidly communicates to the pupil the "quantities" of the syllables, and, on the other hand, the possible inconvenience to the pupils in being compelled to change their pronunciation when they pass from the tutor to the school.

But for the hesitation of one or two Head Masters this system would probably be now in use among all the classical schools; and the next wave of reform in matters educational is likely to re-introduce it with general acceptance; but for the present it must be considered an open question. The Author's experience, however, has been that pupils taught on the new system can, without any difficulty worth mentioning, adopt the old when needed, while retaining much advantage from their knowledge of the new.

Of course, in quoting familiar Latin proverbs and phrases that are, as it were, Anglicised, the English pronunciation would naturally be adopted.

54. GEOGRAPHY.

The object of teaching a child geography is, firstly, to give him information about the countries and nations of the globe, but secondly (which is the more important object of the two) to implant in him a habit of seeking, and a faculty in acquiring, further information on these points for himself.

Geography may be divided into two kinds: (1) Descriptive and Physical; (2) Historical and Commercial.

The former deals with the phenomena of Nature and their causes, so far as they concern the physical features and climate of the different parts of the earth; the latter deals with the earth as peopled and modified by man, the demarcation of countries, cities, populations, and exchangeable products. So far as it deals with physical causes, geography trains the reason; and so far as it is descriptive, it creates interest in the variety, and admiration at the beauty of the world. Again, historical geography supplies information without which it is difficult to understand history; and commercial geography shows us how the different countries of the earth are connected together by the natural exchange of their several products.

It is evident that, until a boy is fairly advanced in history, historical geography cannot be taught except in outline; or, if taught in detail, cannot be easily recollected for want of the necessary associations with historical facts; and in the same way the details of commercial geography, for a boy unacquainted with the details of the commercial relations of different countries, will be dull and difficult to remember.

The conclusion from all this is, that it is not wise to overload the young memory with lists of statements about populations, commercial products, minute details of boundaries, lengths of rivers, heights of mountains, and the like, until the mind, by familiarity with history and the facts of commerce, is made duly receptive of such teaching. The teacher of geography should avoid, as far as possible, teaching any fact that is not (somewhat obviously) worth remembering; otherwise, it may be taught, but will not be permanently remembered. And as historical and commercial geography do not appeal to the reason, but to the memory, the facts which they teach are of no use as an exercise of the rational faculty; and, unless they can be remembered, it is better that they should not be taught at all.

The following detailed rules spring from the above general considerations.

1. Begin early by stimulating the child's imagination with pictures of Tropical and Arctic regions, as different as possible from our own country, so that the child may realize something of the greatness and grandeur of the world, and may be curious to know as much as possible of its wonders and varieties.

2. Teach him how to make a map of his street and the immediate neighborhood (or, if he is very young, begin by showing him how to make a plan of a room or a garden). After he has made several attempts on slips of paper of different sizes, show him an enlarged ordnance map of the same neighborhood, and make him understand how the same place may be represented by maps on a different "scale."

3. Pass at once to a map of England, on which mark the town and county in which the pupil lives. Then show him England in a map of

Europe. The object of this is to prepare him to realize in some degree the relative size of the objects to which geography will introduce him.

4. Then tell him that Europe itself is but one among several continents that cover the surface of the earth, which is not flat, but a globe. And here produce a small globe, which the boy may take out of its frame and handle; and help him to recognize England upon it.

5. By means of a compass, show how to determine the North and South; and point out that the sun is always South about twelve o'clock, Southeast about nine A. M., Southwest about three P. M., etc. Encourage the child to make for himself a rough kind of sun-clock, by means of a vertical stick casting a shadow.

6. When the child has thus arrived at the conclusion that the sun moves, point out to him (using the illustration of two railway trains) that the phenomenon he sees might be caused by the earth's moving.

Then, either with the portable globe and a candle—or (far better) with the aid of the interesting model called a Tellurium,[1] if one can be procured—which exhibits the earth revolving on its axis and in its orbit, round a light representing the sun—show him the causes of the phenomenon of day and night, summer and winter, and how the earth is but as one of the planets which he may see by night moving in the heavens.

7. Hence show that it is day in New Zealand when it is night with us, and that at noon in New Zealand the sun is in the North, not in the South.

8. Now returning to earth, draw attention to the natural features, mountains, rivers, lakes, and seas.

Show the pupils how miniature rivers are to be seen in the walks of gardens and of parks, or of hedge-sides, where they may see on a small scale winding streams, cataracts, lakes, and deltas. Then show them one of the best kind of raised maps; or, better still, model a mountain region for them yourself in clay,[2] and show how the passage of the water may be determined by the shape of the land. Hence, make them clearly understand the nature of a watershed.

9. Draw for your pupils, and teach them to draw, the course of a river from the source to the mouth, fed by tributaries, showing them that a river's course always chooses the lowest ground, so that it cannot be straight, like that of a canal; and warn them that a river must never be represented (as some boys represent it) flowing up hill.

10. Passing now to the map of Europe, call attention to the principal mountain ranges, rivers, etc., and at the same time indicate something of their historical importance in determining the boundaries of nations. Then rapidly teach the names of the different countries.

Show, in the case of England, Switzerland, the Netherlands, Germany, and Russia, how the existence of a large extent of sea-coast, or

---

[1] To be seen at Messrs. Laurie & Co., Publishers, Paternoster Row, London.
[2] This suggestion is borrowed from Mr. Fitch's *Lectures on Teaching*.

its absence, how plains or mountains influence the history and character of a people.

11. Next take the principal rivers, and, making imaginary journeys down them, mark the principal cities on their banks, associating each name with some intelligible and interesting fact of history or commerce. Also point out the commercial importance of navigable rivers.

12. Now, taking ship, make a number of imaginary voyages from port to port, naming the seas traversed, the islands and some of the points passed by, and the straits passed through.

13. Next arrange the countries of Europe, first, in order of magnitude, and second, in order of population, pointing out how the order differs in the two cases.

It is quite unnecessary that the pupils should commit to memory the numbers of the populations of all the countries in Europe; but they will find much less difficulty in remembering the *order* in which the different countries stand; and then if they can remember the exact population of two or three, they will have a fair notion of the rest.

14. After this, the teacher may be guided by circumstances as to the direction his lessons shall pursue. But, for an English boy, the British Colonies may naturally be presented as the next subject for study.

15. In order to show the pupils how to utilize and augment their knowledge of Geography, the teacher should now take a brief sketch of the wars of Napoleon, and show them how to follow the outline of the history rapidly in their maps, omitting details; or he might do the same thing more simply with a brief life of Hannibal.

16. It will be seen that in all these lessons sketched above, not much room is left for the " text-book."

Geography is really a very difficult subject to teach, especially for Oxford and Cambridge men, not trained to teach, and unaccustomed to the use of the blackboard; and because of its difficulty, many teachers prefer to trust entirely to the book, " setting lessons " out of it, which are to be " repeated " to the teacher.

Thus taught, Geography is of very little value. The text-book, in order to be complete, generally arranges all the facts and objects of one kind together, *e.g.* the capes, cities, lakes, rivers, etc. Hence the order of the text-book is not the order of the traveler. But the child who is learning geography ought to learn it, as far as possible, in the same order and with the same interest as though he were traveling across the country.

Moreover, in the complete lists of the text-books many unimportant facts are mixed with some that are important, and if the child learns all these promiscuously, he learns too much, and a great deal more than he can associate with intelligible and interesting ideas. Hence whereas he might have remembered a few things, if a few had been well selected, he now forgets everything, because the teacher has eliminated nothing

Nor is this loss of information the only evil. He has also failed to form the valuable habit of connecting the names of places with characteristic events and facts, and has lost the active curiosity and interest which would have stimulated him, all through life, to ask, whenever he heard or read about some striking incident, "Where is that *place?* How did the *place* influence the *event?*"

17. Map-drawing may be made a useful exercise if it accompanies a study of the history of the country, and if the pupil is limited to a few of the more important towns, and *obliged to state, in writing, his reasons for selecting them.* Without some such precaution, boys will put in names wherever they will produce the prettiest pictorial effect, without the slightest regard to their historical or commercial importance; and it is needless to say that maps so constructed are positively mischievous.

More useful than elaborate map-drawing is the art of drawing rapid sketch-maps from memory, the pupil inserting only such towns as are prescribed by the teacher.

18. The last, but most important conclusion to be deduced from the foregoing remarks is that no one should teach geography who is not perfectly familiar with it himself.

The speaker should never need to take his eyes off the class or off his pupil *to look at the book*, and should be able rapidly and unhesitatingly to draw a map upon the blackboard without reference to an Atlas.

To make one's pupils see anything—and that is a principal object of geographical instruction—it is necessary that the teacher should (either with his eyes or with his imagination) have previously seen it himself; and the ideal Instructor in geography is one who, with all the qualifications of a teacher combines the experience of a traveler, who has actually seen what he describes; but next to this comes he who has, by reading and study, so completely mastered the outlines and coloring of the region he is describing, that he can speak of them as if he had seen them.

55. HISTORY.

"My own experience as a child," writes Preceptor, of early teaching in History, was derived from the mere reading of text-books, the result being that, after I had read two of them from beginning to end, I retained nothing except one or two mental pictures of little Arthur being blinded, Essex receiving a box on the ear, Rufus shot with a chance arrow, the original Briton colored and tattooed; and as my one interesting historical problem—a perplexity with regard to the important part played in history by what was called in my books a 'cabinet,' but at home a 'chiffonier.'"

Preceptor proceeds to pour contempt on the early teaching of History, declaring that it "goes in at one ear and out at the other." A great number of good teachers will endorse his opinion; but the legitimate inference appears rather to be that History, as commonly taught to young children thirty years ago, was unsatisfactory, and not that more satisfactory results may not be obtained by more satisfactory methods.

Indeed, Preceptor himself suggests a method which must be undoubtedly more interesting, and the results of which are likely to be more permanent, than those of the old text-book teaching. "Begin," he says, "if you are to begin early at all, with the soldier, the policeman, the tax-gatherer, and—if you live in London—with the Palace of Justice, Westminster Hall, and the Houses of Parliament. The use of the soldier and the policeman will be one of the necessities of the body politic most easily comprehended by children, and the need of paying them supplies a natural introduction to the consideration of taxes.

"Then, since soldiers and policemen must be paid, roads repaired, lighted, and swept, the questions will arise, Who is to keep the money which the tax-gatherer collects from us? Who is to settle how much money shall be collected? Who is to tell the soldiers what enemy is to be attacked, and when? Who is to make rules for the policemen, that they may know when to take people up? And who is to decide what is to be done with the people thus taken up? Shall it be one ruler, or fifty rulers, or shall all the rich people rule, or shall all the people, without exception, meet together and rule?

"Here, by way of inculcating the need of some kind of rule, I remember drawing for some young people (in very rude and rough sketches) a picture first, of 'no ruler at all,' depicting a rabble in wild confusion fighting among themselves; second, a picture of 'one ruler,' Solomon seated on a throne deciding the case of the disputed child; third, a picture of fifty men in armor, stout and comfortable, surveying the execution of a lean poor man on the chopping-block before them. After these pictures followed others, of the tax-gatherer calling for the dog-tax (a mistake of mine, by the way) with the dog looking out of the window; of a ship putting into the docks, and the custom-house officers collecting their dues; of a law court with a judge and jury trying the accused; of a disciplined army contrasted with an undisciplined mob of armed men; of a representative assembly of some 400 or 600 making laws, addressed by an orator, with one hand in his pocket and the other holding his hat; of a vast popular assembly, such as in Athens, met for the same purpose, and being harangued by a speaker of Demosthenic action—and so on. What may have been the residuum of all this in the minds of my pupils I do not well know, for I had not leisure to continue the study of History with them when they grew a little older; but I remember that the lessons appeared to be interesting, and my impression is that they disposed the young people to approach the study of History as something very different from a bundle of dates or statistics, and also (which is not unimportant) as something different from a series of picturesque biographies."

Certainly it would be an interesting experiment to try the effect of a course of Historical lessons of this kind on young children. There seems no reason why boys of ten years old should not understand them and retain at least parts of them. Even a boy of eight or nine can understand the use of a soldier, a policeman, a law court, and a legislative assembly, and can be taught to divide the functions of government into law-making, judging, and law-executing, or, in other words, the legislative, the judicial, and the executive. He can even understand, either then or not much later, how, in some nations, these functions have all been discharged by one, in others by two, in others by three, bodies; and it will not be difficult to make him understand the advantages of assigning them to three; so that the same men may not both make laws and execute them, or make laws and judge those who are accused of breaking them. In this way, when he is introduced to the history of a new nation, he may be trained from the first to ask, Who made the laws? Who judged? Who executed the laws? and to classify nations in the same way in which he would classify birds, beasts, and fishes. And thus he will be prepared to estimate the importance of historical events by their influence on the legislative, judicial, and executive functions of the state; and he will be better able to understand the motives of the kings and statesmen with whom the study of History is to bring him into contact.

Nor need we stop here, if we are to accept Preceptor's further suggestions, which have at least the merit of being vivid, though many will pronounce them unpractical. "Set before the pupil," he says, "a large picture illustrative of the feudal times, showing the exaction of fines for the right of holding markets, the tolls taken at the gates of every city, at the passage of every bridge, at the boundaries of every petty feudal lord; and make the child understand how restrictions of this kind—checking commerce, hampering industry and enterprise, diminishing comfort, and preventing that leisure which enables people to think of other things besides bread-winning—might thus indirectly hinder the diffusion of knowledge, taste, and art, and enforce a people to remain in brutish ignorance. Or by reference to the paper-tax or the window-tax (the latter of which might be simply and forcibly illustrated) in our century, show how a nation, by an injudicious burden, may be mentally or physically enfeebled.

"Then point out how important it is that laws should be wise and just, and how unwise laws (as well as unjust laws) have, for the most part, been made for the poor by the rich and powerful, who did not belong to the poor for whom the laws were made, and therefore did not understand what the poor needed. Hence let the child understand how important it is that the poor should have a voice in the framing of those laws which they themselves are intended to obey.

"When this course is completed—which may be described as Historical Statics—I should proceed to teach them something of Historical Dynamics. Nor should I begin with the details of English History; for, indeed, early English History is much more difficult for children to understand than the history of Xerxes, Alexander, Attila, or Charlemagne. As, therefore, in Geography, after teaching the pupil about the elements of land and water, you passed to the map of Europe, so in History I should pursue the same course. To do justice to it, especially with a large class, one should have very large pictures (or dissolving views would be still better) each illustrated with a few striking sentences, not a word of which would ever require to be retracted, so as to produce on the mind of the child, through ear and eye together, a quite indelible impression.

"Failing dissolving views, we should have a series of brightly-colored maps exhibiting the changes that have passed over Europe and Asia Minor since the time of Xerxes to the present. There should also be pictures, not only of the decisive battles, but also of various incidents or objects that may be best suited to let the boy into the secret of the character of the nation or period that he is studying: Greek sculptures; Roman camps and armies; German forests; the death of Alexander; Cæsar crossing the Rubicon; the martyrdom of the Christians under Nero; the Nicene Council; the sacking of Rome by Alaric; a squadron of Huns with Attila; Mohammed purifying Mecca; the Saracens invading Spain; Charlemagne crowned by the Pope; William the Conqueror at Hastings; Henry IV at Canossa; Michael Schwartz inventing gunpowder; Columbus encouraging his crew; Luther burning the Pope's bull; the Armada; Plassy; the execution of Louis XVI; Waterloo.

"If in this way the principal epochs in European history could be once vividly impressed on the pupil's mind in their chronological order, he would certainly find no difficulty at all in retaining their relative positions in his mind, and probably find very little difficulty in committing to memory the exact dates of the most important events. This definite outline, besides being of subsequent value when the pupil comes to the study of the history of nations, is also of immediate use in giving precision and order to the study which ought now to begin, I mean Historical Biography.

"Biography, no doubt, is not history; but the life of a man is so much more attractive to children than the life of a nation that the indirect historical teaching of the former is often far more effective than the direct teaching of the latter. The same remark applies to novels. They may occasionally take liberties with chronology, and distort or adorn a fact; but in accustoming children to fill up historical outline with color, and in dissipating the notion that history is 'a dry study,' they are of such great value that a systematic course of novel reading may well be made an adjunct to the study of historical text-books, at all events for the young.".[1]

---

[1] See the very copious *Descriptive Catalogue of Historical Novels and Tales*, compiled by H. Courthope Bowen, M.A. (London, Stanford, 1882); also Bulletins of Boston Public Library, Historical Fiction, and English Prose Fiction, 1875-77.

GEOGRAPHY.

In favor of Preceptor's novel suggestion that the outlines of European history should precede the study of English history, thus much may at least be said, that it is in accordance with the ordinary method of studying Geography, where Europe (in outline) generally comes first, and England second. And certainly the succession of picturesque and striking scenes suggested by Preceptor might do for history what the pictures of tropic and arctic regions (see § 54) were intended to do for Geography. The difference, however, is, that while any boy can understand a mountain or a glacier, it is not so easy for the young to realize the importance of the death of Alexander, or Cæsar crossing the Rubicon, or Luthur burning the Pope's bull; and it is just possible that, in very young and dull children, Preceptor's pictures, though they might give pleasure, might cause some bewilderment as well. Yet, on the whole, in the hands of a good teacher, who could temper enthusiasm for his subject with sympathy for his pupils, it seems not improbable that such a preliminary course might be of use.

When the pupil (with or without the previous training suggested above) is introduced to the more detailed study of the history of his native country, a text-book will, for the first time, be placed in his hands. Here must be repeated what was said above as to the use of text-books in Geography, that the main use of the book should be to enable the pupil to revise, amplify, and master what the teacher has said, and not to dispense with the teacher's saying anything. A text-book cannot very conveniently (without the aid of different sizes of type, which are perhaps somewhat confusing to children) touch lightly enough on unimportant incidents, or give to narrative so picturesque a shape as a teacher can give in oral instruction. On the other hand, if a teacher relies entirely on oral teaching, he will find that, unless his pupils are above the average in retentiveness, only a small residuum of his lessons will remain in their memory.

The best plan seems to be to begin with a short sketch or Primer, which will contain none but the more important features of the period under study; then to supplement this by reading biographies, and by giving extracts from larger histories bearing on the more important epochs; and lastly, to revise the history of the period in a larger text-book.

In the learning of dates, Memoria Technica should be rejected, for the reasons given above (§ 50), but great care should be taken by sight, sound, and association, to fix the more important dates in the memory. None but very important dates should be at first required; but these should be thoroughly mastered. The reasons for their importance should be explained; and hints may be given to help the learner to remember the sequence (§ 51); but when the repetition is once begun, there must be no appeal to reasons; they are to be learned and repeated by ear, like the Multiplication Table. Then the less important may be grouped round these as centers. But the minor dates must not be so numerous nor so often repeated as to interfere with the central ones, which must be repeatedly revised. The dates of the accessions of sovereigns are of importance where the personal character of the sovereign has had so much influence as to make a great change in the history of the nation; but as they have not always this importance, it is a pity to make these first dates committed to memory by a child. The dates of the signing of Magna Charta, the summoning of Montfort's Parliament, the Black Death, the recognition of English in the Law Courts, the death of Chaucer, the publication of the first printed book in England, the defeat of the Armada, and the loss of America, are very much more important than the dates of the accession of Henry I or Stephen.

Not much can be done to show the beginner how the English language and literature have changed and grown with the English nation. But whatever is done should carefully avoid the danger of "cramming." The text-books which relate that "in this reign Sir Thomas More wrote his celebrated *Utopia*," and there make an end of it, are hardly to be blamed if regarded as mere outlines and skeletons of history, suggesting to teachers what they should teach, and to pupils what they must revise of the instruction received from their teacher; but they are manifestly in themselves inadequate, and the information given in the sentence last quoted is, by itself, clearly of the nature of "cram." If, therefore, the teacher mentions any author at all, he ought to give such a sketch of him and his surroundings, illustrated, perhaps, by one or two characteristic anecdotes, as will enable his pupils in some sort to make a mental picture of the man. Then he may read a short extract from his works which shall have some kind of unity and interest.

For example, after telling his pupils that the History of Utopia means the "History of Nowhere," he may illustrate the "no-whereness" of the book by reading the passage which describes how the Utopians esteemed gold as less valuable than iron, making fetters of it for prisoners and playthings for children. Similarly, in dealing with Chaucer, instead of describing all the characters of the *Canterbury Tales* at the same length, and all very briefly, the teacher should give the shortest possible summary of the poem as a whole, and then read the description of the Knight or of the Clerk in full.

Some notion, also, of the changes of the English language may be given by writing down for one's pupils a few sentences in the New Testament from translations of different periods, thus:

1. A.D. 1000 and fellen gyrdel waes ymbe his lendenu.
A.D. 1150 and fellen gyrdel waes embe his lendene.
A.D. 1380 and a girdil of skin (*i.e.* fell) about his loins.

2. A.D. 1000 and he bodede and cwaeth (compare the later *quoth*), Strengre cymth aefter me.
A.D. 1150 and he bodede and cwaeth, Strengre kymth aefter me.

A.D. 1380 and prechid (*i.e.* boded) seyinge, A strengere than I schal come aftir me.

It will not be necessary to call the young pupil's attention to the differences of inflections. But the mere reading aloud of these sentences will suffice to make him realize how little the English language changed from 1606 A.D. to 1150 A.D. (during which period the English-speaking and French-speaking classes had comparatively little intercourse with each other) as compared with the change between 1150 A.D. and 1380 A.D., when the two classes had learned to co-operate against the crown, and to recognize a community of interests. Thus he will be prepared for hearing that in 1362 A.D. French had become so unintelligible that it was supplanted by order of an Act of Parliament, which enacted that all pleadings in the law-courts should be conducted in "English, not French," inasmuch as French had become "much unknown in the realm"; and thus he will more easily realize the importance and remember the date of one of the most important events in the history of his native country.

For those who live in London, or other places of historical interest, it is scarcely necessary to say how valuable a stimulus for the study of history may be derived from a visit to Westminster Abbey or the Tower of London, especially after a little preliminary reading and study has prepared the pupil for what he is to see.

56. GEOMETRY.

Geometry is so much more easy and interesting for the young than Algebra, that it may be properly included in the present treatise, although Algebra will be excluded.

The principal reason why so many young pupils fail in Geometry is that they are left to rely upon a book, instead of following and retaining the oral instruction of their teacher.

"I remember," writes Preceptor, "that after I had taken a young pupil successfully through the first six or seven Propositions of Euclid without the aid of a book, one day when I found myself obliged to go out, and unable to give the usual lesson, I ventured to place the book in the boy's hands, telling him to study the seventh or eighth Proposition by himself. To my horror, as I passed the door soon afterwards, I heard him *singing* the Proposition. I immediately anticipated the worst. My anticipations were fulfilled when I returned and found that he had learned the Proposition by heart, and could readily repeat it, without being able to understand a word of it. My neglect on this occasion caused a week's retrogression, and I felt that it would have been much better if the half-hour had been spent in play."

Very similar is the Author's experience. Boys have so strong a memory and so great an aversion to think—where memory can serve as a substitute for thought—that it is most important, in teaching Geometry, not to leave the pupil to himself till he has formed the

56. GEOMETRY.

Geometry is so much more easy and interesting for the young than Algebra, that it may be properly included in the present treatise, although Algebra will be excluded.

The principal reason why so many young pupils fail in Geometry is that they are left to rely upon a book, instead of following and retaining the oral instruction of their teacher.

"I remember," writes Preceptor, "that after I had taken a young pupil successfully through the first six or seven Propositions of Euclid without the aid of a book, one day when I found myself obliged to go out, and unable to give the usual lesson, I ventured to place the book in the boy's hands, telling him to study the seventh or eighth Proposition by himself. To my horror, as I passed the door soon afterwards, I heard him *singing* the Proposition. I immediately anticipated the worst. My anticipations were fulfilled when I returned and found that he had learned the Proposition by heart, and could readily repeat it, without being able to understand a word of it. My neglect on this occasion caused a week's retrogression, and I felt that it would have been much better if the half-hour had been spent in play."

Very similar is the Author's experience. Boys have so strong a memory and so great an aversion to think—where memory can serve as a substitute for thought—that it is most important, in teaching Geometry, not to leave the pupil to himself till he has formed the habit of reasoning, and has learned enough to make him understand that it *pays*, in Euclid, not to try to remember, but to reason.

Many excellent teachers object to Euclid as being cumbrous, circuitous, and artificial. But until some other text-book is uniformly or generally adopted, it seems likely that he will maintain his present position. Leaving, therefore, to specialists the task of suggesting better methods or text-books, the Author will merely mention two or three expedients which he has found useful in teaching Euclid, pure and simple, to young children.

1. *The Definitions and Axioms.*—To begin by learning all the definitions and axioms is both tedious and bewildering.

Begin by doing or proving something definite; and then, in the course of your theorems or problems, introduce your definitions, axioms, and postulates, *as you need them*. Let the pupil collect them as they arise, and write them down for himself in a book.

They must undoubtedly be finally learned by heart; but before learning them, let the pupil understand their utility; and, so to speak, instead of regarding them as Euclid's axioms, let him be led to feel that they are his own axioms, which he has himself seen to be self-evident, and of which he himself demands the concession.

Thus, instead of beginning with Euclid's definition of a point, as "that which hath no parts and no magnitude," and a line as "length without breadth," we may for a long time appeal to common sense, and take for granted that, in drawing figures the lines are to be as thin and even as possible, and the points no larger than is necessary to make them clearly visible.

But after the boy *has been learning Geometry some time*, you may draw with a thick piece of chalk upon a blackboard a straight line AC, of perceptible and uneven breadth, and point out (proving it by measurement, if you like) that in the triangle ABC, of which the sides AB, AC are *called* equal, it is not exactly true to say that $AB = AC$; for although AB is equal to *one side* of the thick line AC, it is not equal to the other side. Similarly, if AB, AC meet in a *large* point A, which "hath parts and magnitude," it will depend upon *the part of the point* from which you begin to measure, whether AB is really equal to AC.

Hence the pupil may be able to perceive that Euclid's Propositions could not always be exactly true of points and lines, unless points were "without magnitude" and lines "without breadth." But until he is able to perceive this, it will be best not to trouble him with Euclid's definitions of a point and line, but to leave him to "common sense."

2. *The use of Rules and Compass.*—Before proceeding to the Propositions, he should be taught how to draw triangles and circles neatly, so as to familiarize him with the use of the ruler and compasses.

When he has drawn several circles he should be told to measure the distance from the center to two or three points in the circumference, and to ascertain whether they differ in length; and an oval, or ellipse, having been drawn for him by the teacher, the pupil should be shown how this equality of the radii distinguishes the circle from the ellipse. But I should not as yet trouble him with the definition of a circle.

3. *The First Proposition.*—We now tell the child that we allow him a compass and a ruler, but not a measuring-rule; and he is to try to describe, on a given straight line, a triangle with three equal sides.

After criticising his hap-hazard attempts, and pointing out that, even when the pupil is near the mark, he is proceeding by "guess-work," we offer to describe one in which the sides shall be exactly equal. It will be found that the First Proposition, thus introduced, will present no difficulty, and the child ought to be able speedily to work the Problem himself.

In the course of this Proposition, call attention to the fact that we have *assumed* that "things that are equal to the same thing are equal to one another." Tell the boy that an assumption of this kind is called an Axiom (which means "assumption") and bid him write it down in a manuscript book as the first of Euclid's Axioms.

4. *The Second Proposition.*—The Second Proposition presents more difficulty. For when the child learns that he is "from a given point to draw a straight line equal to a given straight line," he naturally replies that he can do it at once, by *measuring with his pencil* from the given point a distance equal to the given straight line.

We must therefore introduce this Proposition as a test of ingenuity, by saying that "of course any one can do this *with the use of a measur-*

ing-rule, but we are expected to show our ingenuity *by doing it without a measuring-rule*, and with the aid of a compass used merely for the purpose of describing a circle."

When the construction is completed, before proceeding to Euclid's proof, it will simplify matters to go backwards from the conclusion, and to say, "Now you see that BG is equal to BC, do you not?" Yes.

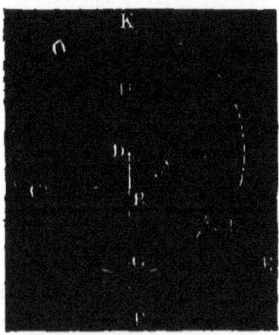

"Then if we can show that AL is equal to BG,[1] the thing required will be done; for AL will have been drawn from A, equal to CB, will it not?" Yes. "Well, then, we shall show that AL and BG are equal in the following way: First, we shall show that DG and DL, the radii of the large circle, are equal, and then that DB and DA, sides of the equilateral triangle, are also equal; and subtracting the small equal lines from the large equal lines, we shall show that the remainder BG is equal to the remainder AL."

Probably the boy will find no difficulty at all in this reasoning; but it should now be pointed out to him that here we are *assuming* that "if equals be taken from equals, the remainders are equal"; and this statement having been illustrated from the subtraction of numbers, lines, and spaces, must be written down as another of Euclid's Assumptions, or Axioms.

This Proposition will need to be repeated perhaps two or three times by the teacher before the pupil can easily work it himself. But he may be helped by being accustomed to a summary of it in dialogue, thus: After he has completed the construction, he may be asked, "What are you going to prove?" That AL is equal to CB. "How are you going to prove it?" By proving that AL is equal to BG, and that BG is equal to BC.

When the teacher is repeating this proposition the second time, he must occasionally stop in the midst of a sentence and let the pupil complete it, to see whether he can take up the reasoning; nor must

---

[1] AL and BG may be drawn in red ink, or otherwise distinguished from the rest of the figure, so as to call special attention to them.

the pupil be asked to work the problem himself till the teacher has good reason to think that the task can be successfully accomplished.

5. *Tests of Understanding.*—When the first three Problems are mastered, they should be drawn upside down; or numbers should be substituted for letters, so that the pupil may be habituated to recognize the truth of the process in all circumstances, and to depend entirely on the reason, and in no respect on memory.

It should be needless to add that the pupil must not have the figure before him to begin with, nor should he be allowed to draw the figures in silence, and then state what he has been doing. Before he is allowed to draw a line, or join two points, or describe a circle, he must state precisely what he is intending to do.

Very often it is a good plan that the pupil should dictate the construction while the teacher executes it. The advantage of this is, that, if the pupil dictates inaccurately, the teacher can correct him silently by carrying into effect the inaccurate instructions, and showing their absurdity. For example, in the First Proposition, the pupil perhaps says, "Let AB be the given line" (omitting the word straight), upon which the teacher will draw a curved line. Or again, instead of saying, "from the center A, *at the distance* AB, describe the circle BCD," the pupil may say, "from the center A describe the circle BCD"; upon which the teacher will proceed from center A to describe an absurdly large circle BCD, passing through a second B, with a radius of eight or nine inches, or (if on a blackboard) of one or two feet.

6. *Angles.*—Before proceeding to the Fourth Proposition, we must now introduce the pupil to angles. Great care is here needed to prevent him from falling into the error of confusing angles with triangles.

For this purpose, Euclid's definition is of little use. "A plane rectilineal angle is the inclination of two straight lines to one another, which meet together, but are not in the same straight line." For, replies the boy, "What is the meaning of 'the inclination of two straight lines to one another?' I thought I knew what an angle was like; but I am sure I do not understand what 'inclination' is." To such a boy, at the present stage, Euclid's definition conveys no meaning, and tends rather to confuse him.

The best means of introducing a boy to the notion of an angle is to lay a stick AB upon another CAD, and then gradually make AB revolve upon the pivot A, so that it passes from a position (AB_1) of coincidence with AD to a position (AB_3) where it is in a straight line with AD. Point out, as you move the stick away from AD, that the moving line is *sloped* or *inclined* more and more to the fixed line AD; and that when the moving line is half way (AB_2) it is sloped equally with respect to AD and AC. Placing the moving line in different positions, e.g. AB_4 (half way between AD and AB_2) elicit from the pupil that AB_2 is *more inclined* to AD than AB_4 is, and that AB_3 is more inclined to AD than AB_2 is. Then show him that, if the line (AB_4) is half way between AD and AB_2, AB_2 is *twice as much inclined* to AD as AB_4 is. Then tell him that, when we wish to describe *how much one line is inclined* to another, we generally speak of the *inclination* of one line to another, and show him how "inclination" is meas-

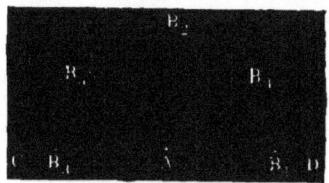

ured by degrees. Tell him that, in passing from AD to AC, the moving line passes through one hundred and eighty degrees (180°); in passing from AD to AB_2, through 90°; in passing from AD to AB_4, through 45°.[1]

In this way the pupil will be saved from connecting the notion of *inclination* with the notion of enclosed space; and there will be nothing in what he has heard that can make him confuse angles with triangles, while there will be much that will prepare him for Euclid's definition of an angle.

After this it is well to construct a dial-face of card-board with moving hands, the circumference being divided into 360°, and to teach the pupil to incline the hands at different inclinations, 60°, 120°, 90°, etc. We may now tell him that the amount of inclination is called *angle*, so that we speak of an angle of 90°, 120°, 60°; and we may then give him Euclid's definition.

Even now the difficulty is not over; for beginners are often perplexed by the "reading" of angles, and unable to see that a single angle may be composed of two or more smaller angles. Taking, therefore, an angle of 90° (BAC), we may bid the pupil divide it as neatly

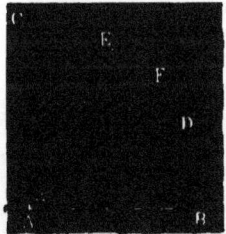

as he can into three equal parts, BAD, DEE, EAC; and then to divide the same angle BAC into two equal parts, BAF, FAC; and we may put the pupil through a series of questions: (1) Trace with a pointer the angles BAF, BAD, DAF, FAE, DAE, DAC, etc. (2) What are the two angles that make up the angle BAF? (3) What are the two

---

[1] In practice it will be found that sticks, pen-holders, rulers, etc., are more intelligible illustrations than any diagram can be

that make up *EAD?* (4) What are the three that make up *EAB?* (5) What are the four that make up *BAC?* (6) Subtract the angle *DAF* from *BAF*, and what is left? (7) *DAF* from *DAE*, and what is left? (8) How many degrees are there in *BAF?* (9) How many in *DAB?* (10) Then how many in their difference *DAF?* (11) How many in *EAD?* (12) How many in *DAF?* (13) Then how many in their difference *EAF?* (14) How many in *CAF?* (15) How many in *FAD?* (16) Then how many in their sum *CAD?*

Not till the pupil is thus familiarized with the reading and reckoning of angles, will it be wise to proceed to the Fourth Proposition of Euclid.

7. *The Fourth Proposition.*—This proposition requires even more care than the Fifth.

The teacher should begin by explaining the method of " applying." "Put a straight line *AB* on *DE*, so that the point *A* shall fall on the

point *D*, and *AB* shall lie on *DE*. Then if *AB* is the larger of the two, where will *B* fall?" On *DE* produced. "And if *AB* is the shorter?" *B* will then fall between *D* and *E*. "And if *AB* happens to be just equal to *DE?*" Then *B* will fall on *E*.

Now let the pupil take two triangles that are not equal to one another in any respect, or that have merely one side of the one equal to one side of the other, and let him "apply" one to the other. Thus he may realize that in these cases the two triangles will *not* coincide with each other nor be equal to one another.

This having been mastered, the teacher should make the pupil cut out in paper two triangles *ABC*, *DEF*, having two sides and the included angle equal; or, better still, make triangles of frame-work,

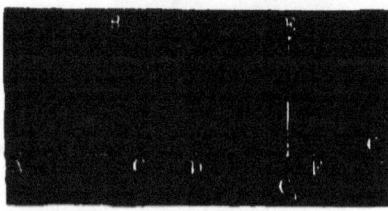

such as may be fashioned from the frame of a broken slate.

This done, the process of applying should be performed, not all at once, but bit by bit, as Euclid prescribes.

A is first to be placed on D and AB made to lie along DE; and (by the preceding demonstration of the method of "applying" one straight line to another) the pupil will realize at once that B must coincide with E, and AB with DE. Here the teacher must pause. "We have now made AB coincide with DE. Now if the angle ABC were smaller than DEF, BC would fall inside, thus (EC_1), and if the angle ABC were greater than DEF, BC would fall outside, thus (EC_2); but since

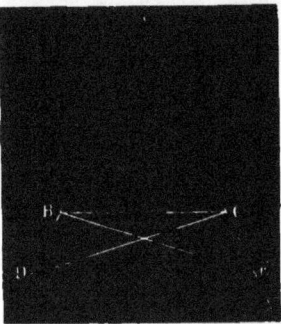

the angle ABC is exactly equal to the angle DEF, where must BC fall?" This reasoning, together with the actual application of the paper or frame-work triangles, will probably make it quite clear to the pupil that BC will fall neither inside nor outside of EF, but *on* EF. If this is understood, the rest presents little difficulty.

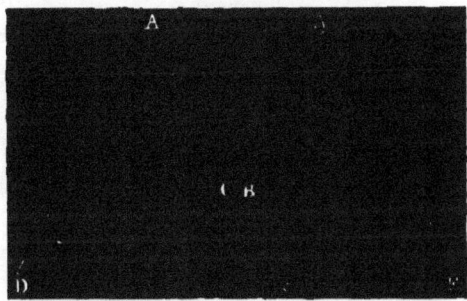

FIG. 1.

8. *The Fifth Proposition.*—The difficulties of the Fifth Proposition arise, 1st, from the overlapping of the triangles, about which the boy has to reason just as though they did not overlap; 2d, from the length of the chain of argument.

To meet these difficulties the teacher must resort to the first principle of teaching, viz., "Divide": 1st, he must exhibit the triangles not overlapping, but apart; 2d, he must break up the chain or argument into its several links and make the connection between them seem easy and natural.

First, therefore, let the teacher draw two triangles (as in fig. 1),

ACD, ABE, which have the two sides AD, AC equal to the two AE and AB, and the included angle DAC equal to the included angle EAB; and in this position let the triangles be reasoned about by the

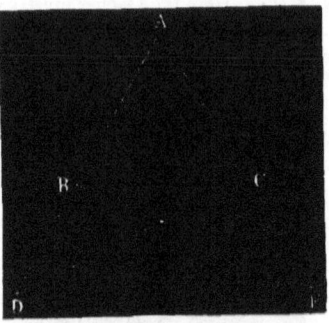

FIG. 2.

pupil, who must deduce about them the conclusions of the Fourth Proposition, viz., that the angles at the bases of these two triangles are equal, and their bases are equal.

Afterwards the boy must go through precisely the same method of proof, when the triangles are made to overlap (as in fig. 2). The only difference will be that, instead of saying that the angle BAE is *equal* to the angle CAD, we shall now have to say that the angle is *common* to the two triangles.

Next let him apply the conclusions of the Fourth Proposition to two triangles BCD, bcE (as in fig. 3), which have the two sides BD, DC

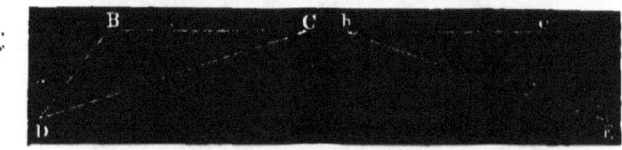

FIG. 3.

equal to the two sides cE, Eb, and the included angle BDC equal to the included angle bEc.

Lastly, let him apply the same conclusions to the same triangles, only now (as in fig. 4) overlapping. The only difference in the argu-

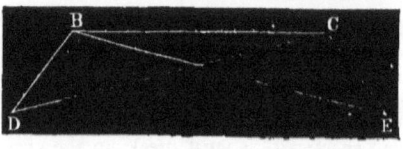

FIG. 4.

ment need be that, instead of saying (as in fig. 3) "therefore the base DC is equal to the base bc," we must say, "and if the base BC were not the same for the two triangles, we could have shown that the two bases were equal."

We now come to the Fifth Proposition itself. As soon as the construction is completed, and the pupil has stated the thing to be proved, viz., that the angle ABC is equal to the angle ACB, we must say, "Now the first of these angles is equal to angle ABE *minus* angle CBE; and the second is equal to angle ACD *minus* angle BCD." If the pupil does not readily grasp this, we must go back to the figure on p. 109, and then, showing him what angle is left when a part is subtracted from a whole, we must habituate him anew to take angles from angles, and to recognize the results.

This done, we resume, "We shall therefore first show that the large angle on the left, viz., ABE, is equal to the large angle on the right, viz., ACD; we shall then show that the small angle on the left, viz., CBE, is equal to the small angle on the right, viz., BCD. Then, if we take away the small angle on the left from the large angle on the left, and do the same on the right, the two remainders must be equal (by the axiom which we used in the Second Proposition), *i.e.*, the angle ABC must be equal to ACB."

In this way, the pupil will be taken, as it were, into the secret of the campaign before the war begins, and will not be bewildered by the tactics which might else seem to him unnecessarily lengthy and inexplicable, and impossible to remember.

Proceeding to the actual proof, the pupil may be easily brought to see that it will consist of two distinct parts: I. The first part will prove that the large angle ABE is equal to the large angle ACD. II. The second part will prove that the small angle CBE is equal to the small angle BCD. For the first part, we shall have to use the large triangles ABE and ACD; for the second part, the small triangles CBE, BCD.

I. As for the first part, he will readily accept it, from the practice that he has had with figures (1) and (2).

At the conclusion of the first part, when it has been proved that the base CD is equal to the base BE, and the angle BDC equal to the angle BEC, the teacher may say to the pupil, "Now perhaps you may wonder what is the use of proving these two things. But you will soon see that we shall use both of them in the second part of the Proposition. For the side CD belongs to another triangle besides ADC. To what triangle? Again, the angle ADC belongs to another triangle besides the triangle ADC. To what triangle? And the same is true of the angle AEB and the side BE. To what triangle do they belong, besides belonging to ABE?" Having elicited that these sides and angles also belong to the triangles CBE, BCD, we reply, "We shall now pass to these triangles, and see what we can prove about them."

II. The second part presents a little difficulty, because, in applying the Fourth Proposition to the triangles BDC, BEC, instead of being able to *infer* that "the bases or third sides are *equal*," the pupil is confronted with the pre-existing *fact* that the bases are the *same*. But this difficulty has been met in figures (3) and (4).[1]

9. In giving these ample details of the Author's experiences in teaching these early propositions, it is not meant that other teachers should reproduce these explanations verbatim. The object is rather to show how important it is that the teacher, in the earliest lessons of geometry, should "keep touch" with the pupil. Where the learner can readily accept the proof without these or similar explanations, the teacher may safely pass on without them.

But the teacher must be quick to perceive the least symptoms of bewilderment, and must never allow the pupil to lose coolness and confidence, or to guess and "plunge," like a bad swimmer, out of his depth. Children differ greatly in the habit and manner of assenting. Some, out of a desire to please, will say "Yes," in answer to the question, "Do you understand this?" when, in reality, they do not understand it, but *only remember* it. Therefore, when a child says he understands any statement in geometry, he should be immediately confronted with several exemplifications of that statement in *different shapes*—angles of different sizes, triangles upside down, X and Y instead of A and B, Arabic numbers instead of letters, and so on; and not till he has passed these tests must the teacher be satisfied that the pupil really understands.

Also, in repeating Euclid, the child must not only be compelled to draw his own figures (or to dictate to the teacher how to draw them), but also when he makes a statement he must be constantly called by the teacher's "Why?" to give a reason for it. "Therefore the base AB is equal to the base CD." Why? "By the Fourth Proposition." "Therefore the remainder AB is equal to the remainder CD." Why? "Because if equals be taken from equals, the remainders are equal." "And AE is equal to AD." Why? "By construction," or "Because we made it so." "Now AB is equal to AC." Why? "By hypothesis," or "Because we supposed it to be so from the beginning."

After the Fifth Proposition has been intelligently and thoroughly mastered, Euclid should present little difficulty till the pupil reaches the Sixth Book, which belongs to a stage of instruction beyond the scope of these pages.

But still, up to the Fifteenth Proposition, or further, the teacher will do well to rely mainly on oral instruction, and—particularly if his pupils have good memories—to *beware of the book*.

Deductions, of a very simple sort, should be in use from the start.

---

[1] A shorter method would be, after the figure has been constructed, to say, "Now we are going to use the Fourth Proposition. Enunciate it. What triangles do you see that *look* equal? (Ans., ABE, ACD.) "Then we shall try to prove that these two have two sides and the included angle of the one equal to two sides of the included angle of the other." This done, you say, "Now what other triangles *look* equal?" (Ans. BCD, CBE.) "Then we shall prove the same thing in these triangles." If the boy can readily pick out the two pairs of equal triangles for himself, it may be unnecessary to use the longer method of instruction.

VI. RELIGIOUS INSTRUCTION AND HOME INFLUENCE.

57. RELIGIOUS INSTRUCTION.

1. It is now generally admitted that, in all subjects of education, it is an injury for the young to be taught to repeat language to which they attach no meaning.

Teachers who believe this, and who believe further that Religious Instruction is the most important of all educational subjects, ought to be especially on their guard here lest the desire to train children in this subject early should result in their being trained prematurely, and consequently inefficiently.

2. But the presence of children at short religious acts, such as "saying grace," singing hymns, and other *short* expressions of devotion, is a very different thing from making them learn and repeat long and (to them) unintelligible formularies of religion.

Silence and attention during "grace" afford one of the earliest and most impressive indirect means of helping a child to realize that there is a Power in the Family, never approached but with reverence; unseen and unheard, yet addressed in words; One who is present not only on Sundays, but on all days, and who, though He is far above us, is nevertheless not so high but that we may ask Him to bless our daily bread.

3. The Lord's Prayer—much though we may desire it to be the first prayer because it is the best prayer—ought, in the Author's judgment, to be deferred till the child has been accustomed to the usual simple petition for "father, mother, brothers, and sisters." No words can well be more powerful than these in introducing the child to the conception of One who must be above all things in greatness and goodness, because he is even greater and better than the child's parents.

As to the importance of the circumstances of prayer, enough has been said above (see § 32).

4. Not till after a child has thus realized in some faint degree the human revelation of God, revealing Him as One who can bless and help, should he be introduced to that other revelation through Nature, which reveals Him as the Maker and Sustainer of all things. Suffer the child first to exult a little in the beauty, and to admire the glory and order, of the visible world, before leading his thoughts up from the things made, to Him who made them.

And when the attempt is made, it is best made by the father or mother, not by nurses or servants. "I remember," writes Preceptor, "that on one occasion, during a walk in the country, when I noticed that my son—a child of four or five years old—seemed more than usually impressed with the beauty of what he saw around him, I thought the time might now have come to lead him from things visible to the invisible Maker, and I asked him who, he thought, had made all this beautiful world. He at once replied 'God;' but his emotions of joy were at once checked, and his countenance became blank and inexpressive, as if he were passing from a state of genuine feeling into mere unmeaning speech. It was obvious to me that he did not realize, in any sense whatever, the meaning of what he uttered; and I guessed at once (what I afterward ascertained upon inquiry) that he had been trained to say it by his nurse, and was merely answering by rote.

"I felt that this teaching, however well intended, had been premature. Wesley records it as one of the critical moments of his life, when his mother took him into a room by himself, and there for the first time spoke to him of the Being above, to whom alone worship is due. Not to all parents assuredly is it given so to impress their children as the young Wesley was then impressed by his mother; and very probably I might have failed as the nurse failed. But I felt that I had been deprived of even the chance of succeeding. No great harm had been done; but an opportunity of good—which I might possibly have utilized, and should have liked at least to have tried to utilize—had been irrevocably lost."

5. The name of God ought by no means to be introduced lightly, or on every occasion, to enforce duty. The consciousness of right and wrong in the first place, and where this is insufficient the will of the parents, ought to suffice for the most part without appeal to religion.

Above all things, teachers should avoid accustoming or encouraging children to talk much about religious matters. Such talk, even when accompanied with right action, cannot be wholesome, for it must always express more than the child really feels. Besides, in most cases, it will not be accompanied with right action: it will be a mere safety-valve for unnatural excitement, letting off steam which ought to have been utilized for something better than words. A child who *gushes* generally turns out badly; and it is this type of gushing creature which goes far to justify the proverb, "The greater the saint, the greater the sinner."

6. Yet it should always be tacitly assumed that God is the Author of all duties, the Maker of the ties that bind a household together, that he sees right and wrong, even though unwrought and unuttered, and existent only in the mind; and that He is pleased with what is right, and displeased with what is wrong.

The best time for impressing this upon the child is before his evening prayer. Most children are apt to be more open and disposed to reveal their thoughts at this time; and it therefore affords the best opportunity for the parent or trainers to review the events of the day. "Now have we anything to think of before prayers? Is there anything done amiss to-day which you must try to do better to-morrow?" Many a child who would have resented a sudden scolding, especially before strangers, will be much more open to genuine conviction and contrition if his fault is thus for the first time pointed out; and a resolution thus made, and followed by the usual evening prayer, is more likely to be adhered to than if made at any other time.

7. By this habit of practically reviewing the day—not, however, to be mechanically or invariably adopted—an additional force and meaning will be given to prayer. Acknowledgment of fault and weakness naturally leads the mother to speak of God as the Forgiver and Helper, to whom prayer must be addressed for forgiveness of the past and strength for the future.

8. As regards church-going, it is obvious that what are called children's services must be less tedious and more intelligible for them than the ordinary services; and with discreet management—so conducted in the church, and with the results so moderated at home, as not to produce any unwholesome excitement—they are probably of advantage.

9. But on the other side much is to be said for the presence of children at the religious observances of their elders. In the Law of Moses it is assumed that the child is present at the celebration of the Passover before he is aware of its meaning; and part of the celebration consists of the child's inquiry and the father's reply, thus traditionally handing down the meaning of the institution from one generation to another.

In the same way the presence of a child with his parents at the services of the church (where they are not so long or so dull as to be absolutely intolerable, probably conveys more indirect benefit than is commonly supposed, giving him an early conception of religion as a social and not merely individual influence, and quickening his apprehension of the Being to whom not only his parents but the whole neighborhood unite in all solemnity to pay homage.

10. If a child is fond of reading, and chooses to read the Bible for himself, his instinct will probably guide him to those parts which are most intelligible, or from which he can at least extract a meaning, and there is no sufficient reason for preventing him from this desultory perusal. But it would be a very sad mistake for a teacher to cause children to read through the Bible consecutively as a religious task.

Not to speak of the genealogies, there are obviously many portions of the books of the Law and the Prophets which should be passed over in teaching children, and there are other portions in the historical books treated with a fullness of detail which does not fit them to be used as reading lessons for the young. Yet, on the other hand, the summaries of the Bible frequently employed by those who have to "get it up for examination," for the most part, omit everything that constitutes the life of the Biblical narrative, so that they cannot be accepted as substitutes for the original.

11. The best course seems to be that a child should receive, as an introduction to the reading of the Bible, one or two oral lessons about the early history of religion, illustrated perhaps by a visit (if in London) to the Egyptian and Assyrian rooms in the British Museum, showing how the great nations of antiquity, groping after the great God who

made heaven and earth, typified Him in various imperfect forms, representing His power and wisdom, and how they fell short of the conception of the Eternal Righteousness and the worship due to Him.

12. After this, they may be taught how God in the darkness sent down a ray of light to Abraham the Father of the Faithful, and to his children and descendants, guiding and chastening them, and revealing Himself to them not only as Powerful, but as being One, Eternal, Righteous, Just, Forgiving; and with this introduction the child may read the lives of the Patriarchs and of the deliverers of Israel, understanding (though, of course, very imperfectly as yet) that the great merit of all these heroes was their faith or trust in Right against Might.

13. Not till a later period must the story of Christ be introduced. In prayers and hymns the child will be already familiar with parts of it. But now these parts are to be combined for him into a brief whole; and he is to be introduced to the Incarnation as being the central event in the world's history, wherein God, who had previously revealed Himself through servants, at last revealed Himself through His Son as being our Father in Heaven.

14. Some people maintain that the conception of God as "our Father" is not in itself sufficient, being compatible with self-conceit, foolish hopes for oneself, contempt for others, and an insensibility to justice; and doubtless if a child is taught to realize God as "*my* Father," these objections are well founded. But they disappear if he recognizes the full force of "our," namely, that God is the Father of our enemies as well as our friends, of those whom we are disposed to dislike or neglect as being offensive or common-place, no less than of those whom we admire as exceptionally good and great; and that He cannot be supposed to fall below Plato's standard of justice, which consisted in "giving to *all* what is best for them."

15. It is thought by many in these days an old-fashioned and exploded doctrine to teach that there is an Evil Being in the world resisting the Good. Yet without believing in the existence of the weaker Evil it is scarcely possible to believe in the existence of the stronger Good.

Even to a child the question must suggest itself in his very earliest years, How can the world—being, in part, evil—have been created by a perfectly good God?

Admit at once that the origin and existence of Evil are past all explanation, and constitute a logical difficulty. The reply is obvious, that any theory whatever of the existence or non-existence of a God involves a logical difficulty. It is therefore the right course to adopt that theory which, though logically inexplicable, does least violence to reason and best approves itself to the instinct of Faith.

Not for nothing therefore does the Bible put at the very fore-front of its teaching the doctrine that there is Evil contending against Good; and to suppress this doctrine, even for children, is, in the Author's judgment, to do great harm.

16. For other reasons, teachers should by no means blink the existence of Evil. The fighting instinct is strong in the young; and one powerful means of enlisting them on the side of the Good is to enlist them against the Evil.

There is a great deal in the Christian Revelation that is not, cannot be, and perhaps ought not to be, readily intelligible to children—for example, the full meaning of forgiveness, and still more the appreciation of Love as dominant in the Universe. It is almost as impossible for children to believe that an element of human nature, so close to them as Love is, and so familiar, should be the most potent Power in the immaterial world, as it is to believe that the same electric fluid which makes the hair crackle beneath the comb produces the roar of the reverberating thunder.

All the more necessary is it that the teacher should appeal to that strong and wholesome instinct which leads the young to fight for one side against another, pointing out to them that they, in a certain sense, are soldiers in the army of Light contending against the powers of Darkness.

17. It may seem a hard saying, but it is said with the Author's deepest conviction of its truth, that few boys can be induced to *love* Christ; and if they say they do, they probably say so mainly because they have been taught to say so.

Yet many boys can be induced to feel a *loyalty* to Christ as their Leader in the battle against Evil; and it is therefore in this character of a Champion that the teacher should strive to present Him. There is no stronger antidote against all the evils that spring up for the young from that thoughtless selfishness which is almost inseparable from youth and inexperience, than Christ thus presented by the teacher and apprehended by the pupil.

18. Whatever may be the differences of opinion among teachers as to the exact historical accuracy of certain parts of the various books that make up the Bible, most will probably agree that the Bible was made for man and not man for the Bible. In other words, it is better to be a sincere worshiper of God, while doubting the genuineness or authenticity of certain passages in the Scriptures, than to accept the Scriptures in their entirety, yet neither to love, nor trust, nor reverence their divine Giver.

19. To lead the young therefore to the worship of God, through the study of the Scriptures, should be the object of the teacher; not to produce a belief in the letter of the Scriptures by habituating children to worship the Book itself.

This being the case, even those who may believe that there are no interpolations and no inaccuracies in our versions of the Old and New Testament must be anxious that the young shall so study the Scriptures as to be led thereby to worship God, *i. e.*, to love Him, trust Him, and reverence him with all the strength of human faculty.

For this purpose the teacher will do well to take as the basis of his teaching that famous vision of the prophet Elijah which taught that the Revelation of the Supreme is not contained in the Fire, nor in the Whirlwind, but in the still small Voice.

The minds of children, naturally alive to the marvelous, are so impressed by the stupendous miracles recorded in the Old Testament that they are often disposed to connect the Revelation of God in those pages solely with these wonders; and then, in after days, when they hear the historical accuracy of some of these events doubted by some whose judgment they respect, they lose at once their belief not only in the historical accuracy of these particular incidents, but also in the whole Revelation which they were supposed to convey.

This danger may be met by laying more stress upon the spiritual revelation conveyed to Israel in the Law and the Prophets; and by showing how, by national calamities and individual troubles, the different spokesmen of God who wrote the books of the Bible gradually built up a structure of religious thought and expression such as cannot be found even in the literature of Greece, or Rome, or India, or any other civilized or uncivilized race.

Teachers will of course remember, in dealing with this subject, that, if they are not teaching their own children, they are bound to consider the parents, who may not unnaturally object to negative teaching on religious subjects. But to parents who themselves undertake the religious teaching of their children, or to teachers who have full authority to give such instruction on this subject as may seem best to them, the words of Preceptor may not be without use.

"When I came," he says, "to the account of the battle of Beth-horon and of the sun's standing still, I endeavored, first of all, before telling the story of the battle, to make my children realize the place, time, circumstances, and historical importance of the struggle, that they might have a vivid picture of it before their eyes, and might also know that this battle was one of the great battles of the world; which, if it had turned out differently, might have changed the whole course of history and of religion. Then I began the story of the march and the fighting, and at a certain point I said: 'Here the story goes on to say that Joshua, the general, stretched out his hand to the sun and to the moon, and bade them stand still, so that the people of Israel might continue the pursuit of their enemies; and that the sun and moon stood still, so that there was no day so long as this before or after, in the history of the world. But it is generally agreed by the wisest people that this part of the story must have arisen from some misunderstanding, because we know from astronomy that this could not have happened without causing a great crash and destruction of all the Universe; and different people give different explanations. But one thing is certain—and that is enough for you and me—that on this day the Lord fought for Israel; and that if this battle had been won by the Canaanites, and not by Israel, then the Chosen People would never have entered into the Promised Land; and the children of Israel might have remained wanderers for ever, and there would perhaps have been no King David, and no Psalms, and no Prophets; and being left without the light of true religion, all the world might still be lying in darkness, and so at this moment you and I might not be worshipers of Christ, and perhaps we should be heathens, bowing down before blocks of wood and stone.'"

It is the Author's experience that, without negative teaching, and without entering into polemics, it is possible to lay much more stress than is usually laid upon the essence of Revelation, as distinct from the medium through which the Revelation is conveyed.

20. If, as will probably be admitted by all, it is impossible to be a sincere worshiper of God and yet remain *deliberately* immoral, it would seem also evident that an apparent sanction of immorality in the pages of the Bible is likely to defeat the purpose for which the Bible is read. Let the pupil therefore be very early confronted with that notable saying of our Lord, that certain things were allowed by Moses in the Law "for the hardness of men's hearts;" and let him be told that this saying applies to the whole of the Old Testament; so that he is not to suppose that, because Jael, or Jephtha, or Samson, or David, did certain things which are not expressly blamed by the historian, therefore those things are necessarily good and right for us in our days, or were even right in those days. And, if we believe that the last and greatest of the Prophets, John the Baptist, is inferior to "the least in the Kingdom of God" in the knowledge of the divine nature, it must seem an obvious inference that even the conceptions and judgments expressed by the writers themselves of the books of the Old Testament must not be expected to stand on the level of the morality of the New Testament. As to the future life, one caution at least may be of use. Servants (unless in very exceptional cases) ought not to be allowed to speak to children about this subject. A child's nature may be warped, or an irremediable taint of servility and superstition communicated, by a frequent and voluble mention of "hell-fire."

Almost as unwise, though not so harmful, is the attempt to ignore altogether the existence of a retribution after death, in teaching children. Much better is it to recognize with very rare mention—but very clearly, when mentioned—that there is a future Life, and a future Judgment, of which we know little more than this, that it will be in the hands of One who is perfect Justice as well as perfect Mercy; and that the future Life and future Judgment will differ from the present Life and the present Judgment not in being more lax and indulgent, or more severe and stern, but in being more manifestly and perfectly just and merciful, because hereafter there will be no vestiges of Evil striving to obscure and hinder the Good.

22. On one point more especially the child may be allowed and

encouraged to think definitely of Heaven, viz., as a place where there will be a meeting of those who have loved one another on earth.

Of all the encouragements and helps to a good and pure life, next to the loyal worship of Christ, there is perhaps none so powerful as the mention made in daily prayers of the names of those who have gone before us to the unseen world, with whom we trust and pray that we may be hereafter reunited. Let those who care more about words than about meaning tell us, if they please, that Heaven is not a *place*. Admitted. We will go further and admit that nothing will be, and perhaps that nothing even now is, precisely or even approximately what we suppose it to be. Yet if we believe that our best and noblest aspirations come from One who is able and willing to satisfy them, we must needs think that corresponding to every pure wish that we entertain on earth—and what wish can be purer or more natural than this?—there will be some spiritual satisfaction in Heaven, not indeed the same as we suppose, but differing in being infinitely better. And so, as regards the meeting of friends in the second life, while admitting that there will be no "place" and "no meeting," we may still retain the belief that there will be something corresponding to "meeting" in something corresponding to "place."

58. HOME INFLUENCE ON THE CHILD AT SCHOOL.

1. As to boarding-schools, the writer knows little that is not known to the ordinary run of parents; and therefore the following remarks are intended for those whose children are attending day-schools.

2. But the following rule applies still more to boarding-schools than to day-schools; viz., that the father should warn the boy against some of the temptations to which he will be exposed. Cheating in various shapes, and indecency, or impurity more or less grave, are sure to be found in any large school; and sometimes in small schools these evils are still more prevalent than in large ones. This being the case, it is only fair to warn a boy what he will have to meet. Let him be told that he is to keep out of these things; and, without making himself a "prig," he is to use the earliest opportunity that may be presented to him, when he rises in the school, for setting his face against faults such as these and for helping his school-fellows to check them.

Against evils of the latter and graver kind, the father ought to warn a boy with somewhat more distinctness. Many a boy, even in childhood, goes wrong simply through ignorance and for want of warning.

3. If the parents are selecting a private school, they ought to take great pains to ascertain the qualifications of the teacher.

The expensive preparatory schools intended to prepare boys for the principal Public Schools are many of them of well-known excellence; but the average private school for the middle and lower classes is at present (1882) very bad indeed, and perhaps now hardly equal (in intellectual training) to the average standard of Public Elementary Schools.

4. A day-school presupposes a good home.

What the house-master (who stands *in loco parentis* to the boys in his house) does at a boarding-school for his pupils, that the parents must do for their children at a day-school, if the boy at the day-school is to make the same moral and intellectual progress as at a boarding-school. At a good school boys ought not to need assistance in their studies at home in order to keep up with the class; but they will often make more rapid progress if they have some occasional help at home. Few parents are likely to be able to give this assistance so efficiently as a house-master; but the deficiency is often more than compensated by the general influence of home life and the stimulus of the boy's desire to obtain the approval of his parents.

5. The boy should be encouraged, if possible, to walk to and from school; or at all events part of the way. Walking, especially with an object is good mentally and morally, as well as physically; enabling a boy to be for a time by himself, and to think over matters that have perplexed him in the day.

It is one of the great drawbacks to the great advantages of the boarding-school system that a boy is not enough by himself. Every hour, almost every minute, is filled up either with work or with play; and some boys are in danger of living on from the beginning of term to the end without having half an hour to think. "Calling over," every hour or two, compulsory football or cricket, and abundant Scripture lessons on Sundays, are excellent devices for preventing boys from thinking about mischief; but, if carried to excess, they may sometimes have the effect of preventing a boy from thinking at all.

6. The parents should coöperate with the school by giving their son fit time and place to prepare his home-work, and by seeing that he gets his meals in such time that he may be punctual in attendance.

On first going to school a boy should receive a hint or two from his parents as to the means for ensuring punctuality; *e. g.*, he is to get his papers and books ready overnight, and always to put them in one place where he is sure not to miss them when he starts in the morning.

7. Parents should show their interest in the boy's progress by inspecting his register of marks or places, say once a week, and by asking him questions about his work, his sports, his school-fellows, etc., striving as far as possible still to "keep touch" with the boy, although he has now passed out of the sphere of home-teaching.

8. Yet though the parents should take an interest in "marks," and a "high place" should be held up as a natural object for the boy's honorable ambition, they should never fail to remind him that a "high character" is much more important.

There is now in our English schools perhaps too much, certainly not too little, of emulation, competition, prize-winning, and marking; and for the majority of boys the parental influence will be well exerted in counteracting this competitive tendency. For a quick, ambitious boy the counteraction is useful in preventing his ambition from running to excess; and for a dull and backward boy it is no less useful in showing him that there are other objects and prizes besides medals and book prizes, viz., the approval of teachers, parents, and conscience.

9. If a boy goes to a boarding-school, he may need occasional warning that he is not to become an athletic fool; but if he goes to a day-school, there is on the other hand the danger that he may become an intellectual milksop.

Pupils at day-schools should therefore be encouraged (if they need encouragement) to make the best use of the training afforded by gymnasium, fives courts, etc. For rowing and swimming there are abundant facilities in almost all large towns; and parents should not let their children pass the age of twelve or thirteen without having learned at least these elements of athletics.

10. When a boy is at a private school, or under a young master at some public school, where the classes are too large or the supervision is too lax, he may sometimes waste a whole term, without any misconduct or laziness so flagrant as to bring the matter before the school authorities or arrest the parents' attention.

Therefore for young boys it will be a great advantage if the parents will now and then test their progress by one or two simple questions: "You say you have finished fractions; then what do $\frac{1}{2}$ and $\frac{1}{4}$ make? You are getting on in Latin; then let me hear the future of *rego*, and what is the English of *Naves nautae habent?* You are practicing English composition; then write me a short letter describing what you hope to do in the next holidays."

Parents shrink from doing this, because they think it is out of their line, and above their capacities. Unhappily, the questions that are capable of eliciting the ignorance of boys are generally within the compass of the meanest understanding. But if they have any diffidence themselves, let them take the boy to some competent friend who will do it for them. Five minutes a month, during the first term, will enable them to ascertain whether their boy is learning anything or nothing; and for want of this little supervision how much is sometimes lost! At a Public School the boy wastes a whole term, gets a bad Report, and returns to school morally dejected and intellectually demoralized. Or, still worse, he wastes a whole term at a Private School, gets an excellent Report, and returns to school well satisfied with his failure, and still more intellectually demoralized; and after two or three years of time similarly wasted he leaves school with six excellent Reports, to find every Public School closed against him because of his hopeless ignorance.

11. Without encouraging boys to "sneak," the parents may seize fit opportunities, two or three times in the year, to ascertain whether any moral epidemic appears to be prevailing or springing up in the school; and very often, without mentioning names, they can give such assistance to the school authorities as will enable them to stop mischief almost before it has begun to be mischievous.

THEORY AND PRACTICE OF TEACHING.

BY REV. EDWARD THRING, M.A.

Head Master of Uppingham School, Late Fellow of King's College, Cambridge.

PREFACE.

It is ill protesting too much. Many good resolutions of silence made and confirmed during thirty years of school work, as every hope of a public character which brightened the early days was destroyed, have been broken by the appearance of this book. Success only strengthened the conviction that it was useless to speak; and yet when the conviction seemed strongest some folly has swept it away. Or is it instinct, like the prescient idiotcy of the butterfly, that lays its eggs on cabbage leaf or nettle, forced by a blind impulse to thwart its own experience, and deposit part of its life where no sign warrants an idea that it will be allowed to live? Perhaps a strong belief that anything, which has a touch of true life in it, will live somewhere or other is at the bottom of it all, however overlaid by chiller wisdom. So this bit of life goes forth. And if it does any work or worker good, cheers or helps a single toiling fellow-worker, the writer will have had his reward. It may be that another hand and heart may take this up, enrich it with wealth of his own, fill it full of prevailing power, and send it on, a higher creation, in a fortunate hour, to a happier end.

THE SCHOOL HOUSE, UPPINGHAM, May, 1883.

EDITORIAL NOTICE.

The general principles and many practical suggestions of this little treatise by an experienced and successful teacher, are of universal application, but the book is the production of the Head Master of a classical school, and the illustrations are drawn from the observations and doings of boys in Greek and Latin classes.

The volume is dedicated to our old friend and co-laborer, Rev. R. H. Quirk, on whose urgency it was written.

A glance at the Contents with its characteristic phraseology on the next page, will give a good idea of the volume.

Material to Think about.

"Material to think about." That is the heart of the whole matter. There can be no thought without material for thought. The baby with its wondering eyes for a time gathers material, even as it takes food, by a natural process. It cannot help doing so. After a time, the curiosity excited by novelty without and by life within is somewhat satisfied by familiarity with the outside of the objects most often seen, or repressed by contact with ignorance and commands to stop unwelcome questions. At this point, where the first curiosity ceases, true education begins, by lifting up a little corner of the veil of the world of common things, and showing that there is an inside as well as an outside to be seen. Thus observation, instead of curiosity, or, rather, as a trained development of curiosity, begins the work of intelligent progress.

The first advance on unconscious absorption of material of thought is the implanting a habit of observation, that is, of consciously gathering material for thought. Here, again, is solid ground and good foothold,— leg-work, not wing-work. Observation is only a better name for patient, well-directed work, a name for learning to see by getting, and waiting long on that which is worthy of being known.

It is recorded of Turner, the great painter, that he was seen to spend a whole day in throwing pebbles into the water, whilst others were working away round him. Throwing pebbles into the water! With what contempt a machine-intellect, with its mechanic power of turning all into a kind of philosophic ledger, would visit such a childish proceeding. How the cold calculating fact-machine would scoff. But there are worlds on worlds; higher worlds with their inhabitants; and the great painter, working in the world of life and living thought, knew what he was about. His power of observation was so great, and his patience and love so unwearied, that, with his trained eye, he could find intense interest and gather lessons above all price from the ripple, and the waves, and the play of light, and harmonious discord of varying movements, from the common curves made by a common stone falling into common water, over which an untrained eye and mind could not spend a profitable moment. Before his eyes was spread the ever-stationary, ever-moving mirror, the changeful eternity of light that flows, the gliding earth-born light of water, with its strange memories of higher worlds, and strange affinities to cloud and sky, free beyond all earthly things to come and go, still loving to borrow, as it moves, brightness from sky and gleams from cloud or shore, and welcoming in its bosom, like a living thing, all images that reach it in its course. He stood and looked upon it, and tried to unlock its secrets, and, conscious or unconscious of the full interpretation, caught some glimpses of the great illuminated text of the book of the thoughts of God, appreciated the exquisite subtlety of the handwriting of speech divine, became a kind of living microscope in his power of seeing unknown beauty, and then handed on to us non-seers the gain of new discovery, to be henceforth part of the possession of the world. A common stone thrown into common water could thus become a prophet revealing truth. But to whom does the prophet-voice of stones and water speak? A careful analysis will show that the great painter, the genius, could see and understand, because he had learnt by years of patient work to observe more than other people. The child begins its first attempts at drawing by a few bounded lines from an unpracticed hand, that will not do its owner's bidding, and an unpracticed mind, that as yet has not much bidding to give; and under it he writes cat, or dog, or cow, as the case may be, and the writing is necessary. And unless hand and mind practice, that is, work, they will never do more. Turner himself, had he been debarred from practicing his hand, and not permitted to exercise his eye, could have done no more. It is quite immaterial to this argument what the difference may be between any pupil and Turner before they end. The all-important fact remains, that, for a long time, the path of both is the same, and the still more important fact, that the teacher has, as his province, that path, and that path only, as far as the external aspect, both of his own and his pupil's work, is concerned. The teacher has no concern with the beyond; but the fact that the vast majority never get within sight of the point where a beyond begins, but remain in the limbo of little-boy drawings, and such like, does concern him very much indeed. The point at which observation begins, and at which it stops, a point very often but little in advance of the unconscious vision of the child, is his business.

Genius and Work.

Genius is an infinite capacity for work growing out of an infinite power of love. Observation is work; without observation there is no thought; without material to build there is no building. Whether it is pleasurable or otherwise, poet's or schoolboy's, observation still is work. And the ideal, after all that foggy enthusiasm can do to mystify, or blowers of glittering bubbles can blow, is but the final expression of the highest thought produced by the greatest knowledge and feeling; and the greatest knowledge and feeling is produced by years of patient, loving work, in a mind originally strong and susceptible. No doubt this is a most unsatisfactory and prosaic conclusion for angels, and wings, and the empyreal to arrive at; but intensely comforting, happy, and real, to an earnest man, who is ready to humble himself to watch and wait on what he loves. It gives the absolute certainty of success in proportion to the means employed. Observation, work, love of work—these are the masters of the world. By these that high training is built up which deals with life and mind as all other pursuits are dealt with, and learns faithfully from the first rudiments to the complete end, and no more thinks it beneath his notice to do the lowest kind of work than a musician thinks it beneath his notice to know his notes.

Work, simple, straightforward, intelligent work is everything. The strong and the weak alike, the genius, as well as the slowest mind, must go through the same work till they part company, as perseverance, strength, and love, carry the best minds farther. There can be no thought till there has been observation. There can be no observation without work. The highest form of human existence is the power of working unweariedly and prevailingly, lovingly wooing, and winning power by love. One word, rightly understood, contains it all,—WORK.

How to Learn.

The boys do not know how to set about learning; they ought to be taught. This teaching cannot be given through the medium of the unknown. It will be acknowledged that the power to observe a simple thing and answer a plain question is the very beginning of mental training. But the boys neither observe, nor can answer. That is, they do not know the process by which it is done, and learning new difficulties does not teach them. They ought to be taught. It is the beginning of the knowledge how to learn. This assertion can be proved and remedied at the same time. Let the teacher, for example, ask the boys of an ordinary class to give an account of any well-known object. For instance, What's an apple? Minutes on minutes will be spent before any reasonable description of it will be given. In other words, there will not be a single boy out of hundreds who may be questioned in this way who has ever had the quiet bit of teaching given him, that the moment he is required to answer, his business is at once to picture to himself the thing mentioned in as many aspects as possible, one by one, compare it with the things most like it, and then note the peculiar facts which make it different from everything else. To take a second example somewhat more complex. "The sower went forth to sow his seed." If a really intelligent answer is to be given as to the meaning of the word "seed" under such circumstances, the process is, first to picture in the mind a seedsman's shop, with all its various seeds, none better to the eye than another, hard, dry facts, all of them, and to contrast it with the summer garden, where every flower and plant declare what they are, self-revealed. The main distinctions of the seed stand out at once. Next the seed must be pictured in the ground, all its hard, dry nature vanishing; it is full of new movement, roots penetrating in subtle, tender shapes of change, and, as they change, drawing the secret powers of the ground into fresh vitality, the seed thus growing with a growth of its own, and so on. All this kind of truth and power of answer proceed, to a very great extent, by rule, the very simple rule of at once picturing the object named, contrasting it with its nearest neighbors, and noting the peculiarities, which present themselves as things seen, rather than as researches of thought.

To apply this to words. What is the construction of the word "when," we will ask. This is only another form of asking, What is the real meaning of the word "when"? The meaning of the word "when" can only be discovered by framing sentences to show its meaning. A little trouble will make it clear that the word "when," in such a sentence as, "When the end has come, all is over," means, "The moment the end has come, all is over;" and again, in the sentence, "When he was in India, he hunted," that the word "when" means, "at various uncertain times." Nothing can be more different than these two meanings; and, accordingly, the constructions used will be very different in every language in which shades of mood are marked.

Sight supplies the place of thought, as soon as a few plain instructions are given as to how to learn. The fact is, it is impossible to examine and report on—nothing. The beginner has no definite object before his mind's eye, and till he is taught the plain common-sense rule, that he must have a definite object before him, and is shown how to have a definite object before him, he has not learnt how to set about his work. Years of useless toil might be saved if the learners only knew how to set about their work. Many other devices to make learning skillful and effective wil. occur to the practical teacher; but, as this is not a teacher's manual, it is sufficient to point the way.

What things the attention ought to be fixed on, and in what way, what to forget, and what to remember, unobtrusive peculiarities that require notice, obtrusive excellences that stick of themselves, these, and many like instructions which experience suggests, can shorten labor, and cause time to be employed to the best advantage. But even to draw attention to the science of learning and the intelligent skill that can exist and may be imparted in the process of setting to work intelligently will be a wondrous advance. As yet, the boy-world, at all events, knows nothing of it. Again, there is another aspect of the not-having-been-taught-to-learn question. No one who has not examined his own class on the work of the past term, and had continued, aye, long-continued experience, could possibly believe that a teacher might spend weeks and weeks in. laying down a few principles of work, and questioning, in and out, of the boys a few elementary beginnings of intelligent treatment of sentences, and have those questions answered, and yet at the end find that no single boy had paid any real attention, and that the work had all to be done over again. If this is the case, as it is, with the most carefully worked-out plan, what happens when there is no plan at all, and a mere farmer's-wife scattering represents the work of the operator, and a punishment lottery the condition of the boys? The fact is, the sole idea of work that a great many good boys have is the filling the knowledge shop; and the work they do themselves is their only idea of the process. It never enters their minds that the teacher is there not merely to correct mistakes, hear lessons, and show them word-tricks and examples of successful work, but to point out the way in which they ought to prepare their minds for doing any work at all. And as this never enters their minds, they naturally reject it even when it is done, and, like a bad player of a familiar game, are only conscious of their misses and hits, and superbly blind to the wrong attitude and the clumsy position, which the scientific player knows will leave them comparative failures to the end of time. The art of learning has no existence for them, and they cannot see that they ought to readjust their crooked, self-willed mental postures at the teacher's word; that is not their idea of being taught, and they cannot bring themselves to receive it. They will not take it. This is a very serious evil. Bad work is one thing; but working in the wrong way is another. Every teacher who is a teacher ought to draw a strong distinction between faults of ignorance, which may be pardonable, and faults of refusing to be taught, and persisting in doing things the wrong way in spite of teaching. A sharp, unmistakable line ought to be drawn between the two. The class ought never to be able to confound for one moment the not doing what they can do, and are shown how to do daily, with any mistake, however gross and startling, which is of ignorance, however culpable. But the misfortune is, the mistakes are gross and startling; they get up and hit the master, as it were, in the face, whilst the refusing to be taught is silent, and a planless master does not observe it at all, and accordingly it often escapes scot-free.

Right Point of View—Study of a Cathedral.

A grand cathedral, for example, is a glorious specimen of thought in stone; but to many the stone meets their eyes, and is but stone, with no message of the higher life, of which, nevertheless, it is a most true and living expression. There it stands, vast, immovable, majestic. What is the point of view from which to examine it? It strikes the eye as a great building. The outward form, as it first appeals to the eye, shall claim attention first. When a traveler in the distance, coming to see it, crosses the last hill, ten miles off, the massive walls and towers in the middle of the plain tell him that he has the famous edifice before him; and these are just sufficient characteristics (sufficient expression of thought, that is) to mark it as a building intended for worship. Many are satisfied at this point. Mere distance deprives them of any power to see more; but they have seen enough, and never go near enough to get fuller knowledge, though what they do know may be as familiar to them as their own hands. These are they who, for want of time or inclination, stop short, and always keep their minds ten miles away from their subject. Some go nearer, and at a distance of five miles the cathedral becomes an important feature in the landscape; but the landscape, not the cathedral, is still the main consideration. Many minds never get nearer than five miles. In the precincts all the outside can be seen. Many are satisfied with a definite knowledge of the outside of beauty. But the great purpose does not reveal itself till the reader of mind addresses himself to the inner truth, and lovingly, with a disciple's heart and eye, searches out the history, learns the plan, strives to enter into the secret shrine of the feelings which wrought out the great sanctuary, and to translate out of the stone the speech which in very truth is in it. Then, as he gazes, spirit answers spirit, and voiceless thoughts, breathed out of the fair structure, pass gently into the gazer's soul, and enter there, and there revive the memory of noble minds that built their heart's best into those walls. And all the inventive genius wakes and lives again at the thrill of a kindred touch. Prayers that passed up—words from praying hearts—and were petrified in pinnacle and lofty roof, pour forth their inspiration and their faith once more. Anthems caught in mid-air, as they mounted upwards to the throne of God, column and arch, one blended harmony of worship and praise, peal like great organ pipes in the ear of him whose life interprets life, and roll down all their music, the marvels of the old, old years from the eternal stone, so silent, yet so ready with its story. Thus the dumb walls shall speak, and the beam unlock its secrets, and the cabinet of spirit-knowledge ever open to a spirit that can watch, and wait, and learn. There is solitude no more. Unseen presences sweep to and fro, the void space fills, and all the solid buttresses and towers melt back into the aspirations out of which they grew. The great past lives again, the peopled centuries unfold and throng the quiet scene with countless shapes, as mind reads mind, content to honor, and love, and follow, according as it is led.

Such is the power of getting near, the power of the right point of view, when distance is got rid of, and mind touches mind, and the loving heart of one willing to be led gets closer and closer to the object of its love.

AMERICAN LIBRARY OF EDUCATION AND SCHOOLS.
EDITED BY HENRY BARNARD, LL.D.

Fifty volumes with an average of 500 pages octavo.
Each volume complete, and sold separately for price annexed, on which is made a discount of 15 per cent. on orders for 5 vols.; of 20 per cent. for 10 vols.; of 25 per cent. for 20 vols.; and of 30 per cent. for not less than 30 volumes.
All orders sent at the risk, and expense of purchaser.
Address H. B., 28 MAIN ST., HARTFORD, CONN.

Nature, Aims, and Methods of Education.

1. **Educational Aphorisms, and Suggestions** on Studies, the Conduct of the Understanding, and the right Ordering of Life. 560 pages: $3.50.

Adams, Æschylus, Alfred, Albert (Prince), Cebes, Arnold, Aristotle, Aurelius, Bible Authors, Bacon, Barbauld, Basedow, Blackie, Brougham, Burke, Butler, Carlyle, Chalmers, Channing, Choate, Cicero, Comenius, Confucius, Curtis, Democritus, Diesterweg, Edgeworth, Emerson, Epictetus, Euripides, Everett, Evarts, Fræbel, Farrar, Fellenberg, Fenelon, Fischer, Fox, Galen, Gaston, Gladstone, Goethe, Grimke, Grotius, Guizot, Hegel, Herbert, Herder, Hillhouse, Hippel, Horace, Humboldt, Irving, Jay, Jefferson, Johnson, Kant, Kent, Krug, Lasalle, Leibnitz, Locke, Luther, Lycurgus, Mann, Milton, Melancthon, Montaigne, Moscherosch, Napoleon, Niemayer, Oeser, Ovid, Pericles, Pestalozzi, Pierpont, Plato, Plutarch, Plautus, Pope, Pythagoras, Quintilian, Raleigh, Raumer, Richter, Rousseau, Ruckert, Ruskin, Scherer, Schiller, Schwarbe, Scott, Shakspeare, Solon, Swift, Socrates, Tennyson, Terrence, Tischer, Valerius, Virgil, Washington, Webster, Wellington, Weikard, Winthrop, Wordsworth, Young, Zschokke.

2. **Studies and Conduct:** Letters, Essays, and Suggestions on the Relative Value of Studies, Books and the best Methods of Reading, Manners and the Art of Conversation, the Acquisition and True Uses of Wealth, and the Conduct of Life, by men eminent in letters and affairs. 564 pages: $3.50.

Addison, Aiken, Bacon, Barrow, Bodleigh, Brougham, Burleigh, Bulwer, Burns, Carlyle, Channing, Chatham, Chesterfield, Collingwood, DeQuincey, Dupanloup, Everett, Faraday, Franklin, Froude, Gladstone, Grimke, Hall, Hamilton, Herschel, Humboldt, Huxley, Jameson, Jerome, Locke, Lowe, Macaulay, Mackintosh, Mill, Milton, More, Niebuhr, Newman, Pitt, Pope, Potter, Raumer, Sidney, Southey, South, Swift, Taylor, Temple, Tyndal, Whately, Wordsworth, and others.

3. **Kindergarten and Child-Culture:** Papers and Suggestions by Fræbel, Pestalozzi, and others. Edited by Henry Barnard. 800 pages: $3.50.

Adler, Aldrich, Aristotle, Armstroff, Barop, Batchellor, Blow, Brooke, Buls, Bushnell, Busse, Carlyle, Catechism, Carpentier, Christie, Cicero, Cotton, Comenius, Cooper, Dambeck, Diesterweg, Duncan, Ehrlich, Emerson, Fræbel, Franke, Fichte, Fischer, Gallaudet, Garland, Goethe, Grassman, Guilliaume, Gurney, Harris, Hoole, Hornbook, Hunter, Jarvis, Kant, Kraus, Kriege, Lange, Luther, Luz, Lyschinska, Mann, Manning, Marbeau, Marenholtz-Bulow, Marwedel, Middendorf, Montaigne, New England Primer, Newton, Oberlin, Otto, Ortman, Pestalozzi, Payne, Peabody, Plato, Pollock, Portugall, Progler, Quintilian, Ratich, Richter, Rochow, Rousseau, Ruckert, Ruegg, Schlotterbeck Schrader, Shaw, Sluys, Spetker, Steiger, Wheelock, Walter, Wordsworth, Zch.

4. **Home and School Training:** Hints (124 pages) by Dr. Abbott (Head-Master of City of London School), and Lectures, Essays, and Suggestions, by Farrar, Fitch, Huxley, Laurie, Ross, Taylor, and others. 500 pages; $3.50.

Abbott, Arnold, Aristotle, Barbauld, Browning, Brown, Carpenter, Edgeworth, Farrar, Fitch, Gallaudet, Herbert, Huxley, Landon, Laurie, Meikeljohn, Plato, Plutarch, Quick, Rhodes, Ross, Ruskin, Shairp, Stewart, Taylor, Thring, Wheelock, Wilson, Xenophon.

5. **Primary and Elementary School Methods.—**Object Teaching and Oral Lessons on Social Science and Common Things, with the Principles and Practice of Elementary Instruction in the Primary, Model, and Training Schools of Great Britain. 576 pages: $3.50.

Ashburton, Barnard, Bell, Brougham, Currie, Dunn, Ellis, Hay, Keenan, Knight, Lancaster, Macauley, Mayo, Morrison, Richards, Ross, Shields, Stow, Sullivan, Tainsh, Wilderspin, Young.

6. **Subjects and Methods for Grammar and High Schools:** in Graded Systems of Public Schools in American and European Cities. 624 p.: $3.50.

Baltimore, Berlin, Boston, Brussels, Chicago, Cincinnati, Cleveland, Dresden, London, Louisville, Manchester, Munich, New Haven, New York, Rugby, St. Louis, Paris, Philadelphia, Providence, Toronto, Vienna, Windsor, Winchester.

(477)

National Pedagogy: Manuals and Treatises for Teachers.

7. American Pedagogy and Schools—*First Series:* 576 pages: $3.50.
Barnard, Burgess, Bushnell, Channing, Cowdrey, Dickinson, Doane, Everett, Fairchild, Hart, Hopkins, Huntington, Mann, Page, Philbrick, Pierce, Potter, Sheldon, Wayland.

8. American Pedagogy and Schools—*Second Series:* 592 pages: $3.50.
Barnard, Brewer, Bushnell, Camp, Cotton, Chauncey, Cushing, Dickinson, Eaton, Edwards, Eliot, Emerson, Garfield, Gilman, Hall, Harris, Hawkins, Mann, Mayo, Mather, Mill, Northend, Newton, Payne, Peabody, Philbrick, Oliver, Parker, Porter, Sears, Sheldon, Smith, Sprague, Runkle, Thayer, Thompson, Walker, Welles.

9. English Pedagogy and Schools: Treatises and Thoughts, Old and New, on Education, the School, and the Teacher. 480 pages: $3.50.
Ascham's Schoolmaster; Cecil's Advice to his Son; Bacon on Education and Studies, with Annotations by Whately; Wotton's Apothegms on Education; Milton's Tractate on Education; Hartlib's Plan of an Agricultural College; Petty's Trade School; Locke's Thoughts on Education; Spencer's Education; Fuller's Good Schoolmaster; Shenstone's Schoolmistress; Cowper's Review of Schools; Crabbe's Schools of the Borough; Hood's Irish Schoolmaster; with Index to Subjects.

10. English Pedagogy and Schools—*Second Series:* 560 pages: $3.50.
William of Wykeham, Dean Colet and the Public Schools of Winchester, Eton, St. Pauls, Christ Church, Westminster, and Harrow, with Report and Action of Royal Commission in 1866; Cardinal Wolsey's Course for Ipswich Grammar School; Elyot's Governor; Mulcaster's Positions; Hoole's New Discovery of the Old Art of Teaching; Cowley's Plan of a Philosophical College; South, Steele, and Pope on Schools and Education; Goldsmith's Essay and Thoughts on Education; Johnson's Plan of Studies; Pedagogical Views of the 19th Century, by Arnold, Carlyle, Faraday, Froude, Gladstone, Hamilton, Huxley, Lowe, Lyell, Masson, Mill, Russell, Southey, Temple, Tyndall, Whewell.

11. English Pedagogy and Schools—*Third Series:* 592 pages: $3.50.
Adams, Bartley, Bowen, Browne, Browning, Dennison, Farrar, Foster, Gladstone, Grey, Laurie, Lord Reay, Meikeljohn, Mulcaster, Quick, Riggs, Roe, Ross, Shairp, Wilson.

12. German Pedagogy and Schools—*First Series:* 724 pages: $3.50.
Early Christian Teachers, Basedow, Comenius. Ernesti, Erasmus, Franke, Gesner, Hayne, Hecker; Herder, Hieronymians, Luther, Melancthon, Neander, Ratich, Rochow, Sturm, Trotzendorf, Felbiger, Kindermann, Duke George, Frederic II., Maria Theresa.

13. German Pedagogy and Schools—*Second Series:* 640 pages: $3.50.
Abbenrode, Benneke, Diesterweg, Fichte, Fræbel, Gœthe, Graser, Hentschel, Hencomp, Herbart, Hentz, Jacobs, Meierotto, Raumer, Riecke, Rosenkranz, Ruthardt, Wichern, Wolf.

14. French Pedagogy and Schools—*First Series:* 572 pages: $3.50.
Early Christian Teachers and Schools; Jesuits, Christian Brothers and other Teaching Orders; Rabelais, Ramus, Montaigne, Port Royalists, Fenelon, Rollin, Montesquieu, Rousseau, Talleyrand, Condorcet, Daunau, Napoleon, Oberlin, Cuvier, Cousin, Guizot, Ravaisson, Remuset, Marcel, Duruy, LeVerrier, Dupanloup, Mayer, Marbeau, Wilm.

15. French Pedagogy and Schools—*Second Series:* 608 pages: $3.50.
Bossuet, Bréal, Buisson, Christian Brothers, Compayre, Fenelon, Lamy, Le Vayer, Oratorians, Ramus, St. Vincent de Paul.

16. Swiss Pedagogy and Schools. Pestalozzi and his Assistants; Fellenberg, Vehrli, and the Industrial Element. 736 pages: $3.50.
Agassiz, Buss, Calvin, Denzel, Dinter, Fellenberg, Fræbel, Girard, Harnish, Niederer, Pestalozzi, Pfeffer, Ramsauer, Rousseau, Zeller, Zwingli, Wherli, with *Leonard and Gertrude, Evening Hour of a Hermit,* and Selections from other Treatises of Pestalozzi.

17. Greek and Italian Pedagogy and Schools, Ancient and Modern. 560 pages: $3.50.
Acquaviva, Aristotle, Boccacio, Botta, Cassiodorus, Dante, Ficinus, Jerome, Manuals of Religious Teaching Orders, Picus, Petrarch, Politian, Tasso, Valla, Victorino.

18. Belgian, Dutch, Scandinavian, and Spanish Pedagogy and Schools. 464 p.: $3.50.

19. Hebrew, Persia, India, Mohammedan, and other Oriental Pedagogy and Schools, Ancient and Modern. 464 pp.: $3.50.

20. Reminiscences of School, Academy, and College Life—Buildings, Teachers, Studies, Methods, Discipline, and Books as they were in different countries. 464 pp.: $3.50.

	PRICE.		PRICE

B C Books and Primers........................ 25
B C-Shooters, and School Life in 15th Century. 25
BENRODE, Teaching History and Geography.. 25
Academies of New England.................... 25
ACAVIVA, Ratio et Institutio Studiorum 25
AMS, J. Q., Normal Schools, Schools of Silesia 25
nit and Supplementary Schools.............. 25
APSIZ, L., Educational Views. 25
NICOLA. R., School Reform in the Netherlands 25
BOYD, E., Improving a Factory Population.... 25
BERT, PRINCE, Science in Education.......... 25
BOTT, A. B., Schools as they were 50
BOTT, WILLIAM A., Memoir and Portrait...... 50
Slate and Black-board Exercises................ 25
DREWS, S. J., The Jesuits and their Schools.. 25
DREWS, LORIN P., Memoir and Portrait....... 50
Anglo-Saxon Language in Study of English.... 25
HALT, System of Public Instruction 25
BERLM, and other Teachers of the 12th Century. 25
Aphorisms on Principles and Methods of Educ'n 2.50
Babic and Mohammedan Schools................. 25
ARISTOTLE, Educational Views................ 25
Arithmetic, Methods of Teaching............. 25
ARNOLD, MATTHEW, Public Schools in Holland. 25
Secondary Schools in Prussia......./........ 50
ARNOLD, THOMAS K., Memoir and Portrait...... 50
Arts and Science, Schools of.................. 5.50
BACHAM ROGER, Memoir, and the Schoolmaster. 50
BURTON, LORD, Teaching Common Things.. 25
Bavaria, Public Instruction—Primary & Secondary 50
Military Schools and Education................ 25
Technical Schools............................. 25
BACHE, A. D., National University............ 25
BACON, FRANCIS LORD, Memoir and Influence... 25
Essay on Education and Studies............... 25
BACON, LEONARD, Memoir of Hillhouse......... 25
Baden, System of Public Instruction.......... 25
Technical Schools............................ 25
BAILEY, EBENEZER, Memoir and Portrait...... 50
BARNARD, D. D., Right of Taxation for Schools. 25
BARNARD, F. A. P., College Improvements..... 25
Elective Studies in College Course.......... 25
BARNARD, J. G., The Problem of the Gyroscope. 25
BARROW, ISAAC, Studies and Conduct.......... 25
BASEDOW, Memoir, and the Philanthropinum... 50
BATEMAN, N., Educational Labors and Portrait. 50
BATES, S. P., Memoir and Portrait............ 50
Liberal Education............................ 25
BATES, W. G., Training of Teachers.......... 25
Bavaria, System of Public Instruction........ 25
Technical Schools............................ 25
BEECHER, CATHERINE E., Educational Views.. 25
Belgium, System of Public Instruction........ 25
Technical and Special Schools................ 25
BELL, ANDREW, Memoir and Educational Views 50
BENEDICT, ST., and the Benedictines........... 25
BENEKE, F. E., Pedagogical Views.............. 25
Berlin, Educational Institutions.............. 25
Bible and Religion in Public Schools......... 25
BINGHAM, CALEB, Educational Work 25
BISHOP, NATHAN, Educational Work and Portrait 50
BLOCKMAN, Pestalozzi's Labors................. 25
BOCCACCIO, and Educational Reform in Italy... 25
BODLEIGH, SIR THOMAS, Studies and Conduct.... 25
BOOTH, J., Popular Education in England. 50
Boston, Educational Institutions............. 50
BOTTA, V., Public Instruction in Sardinia..... 25
BOUTWELL, GEORGE, Educational Work......... 50
BOWEN, F., Memoir of Edmund Dwight........ 25
BRAINERD, T., Home and School Training in 1718 25
BRINSLEY, J., Ludus Literarius, 1627 25
BROCKETT, L. P., Idiots and their Training.... 25
BROOKS, CHAS., Educational Work and Portrait. 50
BROUGHAM, HENRY LORD, Educational Views... 25
Brunswick, System of Public Instruction...... 25
BUCKHAM, M. H., English Language............. 25
BUCKINGHAM, J. T., Schools as they were in 1800 25
BUCKLEY, J. W., Teachers' Associations........ 25
BURGESS, GEORGE, Religion in Public Schools... 25
BURROWES, T. H., Memoir and Portrait......... 25
History of Normal Schools in Pennsylvania... 25
BURTON, W., District School as it was......... 50
BUSHNELL, H., Early Training, Unconscious Influ. 25

BARNARD, HENRY, Educational Activity 3 50
Address to the People of Connecticut, 1838.... 25
Common Schools in Connecticut, 1838-42..... 1.00
Public Schools of Rhode Island, 1843-49...... 3.50
Higher Education in Wisconsin and Maryland 50
U. S. Commissioner of Education 1867-8..... 5.50
Special Report on District of Columbia..... 5.50
Special Report on Technical Education..... 5.50
Special Report on National Systems........ 5.50
Conn. Common School Journal, 1838-42 4v. each 1.25
Educational Tracts, Number I.-XII., each.... 25
Journal of R I. Institute 1845-49 3v.......... 1.25
Documents on Popular Education, I.-IV., each 1.00
American Jour. of Education, 1855-73, 24v., each 5 00
do. International Series, 1874-5, 1v.... 5 00
General Index, with the Volume Indexes... 2.50
Education in Europe in 1854................. 1.50
National Systems of Education, 10v., each.... 5 50
Elementary and Secondary Schools, 4v., each.. 5.50
 I. The German States....................... 5.50
 II. Continental European States............. 5.50
 III. Great Britain........................... 5.50
 IV. American States......................... 5.50
Superior Instruction—Edition of 1875, 2v..... 7.00
Part I.—Historical Development............. 2.50
 1. The University—Authorities.............. 25
 2. Do. in Greece, Alexandria, and Rome 50
 3. Christian Schools—Cathedral and Abbey.. 50
 4. Teaching Orders of the Catholic Church.. 50
 5. Mediæval Universities (Savigny).......... 50
 6. Universities—Past and Present (Dollinger.) 50
 7. Universities and Polytechnic Schools.... 25
 8. The College in Universities.............. 25
 9. American College & European University. 50
Part II.—Superior Instruction as Organized .5.50
 1. Germany and Switzerland................. 3.50
 2. France, Italy............................ 1.00
 3. Belgium, Holland, Denmark, Nor'y, Swe'n 50
 4. Russia, Turkey, Greece, Spain, Portugal.. 50
 5. England, Scotland, and Ireland........... 1.00
 6. American States.......................... 1.00
Professional and Special Schools, 5v., each.... 5.50
 1. Science and National Industries........... 5.50
  Ditto Great Britain....................... 2.50
  Ditto United States....................... 3.00
 2. Military Schools and Education........... 5.50
 3. Normal Schools and Professional Training 5.50
 4. Female Schools and Education............. 5.50
 5. Reformatory and Preventive Agencies..... 5.50
Supplementary Schools and Agencies........... 5.50
Educational Biography, 6v., each............. 3.50
American Teachers, with 21 portraits......... 3.50
 do. do. second series, 30 portraits 3.50
Benefactors of American Education. 26 port's 3.50
German Educational Reformers and Teachers 3.50
English, French, and other eminent teachers 3.50
Swiss Teachers and Educators................ 3.50
Tribute to Gallaudet, and Deaf Mute Instruction 2.50
Ezekiel Cheever, & the Free Schools of N. Eng. 1 00
Armsmear,—a Memorial of Samuel Colt...... 5 50
School Codes—State, Municipal, Institutional 3.50
School Architecture, with 500 illustrations.... 5.50
Practical Illustrations.................... 1.00
Object Teaching, Oral and other Meth. of Inst. 3.50
American Pedagogy, Principles and Methods.. 3.50
English Pedagogy, " " .. 3 50
 do. Second Series,   .. 3.50
German Pedagogy, " " .. 3.50
French Pedagogy, " " .. 3 50
Swiss Pedagogy " " .. 3 50
Educational Aphorisms and Suggestions...... 3.50
Studies and Conduct........................ 3.50
Educational Associations—National, and State 3.50
Connecticut Educational Institutions 3.50
Connecticut School Fund—Historical......... 25
Common Schools, as they were before 1800.... 1.00
 do.   in 1870..................... 1.00
Compulsory School Attendance................ 1.00
Constitutional Provision respecting Schools 25
School Status of Freedmen & Colored Children 1.00
Providence Schools, Documentary History..... 50
Hartford Public High School, Early History ... 25
Teachers' Institutes, Contributions to History. 25

	PRICE
BROOKS, EDWARD, Memoir and Portrait	50
CADY, I. F., Method of Classical Instruction	25
CALDERWOOD, H., Teaching, Its Ends and Means	25
CALDWELL, C., Education in North Carolina	25
Cambridge University. The Undergraduate	25
CAMP, D. N., Memoir and Portrait	50
CALKINS, N. A., Object Teaching	25
CARLYLE, THOMAS, University Studies	25
Letter on Reading	25
CARTER, JAMES G., Memoir and Portrait	50
Essay on Teachers' Seminaries in 1824	25
Catechism of Methods of Teaching	50
Catholic Church, Schools and Teaching Orders	1.00
CECIL, SIR WILLIAM, Advice to his Son	25
CHANNING, W., Teachers & their Education (1832)	25
Hints on Self Culture	25
CHATHAM, LORD, Letters to his Nephew	25
CHEEVER, EZEKIEL, & Free Schools of N. England	50
CHESTERFIELD, LORD, Studies and Conduct	25
CHOATE, RUFUS, Books and Reading	25
Christian Schools, Earliest Established	25
Cities, Systems of Public Schools	2.50
CLARKE, H. G., Principles & Modes of Ventilation	25
CLARK T. M., Education for the Times	25
COGGESHALL, W. J., Ohio System of Pub. Schools	25
COLBURN, DANA P., Memoir and Portrait	50
COLBURN, W., Educational Work, and Portrait	50
COLE, D., Method of Classical Education	25
COLET, J., Educational Views and St. Paul School	50
COLMAN, HENRY, Agricultural Schools in France	25
COMENIUS, A., Educational Labors and Principles	50
Colleges, Origin and Use in Universities	25
College Code of Honor	25
Competitive Examinations for Public Service	25
Conduct—Suggestions by Eminent Men	3.50
Connecticut, Educational Institutions	3.50
Conversation.—Suggestions by Bacon and others	25
Conversational Method	25
Corporal Punishment—Barbarism of Discipline	25
COUTTS, MISS BURDETT, Prize Scheme for Girls	25
COWDERY, M. F., Moral Training in Pub. Schools	25
COWLEY, A., Plan of Philosophical College, 1662	25
COWPER, WM., The Tirocinium. Review of Schools	25
CRABBE, GEO., Schools of the Borough	25
Crime and Education	25
CURRIE, JAMES, Methods of Early Education	25
DANA, J. D., Science and Scientific Schools	25
DAWSON, J. W., Nat. Hist. in its Educat. Aspects	25
DAY, HENRY N., English Composition	25
Deaf Mute Institutions and Instruction	25
DE LASALLE, A., Memoir & the Christian Brothers	50
Denmark, Public Instruction	25
DEQUINCY, Studies and Conduct	25
Letters on the Art of Conversation	25
DEMETZ, M., Colonies for Juvenile Offenders	25
DICKINSON, J. W., Philos. & Methods of Teaching	25
DIESTERWEG, Memoir	25
Catechism of Methods of Teaching	50
School Discipline and Plans of Instruction	25
Intuitional and Speaking Exercises	25
DINTER, G. F., Memoir	25
DISRAELI, B., Studies and Conduct	25
DIXON, W. HEPWORTH—Swiss Schools in 1870	25
DOANE, GEORGE W., The State and Education	25
DÖLLINGER, Universities, Past and Present	25
DOMINIC, St., and the Dominicans	25
DONALDSON, JAMES, Edu. in Prussia and England	25
Drawing, Methods of Teaching	50
DUAI, A., German Schools in the United States	25
DUCPETIAUX, Agricultural Reform Schools	25
DUFFIELD, D. B., Education a State Duty	25
DUNN, H., Methods of the Borough-road Schools	25
DURFEE, JOB, R. I. Idea of Government	25
DURUY, Secondary Special Schools in France	25
D'ISPANLOUP, Studious Women	25
DWIGHT, EDMUND, Memoir and Portrait	50
DWIGHT, TIMOTHY, Memoir	25
Academy at Green Farms	25
Yale College in 1814	25
Educational Biographies, with Portraits of over 100 Eminent Teachers, Educators, and Benefactors of Educators, each	50
Educational Tracts, Numbers I.-XII., each	25
Edu. Documents for Gen. Circulation, I.-IV. each	1.00
Education and the State	25
Education Defined	25
EDWARDS, RICHARD, Memoir and Portrait	
Normal Schools	
ELYOT, SIR THOMAS. The Governour	
EMERSON, GEO. B., Educat. Labors, with Portrait	
Memorial on Normal Schools, 1837	
Moral Education	
England, Elementary Schools and Methods	
Public or Endowed Schools	
Navigation Schools	
Universities of Oxford and Cambridge	
Military Schools	
Scientific and Technical Schools	
English Estimate of Swiss Public Schools	
Public Schools of the United States	
English Pedagogy, First Series	
Second Series	
ERASMUS, Memoir and Educational Works	
Classical Studies	
ERNEST the Pious, Educational Works	
European Estimate of American Schools	
EVERETT, E., Educational Views, and Portrait	
John Lowell and the Lowell Lectures	
John Harvard and his Benefaction	
Uses of Astronomy	
Address on Normal Schools, 1839	
EVERETT, W., The Cambridge System of Study	
FAIRCHILD, Coeducation of the Sexes	
FELBIGER, J. J., Educational Labors in Austria	
FELLENBERG, Memoir and Principles of Education	
FELTON, C. C., Memoir and Portrait	
Characteristics of American Colleges	
Female Schools and Education	
FENELON, Memoir and Female Education	
FICHTE, J. H. VON, Frobel's Eductional System	
FLIEDNER, Ins. for Deaconesses at Kaiserwerth	
FORBES, E., Educational Uses of Museums	
FOWLE, W. B., Memoir and Portrait	
FOWLER, W. C., The Clergy and Common Schools	
France, System of Public Instruction	
The University of Paris	
The University of France	
Technical and Military Schools	
Special Secondary Schools	
French Teachers and Pedagogy	
FRANCIS, ST., and the Franciscans	
FRANKE, A. H., Educational Views and Labors	
FRANKLIN, B., Maxims of Poor Richard	
FREDERIC THE GREAT, as School Reformer	
School Codes of 1764	
Free Schools of New England, Historical Data	
French Schools and Pedagogy	
FROEBEL, The Kindergarten System	
FROUDE, University Studies	
FULLER, THOMAS, The Good Schoolmaster	
GALLAUDET, THOMAS H., Memoir and Portrait	
Plan for a Teachers' Seminary in 1824	
GAMMELL, W., Memoir of Nicholas Brown	
GARFIELD, JAMES A., Education a National Duty	
GASTON, WILLIAM, Advice to College Graduates	
GERARD-GROOTE, and the Hieronymians	
Germany, National System and Pedagogy, 5v.	
Primary and Secondary Schools	5
Technical and Military Schools	3
Universities, Gymnasia, & Polytechnic Schools	3
Educational Reformers—Ratich, Comenius, etc.	3
Modern German Pedagogy	3
GESNER, J. M., Educational Views	
GILMAN, D. C., Scientific Schools	
GLADSTONE, W. E., Educational Views	
GOETHE, Educational Training and Views	
Cultivation of Reverence	
GOLDSMITH, OLIVER, Essay on Education	
GOODRICH, S. G., Schools as they were in 1800	
GOODRICH, W. H., Plea for Extended Education	
Göttingen University	
GOULD, B. A., The American University	
GRASER, System of Instruction	
Greece, Ancient, Schools and Education	
Greece, Modern, System of Public Instruction	
Greek Language, Subject of School Study	
GREENE, S. S., Object Teaching	
Educational Duties of the Hour	
GREGORY, J. M., The Problem of Education	
GRISCOM, JOHN, Memoir and Portrait	
GUIZOT, Ministry of Public Instruction in France	
GULLIVER, J. P., Norwich Free Academy	

The above Treatises have all appeared as separate articles in Barnard's American Journal of Education. Any Book or Pamphlet on the List will be sent by mail, postage paid, on receiving the price in postage stamps or money order. On orders of $20 a discount of 20 per cent. will be made. Address H. B., Hartford, Conn.   January, 1876.

BOOKS ON EDUCATION.

	PRICE
LE, SIR MATTHEW, Studies and Conduct	25
LL, S. R., Educational Labors and Portrait	50
MANN, J. G., Pedagogical Views	25
WIL, S. M., School Discipline	25
MILTON, J., and the Hamiltonian Method	25
MILTON, Sir W., Mathematics	25
he College in the University	25
MMOND, C., New England Academies	25
hover, System of Public Schools	25
AT, J. M., The American Student at Göttingen	25
RT, J. S., Memoir and Portrait	50
haracteristics of a Normal School	25
nglo-Saxon in the Study of English	25
RTLIB, S., Plan of College of Husbandry in 1651	23
ÜY, V., and the Instruction of the Blind	25
VEN, JOSEPH, Mental Science as a Study	25
WES, JOEL, Female Education	25
DOE, N., Schools as they were	25
IREL, FELIX, Public Instruction in Finland	25
LFENSTEIN. J., Mediæval Universities	25
NBY, J., Common Schools	25
NEY, JOSEPH, Philosophy of Education	25
NTSCHELL, E., Teaching Singing	25
Teaching Drawing	25
RBERT, J. F., Pedagogical Views	50
RDER, Life and Educational Views	25
ese-Cassel, System of Public Schools	25
ese-Darmstadt, System of Public Schools	25
LL, M. D., Reformatory Schools	25
LL, T., True Order of Studies	25
LLIARD, G. S., Boston Public Library	25
LLHOU-E. J. A., Literary Culture in Republics	50
ois and Methods for the Use of Teaching	25
DJINS, J. GEORGE, Education in Upper Canada	25
LBROOK, J., Educational Labors and Portrait	50
The American Lyceum	25
lland, System of Public Instruction	25
OD, THOMAS, The Irish Schoolmasters	25
OLE, C., The Old Art of Teaching, 1659	25
PKINS, M., Educational Labors and Views	1.00
WE, S. G., Memoir and Portrait	50
Laura Bridgman	25
MBOLT, WM. VON, Studies for Old Age	50
MPHREY, HEMAN, Normal Schools	25
Common Schools as they were	25
NTINGTON, F. D., Unconscious Tuition	25
llege Prayers	25
XLEY, T. H., Science in Schools	25
NATIUS LOYOLA, and the Schools of the Jesuits	25
lteracy in the United States	25
iland, English Educational Policy	25
National Schools	25
Endowed Schools	25
Universities	25
ily, System of Public Instruction	25
Revival of Classical Learning	50
Mediæval Universities	25
lant School and Kindergarten	25
COBB, F., Method of Teaching Latin	25
COTOT, L., Memoir and Method of Instruction	25
MESON. Mrs., Social Occupations of Women	25
DVIS, E., Misdirected Education and Insanity	25
ROME, ST., Education of Daughters	25
suits, Society and Schools of the	25
WELL, F. S., Teaching as a Profession	25
HNSON, SAMUEL, Educational Views	25
HNSON. W. R., Educational Labors, & portrait	25
LIUS, DR., Normal Schools in Prussia	50
IENAN, P. J., Organization of Irish Schools	25
NDERMANN. School Reform in Bohemia	25
NGSBURY, JOHN, Memoir and Portrait	25
IGHT. CHARLES, Economical Science	50
RKPATRICK. E., Education in Greece & Rome	25
SY, JOSEPH, Prussian Schools	50
IUSI, Life and Educational Labors	25
LOR, J., Nature and Objects of Education	25
NCASTER, JOS., Memoir and Monitorial Schools	25
WRENCE, A., and Lawrence Scientific School	25
tin Language, Methods of Teaching	50
NON, E., Illiteracy in the United States	25
WIS, DIO, The New Gymnastics	25
WIS, SAMUEL, Memoir and Portrait	50
WIS, T., Methods of Teaching Greek and Latin	25
NDSLEY, PHILIP, Memoir and Portrait	50
CKE, JOHN, Thoughts on Education	1.00
LONGSTREET, Schools as they were in Georgia	25
LOTHROP, S. K., W. Lawrence & N.E. Academies	25
LOWE, ROBERT, University Studies	25
LOWELL, JOHN, and the Lowell Lectures	25
LUTHER, MARTIN, Memoir and Views on Educat.	50
LYON, MARY, Principles of Mt. Holyoke Seminary	50
LYTTON, SIR E. B., Studies and Conduct	25
Money, its Acquisition and Uses	25
LYCURGUS, and Spartan Education	25
LYELL, SIR CHARLES, Physical Science in Educat.	25
MACAULAY, LORD T. B., Educational Views	25
MANSFIELD, E. D., Military Acad. at West Point	25
History of National Land Grants to Ohio	25
MARCEL, C., Conversational Method in Language	50
MARCH, F. A., Study of English Language	25
MARIA THERESA, Educational Reforms	25
MARION, GENERAL, Free Schools for Republics	25
MANN, HORACE, Memoir and Portrait	50
Lectures and Reports	5.50
Teachers' Motives	25
Professional Training of Teachers	25
College Code of Honor	25
Fourth of July Oration, 1842	25
Manual Labor in Education	25
MASON, LOWELL, Memoir and Portrait	50
MASON, S. W., Physical Exercises in School	25
MASSON, D., College and Self-Education	25
Milton's Home, School, and College Education	25
MAY, S. J., Educational Work, with Portrait	50
MAYHEW, IRA, Educational Work with Portrait	50
McCRIE, DR., Universities of Scotland	25
McELLIGOTT, J. N., Debating in School Work	25
MEIEROTTO, Method of Teaching Latin	35
MELANCTHON, P., Memoir and Educational Work	50
Metirey Reform School, Rise and Progress	25
MILL, J. S., University Studies	25
MILTON, JOHN, Tractate on Education	25
Home, School, and University Training	25
MOLINEUX, E. L., Military Exercises in Schools	25
Monitorial System and Method	25
MONTAIGNE, Educational Views	25
MONTESQUIEU, Educational Views	25
MORE, SIR THOMAS, Educational Views	25
MORRISON, T., School Management	50
MULCASTER, R., Positions and Elementaire	25
MURRAY, J. N., English Policy in Irish Education	25
Music, Method for Common Schools	25
NEANDER, M., Educational Views	25
NEWMAN, University Education	25
NIEBUHR, Method of Philological Study	25
NIEMEYER, Aphorisms (other German Educators)	2.50
NISSEN, H., Public Schools in Norway	25
NORTHEND, E., Memoir and Portrait	50
Normal Schools and Teach. Sem., Ed. of 1854	2.00
Norwich Free Academy	25
OBERLIN, J. F., Educational Work	25
Object Teaching, and other Methods	3.50
Oral Methods	50
OLMSTEAD, D., Memoir and Portrait	50
Democratic Tendencies of Science	25
Timothy Dwight—a Model Teacher	25
OVERBERG, B., Educational Views	25
OWEN, R., Educational Views	25
Oxford University in 1873-4	25
PAGE, D. P., Memoir and Portrait	50
Pouring In and Drawing Out Methods	25
Paris, The Old University	25
Superior Normal School	25
Polytechnic Schools	50
PARR, SAMUEL, Educational Views	25
PARTRIDGE, A., Educational Work and Portrait	50
PATTISON, Prussian Normal Schools	25
PAYNE, JOSEPH, Science and Art of Education	25
PEABODY, GEORGE, Educational Benefactions	25
PEIRCE, B. K., Reformatory for Girls	25
PEIRCE, CYRUS, Memoir and Portrait	50
PESTALOZZI, Memoir and Portrait	1.50
Leonard and Gertrude	1.00
Evening Hour of a Hermit	25
PESTALOZZI, and Pestalozzianism	3.50
PESTALOZZI, Fellenberg and Wehrli	25
PETRARCH, DANTE, and BOCCACIO	25
PETTY, SIR W., Plan of a Mechanical College, 1647	25
PHELPS, ALMIRA L., Memoir and Portrait	25
PHELPS. W. F., Memoir and Portrait	50

The above Treatises have all appeared as separate articles in Barnard's American Journal of Education. Any Book or Pamphlet on the List will be sent by mail, postage paid, on receiving the price in postage stamps or money order. On orders of $20 a discount of 20 per cent. will be made.
Address H. B., Hartford, Conn.   January, 1876.

BOOKS ON EDUCATION.

	PRICE.
PAYNE, A., The Science and Art of Education..	25
PHILBRICK, JOHN D., Memoir and Portrait....	50
Work for the National Teachers' Association.	25
Report on Boston Public Schools, 1874.........	50
PLATTER, T., School Life in the 15th Century....	25
PLUTARCH, Educational Views..................	25
POMBAL, MARQUIS, Educa. Work in Portugal...	25
Port Royalists, Educational Views...............	25
PORTER, J. A., Plan of an Agricultural College..	15
PORTER, NOAH, Prize Essay on School Reform..	25
Barnard's Educational Activity in Conn. & R. I	50
Portugal, System of Public Instruction..........	25
POTTER, ALONZO, Memoir and Portrait.........	50
Consolidation of American Colleges...........	25
POTTER, E. R., Religion in Public Schools.......	50
POUCHET, M., French View of Ger. Universities	25
Prussia, System of Public Schools..............	3.00
1. Primary Schools............................	50
2. Secondary Schools.........................	50
3. Universities...............................	50
4. Technical Schools..........................	50
5. Military Schools............................	50
Public Schools, Official Exposition in 1856......	50
QUICK, Educational Reformers—Jacotot.........	25
QUINTILIAN, Educational Views................	25
RABELAIS, Educational Views..................	25
RAMUS, PETER, Memoir and Educational Views .	25
RANDALL, HENRY S., School Libraries	25
RANDALL, S. S., Memoir and Portrait...........	50
RAPHALL, M. L., Education among the Hebrews	50
RATICH, Educational Views....................	25
RAUMER, KARL VON, German Universities..	2.50
Early Childhood..............................	25
Methods of Teaching Latin....................	25
Methods of Teaching Arithmetic...............	25
Physical Education	25
Education of Girls	50
Educational Revival in Italy....................	25
Progressives of the 17th Century...............	25
Ratich, Comenius and Basedow.............	1.00
Loyola and Schools of the Jesuits.............	25
RAUMER, RUDOLF, Instruction in German.......	25
RAVAISSON, F., Instruction in Drawing.........	25
Reformatory and Preventive Schools & Agencies	1.50
RENAN, E., German views of French Education..	25
RENDU, E., Prussian & French School Expenses.	25
REUCHLIN, and Education in the 16th century...	25
Rhode Island Institute of Instruction............	25
RICHARDS, W. F., Manual of Methods.........	50
RICKOFF, A. J., Memoir and Portrait............	50
RIECKE, Philosophy of Early Education.........	25
RIDER, ADMIRAL, Navigation Schools for England	25
ROSS, W. P., Catechetical Method.............	25
ROUSSEAU, Memoir and Educational Views......	25
ROLLIN, CHARLES, Education of Youth..........	50
RUSSELL, SCOTT, Technical University for England	25
Systematic Technical Education..............	25
RUSSELL, WILLIAM, Memoir and Portrait.......	50
Normal Training..............................	1.50
Legal Recognition of Teaching as a Profession	25
Russia.—System of Public Instruction..........	25
Military and Naval Education................	25
Universities................................	25
RYERSON, EDGERTON, Memoir and Portrait......	50
Savigny, Universities of the Middle Ages.......	50
Saxony, System of Public Instruction...........	25
Secondary and Superior Instruction...........	25
Technical and Special Schools..............	25
Saxon Principalities, Public Instruction........	25
SARMIENTO, Memoir and Portrait................	50
The Schoolmaster's Work.....................	25
School Architecture, Revised Edition, with 500 Ill.	5.50
School Architecture, Practical Illustrations.. ...	1.00
Do. Rural and Ungraded Schools........	50
Do. City and Graded Schools............	1.00
Do. Primary and Infant Schools..........	50
Do. Public High Schools................	50
Scotland, System of Public Instruction..........	50
Secondary Schools and Universities.............	1.00
SEELEY, J., Cambridge System of Examinations	25
SEGUIN, Treatment and Training of Idiots.......	25
SETON, S. S., Schools as they were 60 Years Ago	25
SHELDON, E. A., Object Teaching..............	25
SHENSTONE, W., The Schoolmistress...........	25
SILJSTROM, P. A., American Schools...........	25
SIMONSON, L., Cadet System in Switzerland.....	25
SMITH, ELBRIDGE, Norwich Free Academy......	25
SPENCER, HERBERT, Thoughts on Education....	50
SOUTHEY, ROBERT, Hon
Dr. Dove, and the Sch
SPRAGUE, W. B., Influe
Spain, System of Public
SPURZHEIM, Educationa
STANLEY, LORD, Lyceun
State and Education—T
STEARNS, E., Early Ills
STOW, DAVID, Gallery T
STOWE, CALVIN E., Men
Teachers' Seminaries.
STURM, JOHN, Educatio
SULLIVAN, O., Teaching
Sweden and Norway, P
SWETT, JOHN, Educatio
SWIFT, JONATHAN, Man
Switzerland.—Public Ir
Military, and Cadet S
SYBEL, H. VON, The Ge
TAINSH, E. C., Prize Es
TAPPAN, H. P., Memoir
Educational Developm
TARBOX, J. N., America
TAYLOR, HENRY, True
Text Books, Catalogue
THAYER, GIDEON F., M
Letters to a Young T
TILLINGHAST, NICHOLA
TOWN, SALEM, Schools
TROTZENDORF, Educati
Tubingen University..
TUCKER, GEORGE, Educ
Turkey, Schools and S
TYNDALL, Science in Ed
Unconscious Influence—
Unconscious Tuition—I
United States, Systems
Common Schools as t
Common Schools in 1
Colleges and Univers
Military and Naval Sc
Normal Schools......
Universities and College
University Life—Past a
Deposition, Pennalier
Tripos, Prævaricator,
VAIL, T. H., Methods o
VASSAR, M., Memoir an
VEHRLI, J., Industrial
Ventilation and Warmi
Vienna, Educational It
VIVES, L., Memoir and
WADSWORTH, JAMES S.
WASHINGTON, GEORGE,
National Education..
WAYLAND, FRANCES, M
Intellectual Educatior
WEBSTER, DANIEL, Edu
WEBSTER, NOAH, Educa
WELLS, W. H., Memoir
Methods in English G
West Point Military Ac
WHATELY, A., Annotat
WHEWELL, W., Educati
WHITE, E. E., Normal
National Bureau of E
WHITE, S. H., National
WICHERN, T. H., Germ
WICKERSHAM, Educatio
Education in Reconst
WILLARD, MRS. EMMA,
WILSON, J. M., Science
WILLIAM of Wykeham
WILLM, J., Teachers' C
WIMMER, H., Special So
Public Instruction in
WINES, E. C., Memoir a
WINTERBOTHAM, W., A
WIRT, WILLIAM, Profe
WOLF, T. A., Education
WOTTON, SIR HENRY, E
Wurtemberg, System o
Technical Schools...
WOODBRIDGE, W. C., M
WYKEHAM and St. Mar
YOUNG, THOMAS, Manu
Zurich, Cantonal Schoo
Federal Polytechnic I

The above Treatises have all appeared as separate articles in Barnard's American Journal of Education, sent by mail, postage paid, on receiving the price in postage stamps or money order. On orders of $20 a discount
Address H. B., Hartford, Conn.

BARNARD'S AMERICAN LIBRARY OF EDUCATION.

History and Systems of Education and Public Schools.

21. History of Education prior to Christian Era. 512 pages: $3.50.
India, Persia, China, Palestine, Egypt, Greece, Rome, and Arabia.

22. Schools and Education as influenced by Christianity, with the Problem of Religious Instruction in Public Schools. 656 pages: $3.50.

Elementary and Secondary Schools.

23. National Education in Europe, with special notice of Normal Schools in 1850. 890 pp.; $3.50.

24. Public Instruction in German States. 950 pages: $5.50.
Anhalt, Austria, Baden, Bavaria, Brunswick, Hanover, Hesse-Darmstadt, Liechtenstein, Lippe-Detmold, Lippe-Schaumberg, Luxemburg and Limberg, Mecklenburg-Schwerin, Mecklenburg-Strelitz, Nassau, Oldenburg, Prussia, Reuss, Saxony, Saxe-Altenburg, Saxe-Coburg, Saxe-Meiningen, Saxe-Weimar, Waldeck, Wurtemberg, and the Free Cities, with a summary of the Systems and Statistics for the whole of Germany.

25. Public Instruction in Switzerland, France, and other European States. 864 pages: $5.50.
Switzerland (each of the 23 Cantons), France, Belgium, Holland, Denmark, Norway and Sweden, Russia, Turkey, Greece, Italy, Portugal, and Spain.

26. Public Instruction in Great Britain. 864 pages: $5.50.
Historical Development of Education and Schools in the British Isles: National and Intermediate Schools in Ireland; Parochial Schools, Burgh and Grammar Schools, and System of Elementary Schools in Scotland; Schools for the People, Schools aided by Government, and Elementary Schools, and Endowed Grammar Schools in England.

27. Public Instruction in United States: National, State, Denominational, Land Grants, Military and Naval Schools, and Incorporated Schools of different kinds. 1,276 pages: $5.50.
Relations of the General Government to Schools and Education, including the Negro and Indian Races; State Systems and Institutions; Academies and Schools under Denominational and Incorporated Control, with a History of Religious Denominations.

28. State Systems of Public Schools—Historical Development in each State of Common and High Schools, Incorporated Academies and Seminaries, Normal Schools, Teachers' Institutes and Associations, with a History of School Conventions, and other agencies in the advancement of Popular and Liberal Education. 816 pp.: $5.50.

20. City Systems of Graded Schools: Organization, Subjects and Courses of Instruction, Buildings and Equipment, Supervision and Statistics. 832 pp.: $5.50.

30. School Codes, State and Municipal—Examples of Early and Recent Legislation, with Judicial Decisions of Questions affecting the Rights of Teachers, Parents, and Children in Public Schools. 556 pages: $3.50.

31. School Architecture—Site, Drainage, Designs, Construction, Hygienic Arrangement, Decoration and Equipment of Schools of Different Grades, with 500 Illustrations. 816 pages: $5.50.

Superior Instruction.

32. The University, Ancient and Mediæval, and other Institutions of Highest Culture. 464 pp.: $3.50.

33. Universities of Modern Europe—Belgium, Germany, France, Holland, Italy, Norway, Russia, Sweden, Spain, and Portugal. 800 pp.: $5.50.

34. Universities of Great Britain—England, Ireland, and Scotland, with an Account of the Great Public Schools of England. 800 pp.: $5.50.

35. Colleges and Universities of the United States, with the original Free [Endowed Grammar] Schools of New England. 800 pp.: $5.50.

Professional and Special Schools.

36. **Schools of Divinity, Medicine, and Law**—Legal Requirements. Studies, Examinations, and Privileges in different Countries. 476 p.: $3.50.

37. **Professional Training of Teachers:** Normal Schools, Teachers Institutes, Conferences, and Associations; University Chairs and Courses, and other agencies for the special education of teachers. 816 p.: $5.50.

38. **Technical Schools & Education:** European States. 800 p.: $5.50.

39. **Scientific and Technical Schools in Great Britain.** 464 p.: $3.50.

40. **Agricultural, Mechanical and Mining Engineering, Trade** and other Industrial Schools in the United States. 464 p.: $3.50.

41. **Art Schools, Classes, and Museums.** 464 p.: $3.50.

42. **Military and Naval Schools, and Education.** 964 p.: $5.50.

43. **Child-Saving and Crime-Preventing Education,** and Institutions for Juvenile Offenders, Orphan Asylums, Farm Schools, with History of Prisons, Houses of Correction, and the treatment of criminals. 800 p.: $5.50.

Educational Biography, with History of Institutions and Methods.

44. **Representative Educators and Teachers, Ancient and Modern, of Different Nationalities.** 720 pages: $5.50.

I. Confucius, Moses, Christ (the Great Teacher), and other Oriental Teachers. II. Aristotle, Plato, Socrates; Cicero, Quintilian, Cassiodorus, Dante, Valla, Rosmini. III. La-Salle, Ramus, Fenelon, Montaigne. IV. Rousseau, Pestalozzi, Fellenberg. V. Ratich, Comenius, Franke, Hecker, Froebel. VI. Ascham, Mulcaster, Bell, Lancaster, Arnold.

45. **American Educational Biography:** Founders and Benefactors of Systems and Institutions, and Eminent Teachers, *prior to* 1800. 720 p.: $5.50.

Adams, Berkley, Bingham, Blair, Chauncey, Cheever, Collett, Cotton, Cutler, Copland, Davenport, Dust and Ashes, Eaton, Eliot, Franklin, Harvard, Hooker, Hopkins, Jefferson, Johnson, Ludlow, Moody, Morse, Nitschman, Penn, Rumford, Rush, Smith, Stiles, Washington, Webster, Wheelock, Winthrop, Yale.

46. **American Educational Biography:** Founders, Officers, and Benefactors of Colleges and other Institutions of Higher Learning. 720 p.: $5.50.

47. **American Educational Biography:** Organizers and Administrators of Systems and Institutions of Public Schools and Popular Education, State and Municipal. 720 pages: $5.50.

48. **American Educational Biography:** Founders and Teachers of Institutions for Special Classes—Blind, Deaf-Mutes, Orphans, etc. 756 p.: $5.50.

49. **American Educational Biography:** Female Teachers and Educators, with Account of Institutions for Girls. 720 pages: $5.50.

50. **American Educational Biography:** Founders and Officers of Teachers' Associations, and other Eminent Preceptors. 720 p.: $5.50.

Supplementary and Miscellaneous.

51. **Supplementary Schools and Agencies of Education:** Books and Libraries, Evening and Vacation Schools, Associations of Different Aims, Lectures and Reading Circles, and Summer Schools and Classes, Race Schools and Missions and other Special Agencies for Indian, Negro, and Chinese Education. 756 pages: $5.50.

52. **Nomenclature and Bibliography** of Education, Schools, and School Systems, with selected Lists of Books for Professional Reading. 464 p.:$3.50.

53. **General Index to Barnard's Journal of Education,** the American Library of Education, and other Educational Publications. $10.50.

Barnard's Am. Journal of Education, 1856-85; $5.50 per vol. ½ goat, $4.50 cloth.
Connecticut Common School Journal, 1838-42, $4.00.
Journal of Rhode Island Institute of Instruction, 1845-49, $3.00.
Reports as U. S. Commissioner of Education, $5.00 per volume.

Price Lists of over 800 Treatises and Tracts on Education and Schools will be sent per mail, to orders with 5-cent stamp enclosed.

KINDERGARTEN AND CHILD CULTURE PAPERS.
SOLD SEPARATELY OR IN VOLUME.

FRIEDERICH AUGUST FROEBEL AND THE KINDERGARTEN as developed by him and his immediate Associates and Pupils, and the Principles and Practices of Child-Culture by eminent Educators. Papers published in the *American Journal of Education*. Edited by Henry Barnard, LL. D. 752 pages, with Portrait, from steel plate, of Froebel. $3.50.

KINDERGARTEN PAPERS SOLD SEPARATELY,
And sent by mail on receipt of price named, in postage or money order.

MEMOIR OF FROEBEL: Principally Autobiographical, with Aids to the understanding of his Principles of Child-Culture, by Barop, Middendorff, Lange, Payne, Zeh and others. 128 pages, with Portrait. $1.25, in neat cloth and beveled stiff cover.

MEMOIR OF WILLIAM MIDDENDORFF: By Diesterweg, with Biographical Sketch of Diesterweg's Educational Work. 20 pages. 25 cents.

MEMOIR OF BARONESS VON MARENHOLTZ-BULOW, and her Educational Mission. 16 pp. 25c.

MEMOIR OF BARONESS VON MARENHOLTZ-BULOW, with her treatise on Child-Nature and Nurture according to Froebel, translated by *Alice M. Christie from the latest Berlin edition*, with Thoughts on Child-Life in Christ, by Rev. Stopford A. Brooke. 144 pp. $1.25, cloth.

FICHTE (J. H. VON): National Education demanded by the Age, in connection with Froebel's system. Submitted to Congress of Philosophers at Frankfort, 1869. 48 pp. 25 cts.

FISCHER (A. S.) AND GUILLIAUME (JULES): Kindergarten Papers in Brussels Educational Congress in 1880. 32 pages. 25 cents.

BUSSE (F.): Object Teaching—Principles and Methods in the Spirit and Method of Froebel's Kindergarten. Translated from Diesterweg's Wegweisser, edition of 1873, by Mrs. Horace Mann. 48 pages. 25 cents.

SCHRADER (*Henrietta Breymann, niece and pupil of Froebel*): Principles of Froebel as applied in the Kindergarten at 16 Steinmetz Strasse, Berlin, with visits to the Institute, by Henny, Aldrich and Lyschinska. 20 pages. 25 cents.

SLUYS (*A., Director of Model School, Brussels*): Intuition and Intuitive Methods, with notice of Infant and Kindergarten work in Switzerland, France and Belgium, by Pape-Carpentier, Marbeau, Portugall, Buls and Miss M. J. Lyschinska. 32 pages. 25 cents.

MANNING (*Miss E. A.*,): Some Difficulties and Encouragements in Kindergarten Work in England, with suggestions on Early Culture, by Miss Lyschinska. 16 pages. 25 cents.

KRAUS-BOELTE (*Mrs. Maria and Prof. John*): Reminiscences of Kindergarten Work, with account of New York Normal Kindergarten and Associated Model Classes; with Portrait and other Contributions to Froebel's Kindergarten in United States. 48 pages. 50 cts.

PEABODY (*Elizabeth P.*): Froebel's Principles and Methods in the Nursery; Kindergarten Culture in Public Schools. 40 pages. 25 cents.

BLOW (*Susan E.*) The Mother Play, and Some Aspects of the Kindergarten—Lectures addressed to Kindergartners in St. Louis. 44 pages. 25 cents, in neat cloth-bound cover.

GALLAUDET, GARLAND, HUNTER AND OTHERS: Boston Training Class; Early Kindergarten Work in United States. 32 pages. 25 cents.

HARRIS (*William T.*) AND MRS. LOUISE POLLOCK: Kindergarten in the Public School System, and Froebel's Method in Public Primary School. 26 pages. 25 cents.

MANN (*Mrs. Horace*) AND MISS PEABODY: Charity Kindergartens and the Homes of the Poor—Experience in Boston and San Francisco. 32 pages. 25 cents.

SPRING (*Marcus*) AND MISS PEABODY: Clay Modeling and other Kindergarten Occupations, a Training for Art (Ideal and Industrial). 16 pages. 25 cents.

BATCHELLOR (*D.*) : Use of Color in Teaching Children to Sing, and the Analogies of Tone and Color. 16 pages. 25 cents.

NEWTON (*Rev. R. Heber*): The Free Kindergarten in Church Work, and for Neglected Children. 32 pages. 25 cents.

BUSHNELL (*Horace*) *Goethe, Channing and others:* Aphorisms and Suggestions on Early Training, with Hints on Buildings, Grounds and Equipment for Kindergartens. 80 pp. 50 cts.

SUPPLEMENTARY PAPERS will be printed, if called for, viz.: *Use of Stories in Child-Culture*, by Mrs. Mann and Anna Buckland; *The Kindergarten in Relation to Family Life and School*, read to the London Froebel Union by Miss Shirreff; the *Kindergarten in San Francisco*, in Reports of Miss Marwedel, Mrs. Cooper, Miss Virginia Smith and others; *Prof. Hailman* and Kindergarten Work in the West; *The One Hundreth Birthday of Froebel in Many Lands.*

☞ *Liberal discount made on all bills over $10.*

ORDERS ADDRESSED TO *Barnard's American Journal of Education*,
28 *Main Street, Hartford, Conn.*

FROEBEL'S EDUCATIONAL WORK.

 Assistants—Pupils in training for teaching.................................... 63
 Organization of a School of Eighty Pupils—Two Divisions.................. 63
 First Division composed of Children under Eight Years—Nurture............ 63
 Second Division—Lower and Upper Class.. 63
 Upper Class—Study and Productive Industries—Technology................. 64
 Every Subject treated in Organic Unity of the Child and Pupil............... 65
 Every Member of the School must be regular and punctual.................. 65
 Special Educational Aims—Order and Progressive Growth.................... 65
 Possibility of Introducing Pestalozzi's method into Families................... 66
 Connection of Elementary Instruction with higher Scientific Culture........ 67
3. LANGE'S REMININISCENSES OF FROEBEL.................................... 69-80
 Froebel at Hamburg in 1849—Address to Women's Union..................... 69
 What is New in Froebel's Aim and Method.. 71
 Fundamental Ideas of Rousseau, Pestalozzi, and Froebel...................... 72
 Diesterweg's Adaptation of Pestalozzi's Views to Popular Schools........... 73
 Personal Relations of Froebel—Experience in Teaching........................ 74
 Development of Individual Men and the Race—Macrocosm and Microcosm.. 76
 Family School at Griesheim—Institution at Keilhau—Marriage............... 77
 Publication 1819–1826—Institute at Wattensee—F. Froebel and Barop...... 79
 Girls School at Willisan—Official Report of Berne Cantonal Commission.... 80
 Educational Institute for Orphans, and Teacher's Class at Burgdorf......... 80
 Genesis of the Kindergarten at Blankenberg in 1837............................ 81
 Come let us live with our Children—Kindergarten in Dresden in 1839....... 81
4. THE KINDERGARTEN—GENESIS, NAME, AND OBJECTS...................... 82-96
 (1) WINTHUR—Froebel's First Announcement to Barop in 1829.............. 82
 Letter from Burgdorf in 1836 to the Froebellan Circle........................... 82
 Inauguration of plan at Blankenberg in 1837—Sountagsblat................... 83
 Appeal to the Women of Germany at Guttenberg Festival 1840............... 83
 Foundation of the Universal German Institution at Keilhau................... 84
 Publication of *Die Mutter und Koselieder*—Pictures, Play and Songs....... 84
 Explanation of Gifts for Play—Movement, Plays, and Songs.................. 85
 Intercourse with Nature and Social Phenomena................................ 87
 Domestic Education improved by Kindergarten Pupils........................ 88
 Women to be trained as Mothers and Nurses.................................... 89
 Organic Connection between the Kindergarten and School................... 90
 (2) PAYNE—Froebel's Interpretation of the Activity of Children.............. 91
 Play the Natural Occupation of the Child in its normal state................. 92
 Theory in Practice—Gifts for the Culture of Observation..................... 93
 Objections to the System Considered.. 95
5. BAROP—CRITICAL MOMENTS IN FROEBEL'S INSTITUTIONS............... 97-104
 Financial Difficulties in Keilhau.. 97
 Froebel's Training Institute at Marienthal—Marriage......................... 97
 Son of a Prince taken into the Institution—Visit to Switzerland............ 100
 Difficulties from Priestly Opposition—Interposition of Pfyffer.............. 101
 Meeting of the Cantonal Teachers for three months at Burgdorf........... 103
 Origin of the name Kindergarten... 104
6. ZEH—OFFICIAL INSPECTION AND COMMENDATION OF KEILHAU.....105-110
 Disturbance in Government Circles about Burchenschaften.............105-110
 Suspicions of Barop in 1824—Withdrawal of Children....................... 105
 Froebel's Faith in God in the Darkest Hour—Idea of Kindergarten......... 106
 Teachers reported in 1824—Testimony to their Fidelity...................... 108
 Unity of Life in Teachers and Pupils—Institutional Teaching............... 109
7. UNITY OF LIFE—IDEAL AND ACTUAL.. 111-115
8. PRUSSIAN INTERDICT OF THE KINDERGARTEN............................. 116
9. LAST DAYS—MARENHOLTZ, AND MIDDENDORFF.........................117-124
 Teacher's Convention at Gotha—Last Illness—Funeral...................... 117
10. COLLECTED WRITINGS, BY DR. W. LANGE................................125-126
 PREFACE AND CONTENTS... 125
11. PUBLICATIONS RELATING TO FROEBEL AND HIS SYSTEM...............127-128

FROEBEL'S EDUCATIONAL WORK. 5

II. FROEBEL'S EDUCATIONAL SYSTEM.

Educational Views as Expounded by Friends............129-400
- I. **William Middendorff**...129-144
  - Memoir and Educational Work.. 129
  - Thoughts on the Kindergarten—Devotion of a Life........................ 142
- II. **Freidrich Adolph Wilhelm Diesterweg**...................145-160
  - Acceptance and Advocacy of Froebel's Child-Culture................ 151
- III. **Bertha V. Marenholtz—Bulow**................................149-288
  1. Memorial of a Wonderful Educational Mission........................ 145
  2. PUBLICATIONS IN ELUCIDATION OF FROEBEL'S THEORIES............ 159

  THE CHILD—NATURE, AND NURTURE ACCORDING TO FROEBEL.............. 169
  1. THE CHILD IN ITS HELPLESSNESS AND INFINITE CAPACITIES........161-169
     - (1) Relations to Nature—Subject to her Laws................................. 162
     - (2) Relations to Humanity—The Individual shares the Destiny of the Race.. 163
     - (3) Relations to God—Lives and Progress for a Higher Development........ 166
     - Woman—The Educator of Mankind—Develops the Child in all its Relations.... 169
  2. EARLIEST DEVELOPMENTS OF THE CHILD.................................170-179
     - Physical Movements—Prompted by Necessities of its Being................ 170
     - Exercises of the Limbs—Sense of Touch—The Hand......................... 171
     - Shaping and Producing—Constructions in Sand and Clay.................. 172
     - Sense of Sound—Cradle Songs—Rythm—Awakening of Feeling............ 174
     - Material Needs—Gardening—Its Pleasures.................................... 175
     - Desire to know why, whence, and wherefore—Comparison................. 176
     - Social Impulse—The Basis of Moral Cultivation............................. 177
     - Religious Instinct—Follows Social Development............................. 177
     - God through Nature—Natural Phenomena Symbolic......................... 178
  3. FROEBEL'S THEORY OF EDUCATION OR DEVELOPMENT................. 181-189
     - Education is Emancipation—Setting free bound up Forces................. 181
     - Natural Order, or Progress according to Law—Race........................ 182
     - Pestalozzi's endeavor to discover and apply the principle.................. 183
     - Froebel claims to have completed the method............................... 183
     - Chief Aim of Education is Moral Culture.................................... 183
     - All Instruction and Developing Exercises should perfect the Soul......... 184
     - Law of Opposites and their Reconciliation................................... 187
     - Theory requires Freedom, Assistance, and Unity............................189
  4. ERRORS IN EXISTING EDUCATION OF EARLY CHILDHOOD................190 200
     - Physical—Bad Nursing, and Insufficient Food and Exercise................ 190
     - Moral—Improper Surroundings and Treatment............................... 191
     - Intellectual—Want of Direction and over Stimulant........................ 193
     - Requisites for Healthy Growth in well directed Activity................... 194
     - Educative Uses of Playthings and Play—Evolution of Ideal............... 196
     - Necessary Force exists in Mother's Love if properly trained.............. 200
  5. FROEBEL'S METHOD OF DEVELOPMENT...................................... 101-218
     - Meaning of Method—Both General and Special.............................. 202
     - Object of Thought—Perception, Observation, Comparison, Judgment..... 204
     - Comparison or Reconciliation of Opposites.................................. 204
     - Pestalozzi's Fundamental Law—A. B. C., Form, Number, Language..... 205
     - Differences between Education and Instruction............................. 206
     - Feeling and Willing—Good and Beautiful—Self and Others............... 206
     - Insufficiency of Pestalozzi's Doctrine of Form............................... 207
     - Law of Balance, universal and beneficial.................................... 211
     - Mystic side of Froebel's Principles.. 212
  6. THE KINDERGARTEN...219 226
     - The Child World as it appears to an outsider................................ 219
     - Movement Games with explanatory Songs.................................... 219
     - Occupations—in playful work and workful play............................. 220
     - Ideal and useful Art—Cabinet of Collections and Products................ 221
     - Choral melody—affectionate and reverential................................. 222
     - Kindergarten work begins in the Mother's Lap............................... 223
     - Should be continued in all girl schools and education...................... 223

Freedom of Development—Suitable Condition............................ 223
Work or Activity for Development.................................... 223
Unity or Progression—Continuity of Development...................... 224
Hindrances to the Realization of the Kindergarten................... 225
7. THE MOTHER PLAY AND NURSERY SONGS................................... 227
Book for Mothers the basis of Froebel's System...................... 227
Its Philosophy best felt by Children and Mothers.................... 228
First Development goes on in play, which must be assisted........... 229
Examples given based on the instincts of infancy.................... 230
8. EARLIEST DEVELOPMENT OF THE LIMBS.............................. 231-232
Popular Nursery Games originate in the Motherly Instinct............ 231
Exercises of the Hand, Fingers, and Wrist........................... 232
9. CHILD'S FIRST RELATION TO NATURE.................................... 239
Games should deal with Natural Phenomena............................ 233
The Weather Cock—The Sun-Bird—The Child and the Moon................ 234
Farm Yard Gate—Little Fishes—Bird Song.............................. 337
10. THE CHILD'S FIRST RELATIONS TO MANKIND............................. 200
Mother—Family Circle and Life—Neighborhood......................... 240
Froebel's Introduction to their Relationships....................... 241
Finger Games—Physical, Mental, and Moral Uses....................... 242
First Impressions in Critical Moments most lasting.................. 243
First Walk, Fall, Fright, Pain—Game of Bopeep—Confidence............ 244
Cuckoo game—Conditions for Indulgence—Habits........................ 245
First step to moral development—High expels the low................. 247
Sense of Taste—Germs of aesthetic Culture—Moral Freedom............. 249
Handicrafts and other Industries—Movement Games..................... 251
Habitation—Instinct for—Constructive Tastes and Habits.............. 252
Value of Manual Labor—Respect for the Laborer....................... 253
Sense of hearing and vocal organs—Voices of Nature.................. 254
Drawing, ideal and productive—Froebel's Occupations................. 257
Foundations laid for social development in family and life.......... 259
11. THE CHILD'S FIRST RELATIONS TO GOD............................ 261-278
Belief in God, inborn, intuitive, and can be developed.............. 261
First step through the love and trust in its Mother................. 261
Choral Melodies—Gestures, and words of reverence—Prayer............. 262
Personal Activity and Experiences—Symbolic Interpretations of Nature... 263
Froebel's Mother Book—Child's own Story and History Book............ 269
Inner conscious life not possible with children..................... 275
Pictorial Representations deepen Impressions........................ 271
Christ as a Divine Child—God manifest in Man........................ 275
Church services for Children—Analogies in Nature.................... 277
Early Education must be based on religion........................... 278
12. SUMMARY VIEW OF FROEBEL'S PRINCIPLES........................... 279-280
Education begins and ends with Life................................. 279
Follows natural laws, and must be guided by intelligence and love... 279
Mothers and Kindergartners must be trained.......................... 280
SUPPLEMENT TO CHILD'S RELATIONS TO GOD............................. 281-288
Child Life in Christ. By Rev. Stopford Brooke....................... 281
IV. Congress of Philosophers at Frankfort, in 1869............... 289-336
Problem of Popular Education in Pedagogical Section,................ 289
REPORT OF PROF. J. W. FICHTE, EMBODYING CONCLUSIONS................. 291
1. Education the Problem of the Age................................. 291
2. Philosophical Systems in the Educational Problem................. 295
Fundamental Principles of Herbart and Beneke examined.............. 295
3. Psychological Basis of Modern Pedagogy........................... 305
4. Axioms of All Christian Pedagogy................................. 312
5. Pestalozzianism the basis of National Systems.................... 318
6. Froebel's additions to Pestalozzi solve the Problem.............. 322
7. Education of Childhood according to Froebel...................... 327
8. Day Nurseries for Neglected Children............................. 332

V. International Congress of Education at Brussels, in 1880....337-400
  PAPERS ON THE VALUE, AND FURTHER EXTENSION OF FROEBEL'S VIEWS........ 351
  1. FISCHER—PRESIDENT OF FROEBEL SOCIETY IN VIENNA..................339-352
     Grounds on which Froebel's system is assailed, examined................... 339
     Kindergarten should prepare for school.................................. 349
     Kindergartners should have a special training........................... 347
  2. GUILLIAUME—MEMBER OF BELGIAN EDUCATIONAL LEAGUE..............353-368
     Froebel's system extends beyond the Kindergarten age and culture.......... 353
     Cardinal idea of his Education of Man—Force in Nature.................... 355
     Extension of the Gifts and Occupations into the School period necessary..... 358
     Letters to Emma Bothman in 1852—Kindergarten and School............. 362
     Language—How Lina learns to write and read—Excursions.................. 364
     Number—Form and Dimension—Material for Intermediate Class............ 365

III. THE KINDERGARTEN AND CHILD CULTURE.
Progressive Improvement of Manuals and Methods..369-450
  1. A-B-C BOOKS AND PRIMERS...369-378
     Persian—Chinese—Greek—Latin A-B-C....................................... 369
     Primer—Catholic and Protestant... 373
     English Primer of Henry VIII—Horn Book illustrated....................... 373
  2. A GUIDE FOR THE CHILD AND YOUTH... 375
     RULES FOR THE BEHAVIOR...
     Part One—Alphabet, Prayers, Graces and Instructions................... 375
     Symbolic Alphabet. In Adam's Fall, &c..................................... 376
     Rules for Behavior at Home, School and Church............................ 378
     Modifications in New England Primer enlarged............................. 379
  3. THE NEW ENGLAND PRIMER WITH SHORTER CATECHISM................. 379-400
     Historical Data—Webster's Reprint in 1844 of Edition of 1777............... 379
     Illustrations—John Hancock—Adam's Fall—Mr. John Rogers at the Stake... 381
     Infant Songs and Prayers—Letters,large and small—Syllables,short and long.. 382
     Who was the first Man?—Lessons for Youth—Commandments—Creed....... 386
     Mr. John Rogers' Advice to his Children................................... 388
     Shorter Catechism of the Westminster Assembly of Divines................. 390
     Mr. John Cotton—Spiritual Milk for American Babes....................... 396
     Dialogue between Christ, Youth, and the Devil............................. 398
  4. THE PETTY SCHOOLE. BY C. H., 1659..401-413
     How to teach little children to say their letters, to spell, and to read.......... 402
     How children who don't study Latin may be employed....................... 408
     Hints for providing a Petty School, and its daily and weekly routine......... 410
  5. THE ENGLISH SCHOOLMASTER. BY EDWARD COOTE........................... 414
     Title Page—The Schoolmaster's Cautions................................... 414
  6. ORBIS SENSUALIUM PICTUS.. 415
     Janua Linguarum of W. Bateus in 1615..................................... 415
     Janua Reserata of Comenius in 1631....................................... 415
     English Edition by Charles Hoole in 1658................................... 415
     Encyclopedia of things subject to Senses................................... 415
     Woodward's Gate of Sciences, 1658... 416
  7. THE GERMAN TEACHER'S PATH FINDER—BY DIESTERWEG................417-450
     Dr. Busse—Intuitional, or Object Teaching in 1873........................ 417
     (1) Aims and Methods—Teaching by Inspection or Intuition............... 417
     Historical Development from Bacon to Diesterweg......................... 421
     Different kinds of Intuitions for Object Teaching.......................... 430
     (2) The Method and its Rules... 433
     Actual Inspection of real material—and doing............................ 433
     Easy to difficult—Simple to complex—Concrete to abstract............... 434
     Instruction according to Material, and Individual Child.................. 434
     Use of Poetry and Conversation.. 435
     (3) Best Guides and Aids for Observation, Thinking, and Language........ 435

Kindergarten Work in Different Countries............451-736

I. MADAME HENRIETTA BREYMANN SCHRADER..................................451
   Froebelian Institute in Berlin...453
II. MADAME DE PORTUGALL—GENEVA...473-480
   Value and Extension of the Kindergarten Principle.......................473
III. THE CRECHE, AND CHILD CULTURE IN FRANCE............................ 481-488
   Day Nurseries—Infant Asylums—Training Institute........................481
IV. KINDERGARTEN AND CHILD CULTURE IN BELGIUM.......................... 489-512
   1. PUBLIC KINDERGARTENS IN BRUSSELS....................................492
   2. INTUITIONAL TEACHING IN MODEL SCHOOL................................497
V. RECENT KINDERGARTEN PUBLICATIONS IN ENGLAND........................513-528
   1. HINDRANCES AND ENCOURAGEMENTS IN KINDERGARTEN WORK.............513
   2. USE OF NATURAL AND HOUSEHOLD PHENOMENA.............................523
   3. RELATIONS OF KINDERGARTEN TO INFANT SCHOOLS.......................526
VI. KINDERGARTEN WORK IN UNITED STATES................................529-736
   A. EXAMPLES OF TRAINING INSTITUTES AND KINDERGARTENS.................535
   1. BOSTON TRAINING CLASS AND KINDERGARTEN............................535
   2. MRS. MARIA BOELTE-KRAUS.—REMINISCENCES OF KINDERGARTEN WORKS...539
      New York Training Institute and Kindergarten........................537
   3. EXPERIENCE OF NEW YORK FEMALE COLLEGE.............................557
   B. PAPERS IN ELUCIDATION OF FROEBEL'S SYSTEM.........................561-736
   1. FROEBEL'S PRINCIPLES AND METHODS IN THE NURSERY. *Miss Peabody*.561-574
      Helplessness of Infancy—Getting Possession of its Organization..........561
      Froebel's Use of the Natural Instincts—Uses of the Ball................566
   2. THE MOTHER PLAY AND NURSERY SONGS. *Miss Susan E. Blow*.........575-594
      Unity of Human Life—Germs of all Faculties............................578
   3. SOME ASPECTS OF THE KINDERGARTEN. *Miss Susan E. Blow*...........595-616
      Froebel's Dealing with Natural Phenomena..............................595
      Daily Talks—Doing and Expressing—Occupations.........................601
      Laws of Intuitional Teaching..607
   4. FROEBEL'S PRINCIPLES IN PUBLIC SCHOOL SYSTEM. *Miss Peabody*.......617-624
      Quality of Education to be considered—Special Training................617
   5. KINDERGARTENS THE FIRST GRADE IN CITY SYSTEM. *W. T. Harris*....625-642
      Conditions Precedent—Ideal Kindergartens.............................625
      General and Special Disciplines—Transition from Home to School.......629
      Relation to Trades—Moral Discipline—Education of Play................631
      Practical Conditions Necessary to Success............................639
   6. KINDERGARTEN METHODS IN PRIMARY SCHOOLS. *Mrs. Louise Pollock*...643-653
      Lecture to the Public School Teachers of Washington..................643
   7. THE PUBLIC AND CHARITY KINDERGARTEN. *Miss Peabody*..............651-653
      Miss Quincy's Shaw in Boston—Miss Blow in St. Louis..................651
   8. INFLUENCE OF KINDERGARTEN TRAINING ON HOMES. *Mrs. H. Mann*....654-664
      Homes of the extreme Poor—New Element of Sweetness and Light.......658
   9. KINDERGARTEN WORK IN CALIFORNIA....................................665-672
      Miss Marwedel—Young Women's Christian Association..................665
      Silver Street Kindergarten—Kindergarten Workers.....................668
   10. KINDERGARTEN TRAINING FOR ARTIST AND ARTISAN. *Miss Peabody*....673-678
       A Primary Art-School—Play converted into Habits....................673
       Special Training in the Kindergarten...............................676
   11. Clay Modeling for Home and Kindergarten. *Edwin A. Spring*.........679-685
   12. FREE KINDERGARTEN AND WORKINGMAN'S SCHOOL. *Felix Adler*.... 686-690
   13. USE OF COLORS IN TEACHING MUSICAL NOTATION. *D. Batchelor*........ 691-704
   14. FREE KINDERGARTEN IN CHURCH WORK, *R. Heber Newton*..............705-730
   15. KINDERGARTEN FOR NEGLECTED CHILDREN...............................731-736

Barnard's Kindergarten Papers, Hartford, Ct., 736 pages, will be sent by mail on receipt of $3.50

ENGLISH PEDAGOGY—OLD AND NEW: or, Treatises and Thoughts on Education, the School, and the Teacher in English Literature. *First Series.* Henry Barnard, LL.D., Editor. Revised Edition. 656 p. $3.50.

CONTENTS.

I. THOUGHTS ON EDUCATION 1–34
    EDUCATION DEFINED—AUTHORITIES, OLD AND NEW............................ 1
    LATIN AND GREEK LANGUAGES IN PUBLIC SCHOOLS AND UNIVERSITIES.......... 11
    WILLIAM OF WYKEHAM, AND ST. MARY'S COLLEGE, WINCHESTER................ 25
    BISHOP WAYNFLETE, AND ETON COLLEGE................................... 26
    DEAN COLET AND ST. PAUL'S SCHOOL, LONDON............................. 27
    CARDINAL WOLSEY, AND IPSWICH GRAMMAR SCHOOL......................... 29
    ARCHBISHOP CRANMER, PLEA FOR HUSBANDMEN'S SONS....................... 31
    SHREWSBURY FREE SCHOOL 32
    MERCHANT TAYLORS' SCHOOL—PROBATION SCHEME........................... 33

II. TREATISES ON EDUCATION 35–358
    SIR THOMAS ELYOT, 1497 TO 1546....................................... 35–40
      THE GOVERNOR: OR TRAINING FOR THE PUBLIC WEAL..................... 35
    ROGER ASCHAM, 1515 TO 1568.. 49–80
      THE SCHOOLMASTER... 49
      TOXOPHILUS, OR THE SCHOOL OF SHOOTING 77
    RICHARD MULCASTER, 1551 TO 1611..................................... 81–88
      THE ELEMENTAIRE—POSITIONS FOR THE TRAINING UP OF CHILDREN........ 81
    SIR HENRY WOTTON, 1568 TO 1639...................................... 89–102
      MORAL ARCHITECTURE OR APOTHEGMS ON EDUCATION...................... 89
    JOHN BRINSLY, 1587 TO 1665.. 103–106
      LUDUS LITERARIUS, OR THE GRAMMAR SCHOOLE, 1627................... 103
    COOTE—WEBSTER—WASE, 1615 TO 1680................................... 107
      ENGLISH SCHOOLMASTER—EXAMINATIONS OF ACADEMIES—FREE SCHOOLS..... 107
    CHARLES HOOLE, 1618 TO 1677... 109–176
      NEW DISCOVERY OF THE OLD ART OF TEACHING......................... 109
      THE PETTY SCHOOL... 113
      GRAMMAR SCHOOL—THE MASTERS' METHOD.............................. 129
      EARLY ENGLISH SCHOOL BOOKS...................................... 153
    LORD BACON, 1561 TO 1626.. 167–180
      CUSTOM AND EDUCATION—ADVANCEMENT OF LEARNING..................... 177
    JOHN MILTON, 1608 TO 1674... 181–190
      TRACTATE ON EDUCATION.. 181
    SAMUEL HARTLIB, 1610 TO 1665.. 191–196
      PROPOSITIONS FOR ERECTING A COLLEGE OF HUSBANDRY, 1651........... 191
    SIR WILLIAM PETTY, 1613 TO 1666..................................... 191–209
      ADVANCEMENT OF REAL LEARNING, OR COLLEGE OF TRADESMEN, 1647..... 199
    ABRAHAM COWLEY, 1618 TO 1677.. 209–220
      PLAN OF A PHILOSOPHICAL COLLEGE—COLLEGE OF AGRICULTURE........... 209
    SIR MATHEW HALE, 1600 TO 1676....................................... 221–224
      PLAN OF EDUCATION FOR HIS GRANDCHILDREN.......................... 221
    JOHN LOCKE, 1632 TO 1704.. 225–342
      THOUGHTS ON EDUCATION, 1693...................................... 225
      1. PHYSICAL. 2. MORAL. 3. INTELLECTUAL. 4. PRACTICAL............. 226
    ROBERT SOUTH—SIR RICHARD STEELE, 1627 TO 1729...................... 345–368
      DISCOURSE FOR WESTMINSTER SCHOOL—FLOGGING IN PUBLIC SCHOOLS...... 345
    OLIVER GOLDSMITH, 1728 TO 1774...................................... 347–358
      ESSAY ON EDUCATION... 345

	PAGE
III. ENGLISH HOME LIFE AND EDUCATION	369-400
Sir Thomas More—Home School—Letters	359
The Evelyn Family	369
Mrs. Elizabeth Sadler Walker—Mrs. Lucy Hutchinson	385
The Boyle Family—Lady Ranelagh—Countess of Warwick	390
Margaret Lucas—Duchess of Newcastle	391
Anne Harrison—Lady Fanshaw	398
IV. THE SCHOOL AND TEACHER IN ENGLISH LITERATURE.	401-528
THOMAS FULLER, 1608 to 1687	403-408
The Good Schoolmaster	403
OLIVER GOLDSMITH, 1728 to 1784	407
The Village Schoolmaster	407
WILLIAM SHENSTONE, 1714 to 1763	409-426
The Schoolmistress	409
Annotations	417
THOMAS GRAY, 1716 to 1771	427-432
Ode on the Distant Prospect of Eton College	437
Alliance of Education and Government	439
WILLIAM COWPER, 1731 to 1800	433-454
Tirocinium; or a Review of Schools	434
Discipline	453
GEORGE CRABBE, 1707 to 1832	455-463
Schools of the Borough	455
SAMUEL TAYLOR COLERIDGE, 1774 to 1834	464
Love, Hope and Patience	464
ROBERT SOUTHEY, 1774-1843	465-480
Home, and Home Education of Doctor Daniel Dove	465
Richard Guy, the Schoolmaster of Ingleton	470
WILLIAM WORDSWORTH	485-496
The State and Education	493
THOMAS HOOD, 1798 to 1845	489-496
The Irish Schoolmaster	489
Ode on a Distant View of Clapham Academy	495
DANIEL DEFOE, 1661 to 1731	497-512
Essay on Projects—Academies, 1697	497
Plan of a University for London, 1723	501
Military Academy—Academy for Women	508
JOHNSON—BARROW—NEWTON—ADDISON, 1709 to 1784	513-528
Education—Discipline—Wisdom—Travel—Recreation	513
V. SCHOOL MANAGEMENT AND DISCIPLINE	529-576
Scholastic Discipline—By Charles Hoole, 1659	529
The Rod in English Public Schools	561
VI. UNIVERSITY STUDIES AND STUDENT LIFE	577-608
Gray—Pope—Adam Smith—Gibbon—Parr—Jones—Lowth—Knox	577
Warton—Shairp—Wordsworth—Tennyson—Payne—Thornbury	597
APPENDIX—ENGLISH PEDAGOGY AND SCHOOLS—*Continued*	609-640
1. Studies and Conduct—Advice by Eminent Men	609
2. Elementary School Systems and Methods	611
3. English Pedagogy—*Second Series*	615
4. Universities in Great Britain	617
5. Special Schools—Arts of Peace and War	629
6. Teachers and Educators	639
INDEX	643-648

BARNARD'S ELEMENTARY INSTRUCTION IN GREAT BRITAIN. 553

OBJECT TEACHING AND ORAL LESSONS on Social Science and Common Things, with various Illustrations of the Principles and Practice of Primary and Elementary Instruction in the Model and Training Schools of England, Ireland, and Scotland, together with Suggestions on School Organization, Management, and Methods, by Currie, Dunn, Morrison, Richards, Stow, Sullivan, Young, and other practical Teachers and Educators. Revised Edition. 500 pages. Price $3.00. Address P. O. Box "U," *Hartford, Conn.*

INDEX TO OBJECT TEACHING.

ABERDEEN, Ragged Schools, 333.
Abstract Ideas and Terms, 23, 302, 411.
Accidents to School Children, 171.
Accuracy in Answers, 12
Action, suited to the word, in Oral Lessons, 64.
Addition of Numbers, Exercises for Infants, 249.
Adults, Lectures to, 110, 332.
Age of Pupils, 111.
  Borough-road Normal School, 359.
  Irish Infant Schools, 171.
Agriculture in Irish Schools, 144.
Air, necessity of pure in a school-room, 233.
ALBERT PRINCE, Law of Nature, 93.
Algebra, 367, 371.
Allen, William, Aid to Joseph Lancaster, 437.
Alphabet, Methods of Teaching, 279.
  Borough-road Model, 394.
  National Society's Central, 517.
  Cowper's Ivory Letters, 280.
  Currie's Manual, 279.
  Locke's Suggestions, 279.
  Sullivan's Methods, 445.
Althorp, Lord, and Popular Education, 332.
Analysis, defined, 214, 295.
Analytical Method and Processes, 294.
  Borough-road Model, 395, 401.
  Morrison's School Management, 296.
Anger, in a Teacher, 171.
Answer to Questions, 10.
  Conditions of a good, 302.
  Class and Individual combined, 302.
  Pupils, first in his own words, 10, 303.
  All, collectively in the right way, 303.
Animals, Oral Instruction as to, 34, 63, 401, 454, 458.
Apparatus for Elementary Schools, 91, 261, 503.
Aptitude in Teaching, 234, 572.
Arithmetic, Suggestions on the Study of,
  Mental, 363, 412.
  Written, 412
  Preliminary Exercises, 192, 547.
Arithmetic, Place and Methods in,
  Borough-road Normal, 367.
  Borough-road Model, 411.
  National Society's Central, 525.
  Home and Colonial, 459.
  Irish Infant Schools, 191.
  Scotch Infant and Primary, 247.
Arithmetical Tables, 413.
Arithmeticon, 525.
Arnica, Remedy for sprains and accidents, 173.
Arnold, Dr., cited, 8.
Art of Teaching, Principles and Practice in,
  Borough-road Normal, 308, 376.
  Home and Colonial Infant, 462.
  Currie's Principles and Practice, 229.
  Dunn's Hand-Book, 308, 381.
  Irish Training School, 141, 203, 213.
  Morrison's School Management, 21, 294.
  Richard's National Society's Manual, 501.
  Ross's Catechetical Method, 7.
  Stow's Training System, 57. [445.
  Sullivan's Method in National Model School, Dublin,
  Young's Infant School Teacher's Manual, 155.
ASHBURTON, Prize Scheme of Common Things, 101.
Assimilation of Children of Different Creeds, 753.
Attendance, 507.
Attention of a whole class, 9, 301.

Backward and dull children, 17.
Bacon, Lord. cited, 93.
Bather, Archdeacon, Socratic Method, 15.
  Business of a Catechist, 15.
Behavior of Children at School, 172.
Bell-frame in Arithmetic, 255, 411, 525.
BELL, ANDREW, Memoir, 329.
  Madras System of Instruction, 488, 495.
  List of Publications, 495.
  Relations to National Society, 330.
BIBLE, the Basis of Religious Instruction, 446.
  Lessons in Emblems of, 289.
  Rule of Irish Board of Education, 137.
  Rule of British Schools, 439.
Bipartite Plan of School Organization. 210.
Time Table, Boys School—Mixed Schools, 213.
Blackboard. 247, 263, 381, 397.
Body, Lessons on different parts of, 240.
Book-learning in Infant Schools, 231.
Books for Teachers and Pupils,
  Borough-road Model School, 395, 412, 417, 423.
  National Society's Central, 502.
  Object Lessons, and Oral Teaching, 246.
  Infant School Manuals, 274.
  Children's Reading, 276.
Books, care of, 172.
BOROUGH-ROAD MODEL SCHOOL, 373.
  Hand-Book, for Details, 381
  Organization and Instruction, 381.
BOROUGH-ROAD NORMAL SCHOOL, 355.
  Department for Young Men, 357.
  Junior and Senior Divisions, 356.
  Conditions of Admission, 457.
  Organization, Studies, Practice, 359.
  Daily and Weekly Routine, 362.
  Upper Class, or Pupil Teachers, 365.
  Art of Teaching. 368.
Botany, 541.
BROUGHAM, Popular Education in England, 337, 347
  Letter to the Duke of Bedford, 339.
Byron, Lady, Industrial School at Ealing Grove, 335.
BRITISH AND FOREIGN SCHOOL SOC'Y, 330, 355, 435.
  Lancaster's Relations to, 355, 435.
  Manual of System for British Schools, 439.
  Rule for the Society in reference to Religion, 441.
  Modes of promoting National Education, 438.
Bryce, R. J., Art of Teaching in 1828, 139.

Camel, Stow's Gallery Training Lesson on, 63.
Candidates for Teaching, 357, 449.
CARLYLE, THOMAS, Popular Education. 354.
Catechism, in Church of England Schools, 374, 513.
  National Society's Schools, 513.
  Not required in British Schools, 439, 441
  Objectionable for young children, 285.
Catechetical, Defined and Described, 7
Catechetical Method of Teaching, 7.
  Questions, kinds and language, 8.
  Answer, Elements of a good, 10.
  Objections to the Method. answered. 17.
  Estimates of, by Bather, Watts, Dinter, 15, 16, 17.
  Cautions in the use, 13.
Central Establishment of National Society, 500.
  Model Schools, details of, 501.
Chalk, and Blackboard, 404.
Chalmers, Dr., Parochial Schools of Scotland, 222.
Chapel Exercises in St. Marks Training College. 538.

Character, Formation of Moral, 391.
Christ's love to Children, Lesson on, 290.
  Power, Lesson on, 288.
Church of England, and National Schools, 499.
Class-teaching, 399, 491.
Classes, large or small, 505.
Classification, 208, 316, 505.
  Borough-road Model School, 283.
  National Society's Central, 505.
  Madras System, Schools on, 495.
  Keenan's plans for, 208.
  Moseley, Tripartite system, 316.
Cleanliness, Personal, 158, 171.
Coleridge, Derwent, Education of the Poor, 511.
Collective Teaching, 49, 255, 373, 395.
  Specimen Lessons, 49, 50, 52.
  Ashburton's Prize Scheme, 101.
  Borough-road Model School, 425.
  Mc Creedy, 94.
  Currie, 240.
  Morrison, 21, 33.
  Stow's Gallery Training Lessons, 57.
  Sullivan's Prize Scheme, 93, 97.
Color, Lesson on, 187, 239, 459.
  Hay, D. R., Diagram and Lesson, 321.
Common Things, Instruction in, 21.
  Ashburton's Prize Scheme, 101.
  Currie's Subjects and Specimens, 242.
  Stow's Gallery Training Lessons, 57.
  Sullivan's Premium Questions, 97.
Communication, Power of, 534.
Composition, Practice in English,
  Borough-road Model, 415.
  National Society's Central, 521.
Conversational Method for Infant Schools, 229, 454.
Copy-books, 371.
Cornwell's Text-books, 417, 421.
Corporal punishments, 510.
Covered play-space for inclement weather, 383.
Crime and Education, 116, 130.
Criticism-lesson for Pupil Teachers, 369, 386.
Crossley's Intellectual Calculator, 412.
Cruelty to Animals, 447.
CURRIE, JAMES, Principal of Training College, 229.
  Subjects and Methods of Early Education, 229.

Daily Lesson Book, 383, 505.
Dame Schools, 155.
Deference to Authority, 508.
Definitions, 296.
De Gerando, Baron, on Monitorial Instruction, 491.
De Morgan's Arithmetic, 412.
Denmark, Monitorial System in, 492.
Denominational Schools, 151.
Desks and Forms, Arrangements of, 233.
  British and Foreign School Society, 381.
  National Society, 393.
Development, Processes of, 393.
Developing Lessons, 176.
Devotions, School Exercises of, 291.
Dictation in Spelling, 409, 521.
Dividing of Numbers, preliminary exercise, 253.
Doing, the Principle of Training, 65, 121.
Domestic Arrangements in Normal Schools, 357.
Domestic Economy, Knowledge of, 61, 237, 374.
  Prize Scheme for promoting, 103.
Drafts, and Draft-work, 381.
Drawing, Methods of Teaching in,
  Borough-road Normal School, 363.
  Borough-road Model, 426.
  National Society's Central, 529.
  Home and Colonial Infant, 459.
Drunkenness, Training to prevent the habit of, 123.
Duke of Bedford, and Joseph Lancaster, 435.
DUNN, HENRY, Hand-book for British Schools, 381.
Discipline, Principles, and Methods, 171.
  Borough-road Normal, 372.
  National Society's Central, 501.

Early Impressions, 23.
Early Instruction, Value of, 156, 229.

Economic Science, Instruction in, 104.
Economy and Forethought, Habits of, 122.
Education, Defined and described, 461.
EDGEWORTH, MARIA, Teaching the Alphabet, 448.
Ellipses, Value and place of, 68, 304.
Elliptical method, 463.
ELLIS, WILLIAM, Birkbeck School, 106.
  Industrial Life and Social Science, 106, 110.
Emulation, 391, 455, 508.
Encouragements, 378.
ENGLAND, Elementary education, 325, 345.
  Historical Development and Education, 327.
English Language,
  Speaking, 25, 363.
  Spelling, 283, 409, 517.
  Writing, or Composition Grammar, 365, 415.
  Reading, 363.
  Literature, 366.
Errors, Correction of, 315, 373.
Etymology, Method of teaching, 315.
  National Society's Central School, 521.
Evening Schools, 113, 143, 331.
Example, Power of, 169, 511.
Examinations, Value and Method, 305.
  Borough-road Normal, 373, 378.
  Home and Colonial, 465.
  Questions to guide in writing schools, 371.
Excursions to Gardens and Museums, 391.
Exercise, Physical, 169, 235.
Exposition, 546.
Eye, Education of, 260, 490.
Eye and Hand, Training of, 460.

Familiar, or Common Things, Instruction in, 237.
Female Education and Employments, 101, 374.
  School Mistresses, 103, 374.
Fittings for School-buildings, 381, 501.
Flat top, or surface, to Desks, 382.
Fletcher, Joseph, 355.
Fletcher of Saltoun, 217.
Floral Culture for Teachers, 541.
Flower-borders in School-yards, 383.
Formation of Character, 371.
Form, Instruction in, 178, 260, 458.
Forms, or Long Seats, 382, 502.
Fox, Joseph, and Lancaster, 355.
Fractions in Arithmetic, 254, 414.

Gallery, 6, 382.
Gallery Lesson, 86.
Gallery, Training System, 49, 57, 454, 463.
  Specimen Lessons, 63, 68, 71, 74, 369, 454.
Gardening, and simple Agriculture, 145.
  St. Marks Training College, 541.
Geography, subject of Instruction, 269, 298.
  Preliminary work, 260, 270.
  Industrial, 306.
  Physical, 421.
  Pictorial, 270.
  Topical, 598.
  Incidental in Reading Lessons, 424.
Geography, methods pursued,
  Borough-road Normal, 366.
  Borough-road Model, 421.
  National Society's Central, 527.
  Home and Colonial, 461.
Girard's Home Education, 230, 232, 284.
Gibson, John, Mastery of Methods, 297.
Geometry, 267.
Girls, Education of,
  Knowledge of Domestic Economy, 103, 240.
  Needle-work, 104, 374, 432.
God, First ideas of, 204, 457.
  His goodness, Lesson on, 204, 289.
Gonigraph, for Grammatical forms, 179.
Graduated Course of Instruction, 457, 506.
  Home and Colonial Infant and Juvenile School Society, 449.
Grammar, Methods with English,
  Borough-road Normal, 362, 372.
  National Society's Central, 522.

BARNARD'S ELEMENTARY INSTRUCTION IN GREAT BRITAIN. 555

Gray's Inn-road Normal and Model School, 449.
  Course of Instruction for Teachers, 451.
  Graduated Course in Model School, 457.
  Syllabus of Lectures on Education, 462.
  Specimen of Lesson in Model School, 467.
  Number—a Watch—Idea of Crumbling, 471.
  Silver—the Refiner's work—Month of October, 473.
  Remarks of Head Master on the above Lessons, 483.
Gymnastic Apparatus and Exercises, 383.
Guessing, or Random Answers, 12, 66.

Habits of a School, 373.
Habits of Teachers, 378.
Hay, D. R., Lesson on Color, 320.
  Diagram Illustration, 322.
Health, Philosophy of, 425.
Head Master, Duties of, 209.
Hemming, and other Needle-work, 375.
Herbault, M., Monitorial System, 490.
History, Place and Methods in,
  Borough road Normal, 367.
  National Society's Central, 529.
Home Education, 232.
Home and Colonial Infant School Society, 449.
  Normal and Model Schools, 449.
  Qualifications required of Candidates, 449.
  Graduated Course of Instruction, 451.
Honesty, Training to, 123.
Horticulture in Normal Schools, 541.
Hullah's Method of teaching Singing, 427, 530, 539.
  Grammar of Vocal Music, 539.
Human Body, Instruction as to, 458.

Imagination, Exercise of, 229, 277.
Indefiniteness in Answers, 12.
Indistinctness in Reading, 282.
Individuality of each pupil, 300
Individual and Simultaneous Questioning, 300.
Individual Teaching, 298.
Induction, Habit of, 398, 403.
Industrial Element in Schools, 120, 128, 144.
  Borough-road Normal, 374.
  Borough-road Model, for Girls, 432.
  St. Marks Training College, 540.
  Irish National Schools, 155, 144.
Industrial and Social Economy, 237.
  Birkbeck Schools, 107.
Infant Culture and Schools, Estimate of, 155.
  Young, 155.   Oberlin, 332.
  Currie, 229.   Owen, 332.
  Pestalozzi, 162.
  Wilderspin, 162, 170.
Infant Schools, Details of Organization,
  Physical, 169, 229, 233.   Play-ground, 172.
  Moral, 158.   Daily Time-table, 175,
  Intellectual, 162, 236.   451.
  Sanitary Regulat'ns, 172.   Synopsis of Weekly Les-
  Teachers required, 169.   sons, 175, 452.
  Rules and Regulat'ns,171.
Infant Schools, Object Teaching.
  Objects, 458.   Reading, 273.
  Number, 191, 247, 459.   Reading and Spell'g, 277.
  Form, 178, 258, 260.   Spelling, 283.
  Color, 186, 259, 453.   Human Body, 458.
  Size, 188.   Plants, 459.
  Weight, 192   Eye, 460.
  Order and Position, 189.   Ear, 194.
  Singing, 267.   Hand, 460.
  Geography, 269, 461.
  Examples of Lessons on Objects, 193, 259, 453.
  Subjects in Natural History, 239, 253, 458.
  Industrial and Social Economy, 240.
  Physical appearances, 240.
  Drawing and Gallery Lessons, 459.
  Moral and Religious Topics, 158, 284, 288.
Inkstands, 382.
Inspection, in Irish National System, 147, 205.
  English Staff, 342.
Interrogation, Ploughshare of, 305, 546.
Interrogative Method, 371, 408, 497.
  Specimen Lessons, 108, 401.

Internal Organization, or Fundamental Divisions, 208.
  Borough-road Model, 361.
  National Society's Central, 501.
  Bipartite Plan, 209, 310.
  Monitorial System. 487, 495.
  Modified Monitorial System, 210.
Interest of children in their work, 304.
Ireland, System of National Education, 133.
  Historical Development and Condition, 135, 150.
  Syllabus of Lectures on Methods of Instruction, 213.

Jacotot's method, 402, 519.
Juvenile School Society, 449.

Kay, Dr. James Philip, 340.
Keenan, P. J., Head Inspector of Irish Schools, 205.
  Organization and Inspection of National Schools, 205.
  Tripartite—Bipartite—Modified Monitorial, 209.
  Time-table, for Boys', Girls', and Mixed Schools, 212.
  Monitorial System, 488.
Knight, Charles, Economical Science, 104.
Knitting and Needle-work, 432.
Knox, John, First Book of Discipline, 215.

Lancaster, Joseph, and Monitorial System, 355, 435.
Lancasterian Institution and Method, 355, 448.
Language, Training in, 23, 25, 313, 316.
  Conceptive Faculty, 239.   [544.
  Power of Communicating, or Expressive Faculty,
Lap-bags for Needle-work, 374, 433.
La Salle, Use of Monitors in 1680, 488.
Latimer's Sermon of the Plow in 1548, 324.
Latin, in St. Marks Training College, 539.
Latin Derivations, 421.
Laws of Nature, 93, 95.
Lecture and Preachments to Children, 30, 314.
Lesson, average length for young children, 234.
Lessons on Objects. (See Specimen Lessons.)
Lever, Thomas, Sermon in 1550, 325.
Light, Management of, 234.
Lines—Angles—Circles—Solids, 181, 261.   [542.
Literature and Science, Relative value to Teachers,
Location, or site of School Buildings, 501.
Lord's Prayer, Child's Lesson, 290.
Love, the Teacher's Motive, 172.

Madras System of Instruction, 495.
Management of a School, 465.
Manners, 172, 258, 533.
Manual Labor, 540.
Maps—Skeleton and Map-drawing, 422, 272.
Map Geography, 272.
Marcel, on Language, 232.
Marching in Infant Schools, 237.
Mathematics, 307.
Mayo, Dr., Lessons on Number, 248, 524.
Mc Rae, Mrs., Lectures on Teaching, 377.
Meaning of Words and Sentences, 519.
Melodies for Infant Schools, 268.
Memory, 28.
Memorizing Matter well understood, 373.
Mechanic's Institutions, 332.
Method, General Ideas of, 213, 294, 463.
Mental Arithmetic, 353, 413.
Methods, described,
  Analytical, 213, 295, 296.   Mutual, 300, 487.
  Collective, 387, 395. [401.   Pictorial, 272.
  Dogmatic, 214.   Picturing out, 61.
  Elliptical, 214, 403.   Simultaneous, 519.
  Genetic, 30.   Socratic. 214.
  Individual, 298.   Synthetic, 214, 294.
  Interrogation, 401, 447.   Bell, 563.
  Madras, 495.   Jacotot, 448, 519.
  Monitorial, 487.   Lancaster, 488.
  Modified Monitorial, 210.
Misery and Vice, prevented by Education, 117.
Mitchell, M., Ventilation and Light, 234.
Model and Practical Schools attached to
  Borough-road Normal, 373, 381.
  National Society's Central, 501.
  St. Marks Training College, 542.

Monitor, or Pupil Teachers, 210, 487.
  Borough-road Model, 387, 399.
  Borough-road Normal, 372.
  National Society's Central, 503.
Monitorial, or Mutual System, 387.
  Historical Development, 487.
  Objections to, 388, 503.
  Modified in Irish Schools, 210.
Montaigne, on Early Impressions, 155.
MORRISON, THOMAS, Rector of Training College, 21.
  Oral Lessons on Common Things, 21.
  Methods of Instruction, 294.
Moral Education, 158, 288.
MORE, Sir Thomas, Utopia, 327.
Moseley Rev. Canon, Inspector of Schools, 95.
  Tripartite System of Organization, 316.
  St. Marks Training College, 532, 543, 545.
Mother Tongue, 230.
Mulhäuser's Method of teaching Writing, 524.
Multiplication of Numbers, 251.

Nationality of Irish Schools, 150.
National Education, 140, 337
National Schools of Ireland, 140, 205.
National Society for the Ed. of the poor, 331, 499.
  Charter of Incorporation, 499.
  Objects—Increase of Means, and Improvement of Processes, 499.
  Training Schools,—Central Depository, 500.
  Central Model School in Westminster—Monthly Paper, 500.
  St. Marks Training College, 533.
Natural History, School Instruction in,
  Borough-road Normal, 367, 368.
  Borough-road Model, 401, 425.
  Home and Colonial Model, 458.
  Currie—Specimen Lessons, 239.
  Morrison—Oral Lessons, 37, 40.
  Stow—Gallery Lesson, 63, 68.
Natural Philosophy, School Instruction in,
  National Society's Central, 519.
  Borough-road Normal, 367.
  Home and Colonial Model, 478.
Nature's Methods with Children, 22.
Needle-work, Instruction in, 374.
  Borough-road Normal, 374.
  Borough-road Model, 432.
Normal and Model Schools, and Training Colleges,
  British and Foreign School Society, 355, 447.
  National Society, 500, 533.
  Dublin Central Model Schools, 141, 213, 445.
  Edinburgh General Assembly's, 220.
  Glasgow General Assembly's, 220.
  Notes of Lessons, 33, 49. (See Specimen Lessons.)
Number, Exercises, preliminary to the Science of,
  Borough-road Model, 411.
  National Society's Central, 525.
  Home and Colonial Infant, 459.
  Currie's Infant Training, 247.
  Young's Infant Manual, 191.
Numeration, Practical Exercises, 248.

Obedience, Habits of, 392.
Oberlin, J. F., Infant Schools, 332.
Object Lessons, or Real Objects and Common Things, 21.
  Home and Colonial Model School, 453, 458.
  Currie's Early School Education, 239.
  Morrison's Manual, 21, 33.
  Stow's Gallery Training System, 63.
  Young's Infant School Manual, 135.
Observation, Habits of, 176, 238, 486.
Oliphant, Tripartite Organization, 315.
Oral Instruction and Lessons, 21.
  Rule of the Infant School, 231.
  Want of the Infant Mind, 231.
  Separate room essential, 316.
  Qualifications of the Teacher, 27.
  Connection with Mother-tongue, 230.
  Specimen Lessons. (See Specimen Lesson.)
Organizer in Irish System, 208.

Organization of Elementary Schools, 208.
  British and Foreign Colonial Society, 381.
  Home and Colonial Infant and Juvenile School,
  National Society's School, 501.
  Irish System—Bipartite—Tripartite, 259.
  Madras System, 495.
Over-Educating, by the Catechetical Method, 19.
Our Father, the Key-note of Religious Instruction, 284.
Owen, Robert, Infant Schools, 332.

Paid Monitors, 211.
Paidometer, in Madras System, 498.
Parallel arrangements of Form and Books, 502.
Parallelogram, Form for School-room, 381.
Parents, Rules for their guidance, 129, 171.
Parental Authority, Deference to, 392.
Paulet's use of Monitors in 1747, 490.
Pauper Children, and Schools for, 335, 547.
Pause-reading, 497.
Peckham Birkbeck Schools, 107.
Pedagogy, Lectures on, 376.
Penmanship, 363, 410, 524.
Perception, and Perceptive Faculties, 177, 393.
Pestalozzi, Principles of, 462.
  Cited, 157, 163, 170.
Phonic, and Phonetic Method, 281, 519.
Physical Education, 109, 229, 233.
Physical Exercises for Infant School, 235.
Physical Sciences for Children, 237.
Physiology, 237.
Pictures, in place of Real Objects, 270, 272.
Picturing-out Process, 32, 57, 61.
Pietro della Valle, Monitorial Plan in 1665, 488.
Pilans, Principles of Elementary Teaching, 278.
Place in Class, 509.
Platform for Teacher, 381.
Play-ground, 172, 236, 465.
  Circular Swing, and Gymnastic Apparatus, 5, 383.
  The Uncovered School-room, and Children's World, 174, 236.
  British and Foreign School Society's Schools, 383.
  National Society's Schools, 506.
Poetry, Recitations of simple, 167.
Political Economy, Easy Lessons in, 105.
  Syllabus of a course of Lectures, by Mr. Ellis, 110.
Pounds, John, and Ragged Schools, 333.
Practice Schools, for Normal Pupils, 542.
Prayers for School Children, 292, 514.
Predisposition to certain vices, 131.
Prevention of occasions for punishments, 466.
Primary Schools, 21, 57, 455.
Printing on Slate for little children, 246, 394.
Prize Schemes for Knowledge of Common Things, 93, 97, 101.
Prizes and Rewards, 509.
Privilege of the Clergy, 324.
Professional Training of Teachers, 545.
Proportion, how taught, 415.
Progressive Development of Schools for the poor, 327.
Punishments, 466, 509.
Pupil Teachers, 211, 369, 385, 504.

Question, Elements of a good, 9, 301.
Questioning, Art of, 7, 301, 305, 465,
Questions to test a School, 168, 371.
Questions, different kinds and aims of, 7.
  Individual, 168, 302, 392.
  Explanatory, 468.
  Examinatory, 7, 168, 305.
  Recapitulatory, 398.
  Simultaneous and Individual combined, 65, 301.
  Socratic, or Teaching, 8, 16.
Questions and Ellipses, 304.
Quintilian, on Reading, 496.

Ragged Schools, Historical dates, 333.
Raikes, Robert, and Sunday Schools, 328.
Reading, as a mechanical effort, 231, 277.
Reading and Spelling, 277.
  Preparatory Exercises, 278, 281.
  Should be confined to words already known, 277.

Reading, Methods of teaching,
  Borough-road Normal, 363, 371.
  Borough-road-Model, 383, 393, 399.
  National Society's Central, 517.
  Bell's System, 495.
  Currie's Suggestions, 273.
  Young's plan, 175, 204.
  Morrison's Examination on Lessons, 313.
Recapitulatory Exercise, 402, 496.
Reform Schools, 334.
Registration, 373, 498.
Religion and Religious Instruction,
  British and Foreign School Society, 441.
  Home and Colonial Model, 457.
  National Society, 513, 532.
  Irish National Board, 137.
Religious Instruction, Suggestions by
  Bather, 15.   Stow, 87.
  Coleridge, 532.   Tuke, 439.
  Currie, 284.   Watts, 16.
  Morrison, 284.   Wordsworth, 96.
  Moseley, 522.   Young, 198.
  Richards, 512, 515.
  Sinclair, 513.
Repetition, in Training, 67, 466, 493.
Respect for the teacher, 392.
Revenge, Passion of, 126.
Rewards, and Reward-ticket, 390.
Roads, Lesson on, 51.
Roman Catholic Children in Irish National Schools, 137.
Royal Lancasterian Institution, 355, 372, 437.
Ross, WILLIAM, Catechetical Method, 7.
  Adaptations to the Subject, and the Pupils, 8.
  Conditions of a good question, 9.
  Elements of a satisfactory answer, 11.
  Counsels and Cautions as to this method, 13.
  Bather, Watts, and Dinter, on, 16.
Rule of Three in Arithmetic, 415, 526.
Rules for Children at School, 172.
  Candidates for teaching, 357, 358, 449.
  Parents of the Children, 171.
  Teacher, 171.
  Play-ground, 172.
  Ventilation, Cleanliness, Temperature, 173.
  Disease, Accidents, 173.
Russell, Lord John, and Popular Education, 339.

Sanitary Regulations, 172.
School Architecture, I, 381, 501.
Schools, different kinds and grades of,
  Adults, 331.   Mechanics, 332.
  Agricultural, 144.   Monitorial, 329.
  Birkbeck, 106.   Model, 449, 457.
  British, 435.   National, 340.
  Dame, 155.   Normal, 354.
  Evening, 143.   Parochial, 225.
  Grammar, 325.   Ragged, 220, 333.
  Infant, 155, 229, 332. Reform, 334.
  Industrial, 144, 335. Sunday, 328.
  Juvenile, 448.   Sessional, 225.
  Lancasterian, 330.   Training, 142.
  Madras, 495.   Workhouse, 143.
School, Habits of,
School Management, 21, 294.
School Play-ground, 5, 172.
School-room, Rules for, 172.
School-work for the Infant, 232.
Science of Common Things, 58, 237.
Science of Education, 368.
Science and Literature, Relative value, 543.
Scriptures, 427, 457, 513.
SCOTLAND, Elementary Schools, 215.
  Early School Legislation, 216.
  General Assembly of Church of Scotland, 217.
  Wood—Watson—Chalmers—Brougham, 221.
Sewing, Instruction, 376.
Sections and Drafts, in School Organization, 383.
Shields, W. & Peckham Birkbeck Schools, 108.
  Lesson on Wages, 108.
Short, Bishop, School Punishment, 510.
Shuttleworth, Sir James Key, 340.

Simpson, Philosophy of Education, 158.
Simultaneous, or Class Reading, 283.
  Movements generally, 67.
Sinclair, Arch-deacon, Teaching Catechism, 513.
Singing, as a Physical Exercise, 236.
Singing by Ear, and Note, 267, 426.
Singing, and the Choral Service, at St. Marks, 538
Sketching on the Blackboard and Slate, 246.
Slates, for youngest pupils, 394.
Smith, Adam, Wealth of Nations, 327.
Socrates, 16.
Socratic Method, 16, 214.
  Applied to Religious Instruction, 15, 17.
  Defense of, by Watts, and Dinter, 17.
Solids, Lesson on, 185.
Songs, for Infant Schools, 368.
Space for Class-movements, 382.
Specimen Lessons in Oral Instruction and Object
  Teaching, 33, 49, 63, 180, 243.
  Morrison's Oral Lessons on Real Objects,
    The Cow—A Fire—The Elephant, 33.
    Relations of Parts of the Body—Winnowing of
      Corn, 35.
    The Spider's Web—The Common Bat, 37.
    Reaping of Corn—Watering the street, 39.
    The Duck—The Nests of Birds, 40.
    The making of Grain into Meal, 41.
    The Thermometer—The Barometer—Dew, 43.
    Land and Sea Breeze—Why does Ice float? 44.
    Locality and Customs—Rice—Cotton Plant, 45.
    Heat—Mechanics—Pneumatics, 47.
    Ventilation—Cold Water, 48.
  Collective or Gallery Lessons, 49.
    The Palm Tree—Pens, ancient and modern, 49.
    Roads—(1) History, (2) Construction, (3) Uses, 51.
    Weekly Expenses of the Laboring Man—Food, 52.
    Notes of the Lesson—Specimen of Answers, 53
    Climate—Notes of Lessons, 55.
  Stow's Gallery Training Lesson,
    The Camel—The Mole—Air as Conductor of
      sound, 63.
  Natural Science and Common Things, 74.
    Initiatory, or Infant department, 86 subjects, 74.
    Juvenile Department, 220 subjects, 96.
    Senior Department, 31 subjects, 82.
    Miscellaneous subjects, 84.
    Human Body and its Health, 87.
  Specimen Questions for Written Exercises, 97.
    Sullivan's Prizes for Teaching Common Schools,
      For Schoolmasters, 97.   [97.
      For Schoolmistresses, 99.
    Ashburton Prizes—Schoolmasters, 101.
      Schoolmistresses, 103.
  Irish Infant School Manual,
    Primitive Colors, 187.
    Size—Order—Position, 189.
    Number—Weight—Sound, 192, 194.
    Objects—Coal and Chalk, 195.
    Sponge—Bread—Penny, 197.
    Moral Lessons—God—Creator, 198.
    Life—the Mind—Conscience, 201.
    Hope—Love—Fear, 203.
  Currie's Infant and Primary School Training,
    The Sheep—A Bed—The Mouth, 243.
    The Baker's Shop—The Cart—Rain, 244.
    The Elephant—The Sponge—The term "Porous," 245.
    Number—Form—Color, 247.
    The Common Hen—The Common Duck, 245.
    Lessons in Form—Lines—Perpendicular, Horizontal, Parallel, 265.
    Triangles—Parallelograms—Circles—Cylinder and
      Solids, 265.
    Home Geography, 191, 270.
    Religious Instruction, 286, 288, 289.
    Christ's Power—God's Goodness, 289.
    Christ's Love—Lord's Prayer—Truth, 291.
  Borough road Model School,
    Ruminating Animals, 401.
    Scripture Narrative, 428.
    Scripture Emblem, 429.

National Society's Schools,
  Our Lord's Parables, 515.
  Good Samaritan, 510.
  Lesson in Rule of Three, 526.
  England—Geographical, 528.
  Reign of Queen Anne, 529.
  Analysis of a Sentence, 522.
  Syntactical Parsing, 523.
Home and Colonial Infant Model School,
  Objects—Animals—Qualities, 453.
  Form—Color—Size—Weight, 454, 458.
  Objects—Pictures—Animals, 454, 458.
  Plants—Scripture Narratives—Sounds, 454, 457.
  Exercises for the Eye and the Hand, 460.
  Number, 467.
  A Watch, 469.
  Idea of Crumbling, 471.
  Scripture, Natural History, 472.
  Silver—the Refiner's work, 472.
  Month of October, 478.
  Application of Lessons by Pupil Teachers, 483.
Spelling, Methods and Suggestions on,
  Borough-road Model, 371, 409.
  National Society's Central, 517.
  Currie's Infant School Methods, 283.
Spurzheim, Dr., on Monitorial Instruction, 493.
ST. MARKS TRAINING COLLEGE, 533.
  Scope and Design, 532.
  Music—Choral Service—Latin, 538.
  Industrial Occupations of Pupil Teachers, 540.
  Moral purposes of Labor, 541.
  Schools of Practice, 542.
Standard Measures, School Instruction in,
  Money, 256.   Surface, 257.
  Weight, 257.   Time, 257.
  Capacity, 257.
Stanley, E. G., National Education in Ireland, 136.
Stewart, Dugald, Synthesis and Analysis, 295.
STOW, DAVID, Training System, 57.
  Gallery Training Lessons, 57.
  Examples of Method, 53, 68, 71.
  Subjects for Infant Class, 74.
  Subjects for Juvenile Department, 76.
  Subjects for Senior Department, 82.
  Miscellaneous subjects, 84.
  Apparatus for Senior and Juvenile School, 91.
  Sturm, use of Monitors, 487.
  Style in Reading, 497.
  Subtraction of Numbers, Exercises in, 250.
  Sullenness and Ill Temper, 11.
SULLIVAN, PROF., 445, 521.
  Outline of Methods, 445.
  Teaching the Alphabet, 445.
  Prize Scheme for Common Things, 93, 97.
Sunday Schools, 328.
Swimming, 29.
Swing, Circular, 5, 383.
Sympathy with Children, 373.
Syntax, How taught, 419.
Synthesis, 295.
Synthetical Method and Processes,
  Borough-road Model, 395.
  Irish National Training, 213.
  Morrison's School Management, 296.

Tables of Money, Weights and Measures, 413.
TAINSH, EDWARD CAMPBELL, Prize Essay, 116. 132.
  Preventive and Reformatory Agency of Schools, 116.
  Idleness—Drunkenness—Thriftlessness, 117.
  Industry—Sobriety—Economy, 119.
Tasks, as Punishments, 510.
Tate M., Social Science and Revelation, 132.
Teacher, Professional Qualities and Qualificat'ns, 447.
Teachers, Methods and Suggestions for,
  Borough road Normal, 378.
  Home and Colonial Infant Model, 451.
  Irish Model and Training School, 213.
  National Society's Central, 511.
  St. Marks Training College, 532, 539, 543.
Teaching, Art of, 169, 316. 368. 463, 533.
  Theory or Science. 213, 368, 463.
Temperature of the School-room, 234.
Temper, Command of, 512.
Temple, F., Teaching Common Things, 95.
Thinking, Semblance and Reality of, 303.
Time Tables,
  Borough-road Normal, 363, 365.
  National Society's Central, 505.
  Home and Colonial, 451.
  Irish National, 212.
  St. Marks College, 538.
  Young's Infant School, 175.
Topics in Professional Teaching, 369.
Toys in Infant Schools, 458.
Training and Teaching, 121.
Training, Professional, 368, 389, 451, 463.
Trigonometry, 367.
Tripartite plan of Organization, 212, 317.
Trotzendorf, Use of Monitors, 487.   [438.
Tuke S., Denominational basis of National Schools,
Truth, Specimen Lesson on, 291.

Uncovered School-room, 236.

Variety in Activity, 235.
Ventilation, 171, 233.
Vocal Music, 267, 426, 529.
Voice, Gymnastic Training of, 292.
  Monotony, and Inflection in Questioning, 8.

Watson, William, Industrial Schools, 333.
Weight, Lesson in, 192.
Whateley, Archbishop, 173.
Wilderspin, Infant Education, 163, 169.
Willm, Monitorial System, 466.
Windows, and Light, 381.
Wood, Edinburgh Sessional School, 219, 474, 517.
Written Arithmetic, 414.
Written Exercises, 364, 455.
Writing, Instruction in, 384, 410.
Workingmen's Education, 112, 327, 329.

Young Children,
  Characteristics of, 453.
  Special Training of Teachers, 156.
  Physical Conditions, 233.
  Oral Methods, 231.
YOUNG, THOMAS URRY, 155.
  Infant School Manual, 155.

CLASSIFIED INDEX

TO

BARNARD'S AMERICAN JOURNAL OF EDUCATION.

VOLUMES I. TO XVI.

CLASSIFICATION OF SUBJECTS.

I. General Principles and History of Education.
II. Individual Views and Special Systems of Education.
III. Studies and Methods of Teaching; School Organization and Government.
IV. Teachers and their Training; Normal and Model Schools; Teachers' Institutes.
V. State and National Systems of Instruction.
VI. Secondary, Intermediate, Academical, and High Schools.
VII. University and Collegiate Education.
VIII. Special Schools and Departments of Science, Arts, Agriculture, Museums, &c.
IX. Military and Naval Education.
X. Preventive and Reformatory Education.
XI. Education of the Deaf and Dumb, Blind, Idiots, &c.
XII. Moral and Religious Education; Sectarian Schools and Instruction.
XIII. Female Education.
XIV. Physical Education.
XV. Supplementary, Self, and Home Education; Libraries.
XVI. Educational Societies and Teachers' Associations.
XVII. Philology and Bibliography; School-books and Periodicals, &c.
XVIII. School Architecture.
XIX. Educational Endowments and Benefactors.
XX. Miscellaneous.
XXI. Educational Biography and List of Portraits.

18 CLASSIFIED INDEX OF BARNARD'S AMERICAN JOURNAL OF EDUCATION.

CHAPTER I. GENERAL PRINCIPLES AND HISTORY OF EDUCATION.

EDUCATION defined by Eminent Authorities; English, XI, 11-20; Greek, Roman, French, German, Scotch and American, XIII, 7-16.

Educational Aphorisms and Suggestions, from Two Hundred Authorities, Ancient and Modern.—Man, his Dignity and Destiny, VIII, 9. Nature and Value of Education, VIII, 38. Duties of Parents and Teachers, VIII, 65. Early Home Training, VIII, 75-80; XIII, 79-92. Female Education XIII, 232-242. Intellectual Culture in General, X, 116. Subjects and Means of Education, X, 141, Religious and Moral Instruction, X, 166. Discipline, X, 187. Example, X, 194-200. The State and Education, XIII, 717-024.

Education, Nature and Objects of—Prize Essay, by John Lalor, XVI, 33-64.

Education for the Times, by T. M. Clark, II, 375.

Education a State Duty, by D. B. Duffield, III, 81.

Education and the State; Aphorisms, XIII, 717-724. Views of Macaulay and Carlyle, XIV, 403. American Authorities, XI, 323; XV, 5.

Education Preventive of Crime and Misery, by E. C. Tainsch, XI, 77-93.

Home Education—Labors of W. Burton, II, 333.

Intellectual Education, by William Russell.—The Perceptive Faculties, II, 113-144, 317-332. The Expressive Faculties, III, 47-64, 321-345. The Reflective Faculties, IV, 199-218, 309-342.

Lectures on Education, by W. Knighton, X, 573.

Misdirected Education and Insanity, by E. Jarvis, IV, 591-612.

Moral and Mental Discipline, by Z. Richards, I, 107.

Objects and Methods of Intellectual Education, by Francis Wayland, XIII, 801-816.

Philosophy of Education, by Joseph Henry, I, 17-31.

Philosophical Survey of Education, by Sir Henry Wotton, XV, 131-143.

Problem of Education, by J. M. Gregory, XIV, 431.

Powers to be Educated, by Thomas Hill, XIV, 81-92.

Self-Education and College Education, by David Masson, IV, 262-271.

Thoughts on Education, by Locke; Physical, XI, 461; Moral, XIII, 548; Intellectual, XIV, 305.

Views and Plan of Education, by Krüsi, V, 187-197.

Unconscious Tuition, by F. D. Huntington, I, 141-163.

Schools as they were Sixty Years Ago in United States, XIII, 123, 837; XVI, 331, 738; XVII.

Progressive Development of Schools and Education in the United States, XVII.

History of Education, from the German of Karl von Raumer, IV, 149. History of Education in Italy. VII, 413-460. Eminent Teachers in Germany and the Netherlands prior to the Fifteenth Century, IV, 714. Schlettstadt School, V, 65. School Life in the Fifteenth Century, V, 79. Early School Codes of Germany, VI, 426. Jesuits and their Schools, V, 213; VI, 615. Universities in the Sixteenth Century, V, 536. Verbal Realism, V, 655. School Reformers at Beginning of Seventeenth Century, VI, 459. Thirty Years' War, and the Century Following, VII, 367. Real Schools, V, 689. Refurmatory Philologists, V, 741. Home and Private Instruction, VII, 381. Religious Instruction, VII, 401. Methods of Teaching Latin, VI, 5×1. Methods of Classical Instruction, VII, 471. Methods of Teaching Real Branches, VIII, 101-228. German Universities, VI, 9-65; VII, 47-152. Student Societies, VII, 160.

Educational Development in Europe, by H. P. Tappan, I, 247-268.

Hebrews, and their Education, by M. J. Raphall, I, 243.

Greek Views of Education, Aristotle, XIV, 131; Lycurgus, and Spartan Education, XIV, 611; Plutarch, XI, 99.

Roman Views of Education, Quintilian, XI, 3.

Italian Views of Education and Schools, Acquaviva, XIV, 402; Boccaccio, VII, 422; Botta, III, 513; Dante and Petrarch, VII, 418; Picus, Politian, Valla, Vittorino, VII, 442; Rosmini, IV, 479.

Dutch Views of Education, Agricola, IV, 717; Busch and Lunge, IV, 726; Erasmus, IV, 729; Hieronymians, IV, 622; Reuchlin, V, 65; Wessel, IV, 714.

French Views of Education and Schools, Fenelon, XIII, 477; Guizot, XI, 254, 357; Marcel, XI, 21; Montaigne, IV, 461; Rabelais, XIV, 147; Rousseau, V, 459; La Salle, III, 437.

German Views of Education, Abbenrode, IV, 505, 512; Busedow, V, 487; Comenius, V, 257; Diesterweg, IV, 235, 505; Dinter, VII, 153; Felbiger, IX, 600; Fliedner, III, 487; Franké, V, 481; Graser, VI, 575; Gutsmuths, VII, 191; Hamann, VI, 247; Hentschel, VIII, 633; Herder, VI, 195; Jacobs, VI, 612; Jahn, VIII, 196; Luther, IV, 421; Meinotto, VI, 609; Melancthon, IV, 741; Neander, V, 599; Overberg, XIII, 365; Ratich, V, 229; Raumer, VII, 200, 381; VIII, 101; X, 227, 613; Ruthardt, VI, 600; Sturm, IV, 167, 401; Tobler, V, 205; Trotzendorf, V, 107; Von Turk, V, 155; Vogel, IX, 210; Wolf, VI, 260.

Swiss Views of Education, Fellenberg, III, 594; Krüsi, V, 189; Pestalozzi, III, 401; VII, 513; Vehrli, III, 389.

English Views of Education, Arnold, IV, 545; Ascham, IV, 155; Bacon, XIII, 103; Bell, X, 467. Colet, XVI, 657; Elyot, XVI, 485; Hale, XVII, Hartlib, XI, 191; Goldsmith, XIII, 347; Johnson, XII, 369; Lalor, XVI, 33; Lancaster and Bell, X, 355; Locke VI, 209; XI, 461; XIII, 548; Masson, IV, 262; XIV, 262; Milton, II, 61; Mulcaster, XVII, 177; Spencer, XI, 445; Sedgwick, XVII,; Temple, F., XVII,; Whewell, W., XVII.

Early Promoters of Realism in England, XII, 476. Bacon, V, 663; Cowley, XII, 651; Hoole, XII, 647; Petty, XI, 199.

II. INDIVIDUAL VIEWS AND SPECIAL SYSTEMS OF EDUCATION.

Abbenrode. On Teaching History and Geography, IV. 505, 512.
Abbot, G. D., and the Useful Knowledge Society, XV. 241. Educational Labors, XVI. 600.
Ackland, Henry W. Natural Science and Physical Exercise in Schools, XVII.
Acquaviva, and the Ratio Studiorum, XIV. 462.
Adams, John. Education and the State, XV. 12.
Adams, J. Q. On Normal Schools, I. 589. Education and the State, XV. 12. Educational Reform in Silesia, XVII.
Addison, Joseph. Education and Sculpture, XI. 16.
Adelung, J. C. Philological Labors, XI. 451.
Agassiz, L. Museum of Comparative Zoölogy, IX. 615.
Agricola, Rudolf. Life and Opinions, IV. 717.
Airy, G. B. Mathematics and Natural Science in Schools, XVII.
Akerly, S. Deaf-mute Training, III. 348.
Akroyd, E. Mode of Improving a Factory Population, VIII. 305.
Albert, Prince. On Science and Art, IV. 813.
Alcott, A. Bronson. School-days, XVI. 130.
Alcott, William A. Educational Views, IV. 629. Plan of Village School, IX. 540.
Allyn, Robert. Schools of Rhode Island, II. 544.
Anderson, H. J. Schools of Physical Science, I. 515.
Andrews, I. W. Educational Labors, XVI. 604.
Andrews, L. Educational Labors, XVI. 604.
Andrews, S. J. The Jesuits and their Schools, XIV. 455.
Anthony, H. On Competitive Examinations at West Point, XV. 51.
Aristotle, and his Educational Views, XIV. 131. Cited, III. 45; IV. 463; V. 673; VII. 415; VIII. 40-79; X. 132-195.
Arnold, Matthew. Tribute to Guizot, XI. 281. Schools of Holland, XIV. 712.
Arnold, Thomas, as a Teacher, IV. 545-581.
Ascham, Roger. Biographical Sketch, III. 23. Toxophilus; the Schoole of Shootinge, III. 41. The Schoolmaster, IV. 155; XI. 57.
Ashburton, Lord. Prize Scheme and Address on Teaching Common Things, I. 629.
Austin, Sarah. Ends of a Good Education, XI. 20.
Aventinus. Study of German, XI. 162.

Bache, A. D. On a National University, I. 477. Education in Europe, VIII. 435, 444, 455, 564, 609; IX. 167, 210, 569; XII. 337; XIII. 303, 307.
Bacon, Leonard. Life of James Hillhouse, VI. 325.
Bacon, Lord. His Philosophy and its Influence upon Education, V. 663. Essays on Education, and Studies, with Annotations by Whately, XIII. 103.
Bailey, Ebenezer. Memoir, XII. 429. Girls' High School in Boston in 1828, XIII. 252.
Baker, T. B. L. Reformatory Education, III. 789.
Baker, W. S. Itinerating School Agency, I. 729.
Barks, N. P. Museum of Zoölogy, IX. 619.

Bard, Samuel. Schools of Louisiana, II. 473.
Barnard, D. D. Right of State to establish Schools, XI. 323. Memoir of S. Van Rensellaer, VI. 223.
Barnard, F. A. P. Improvements in American Colleges, I. 269. Influence of Yale College, V. 723. Memoir, V. 753-780. Titles and Analysis of Publications, V. 763-769. Value of Classical Studies, V. 763. Open System of University Teaching, V. 765. Post-graduate Department, V. 775. Oral Teaching, V. 775.
Barnard, H. Educational Labors in Connecticut from 1837 to 1842, I. 669; Speech in Legislature in 1838, 678; Address to the People of Connecticut, 670; Analysis of First Report in 1839, 674; Expenditures for School Purposes, 679; Measures and Results, 685; Schedule of Inquiries, 686; Topics of School Lectures, 709; Plan of State Institute, 721. Labors in Rhode Island from 1843 to 1849, I. 723; XIV. 558; Institute of Instruction, 559; Series of Educational Tracts, 567; Educational Libraries, 568; Correspondence with Committee of Teachers, 579. Labors in Connecticut from 1850 to 1854, XV. 276; Plan of Public High School, 279; Public and Parental Interest and Coöperation, 285; Legal Organization of Schools, 289; School Attendance, 293; Agricultural Districts, 303; Manufacturing Districts, 305; Cities, 309; Gradation of Schools, 316; Private versus Public Schools, 323; Teachers' Institutes, 387. Arguments for, VIII. 672. Normal Schools, I. 753; X. 15. Plan of Society, and Journal and Library of Education, I. 15, 134. Principles and Plans of School Architecture, I. 740; IX. 487; X. 695; XII. 701; XIII. 818; XIV. 780; XV. 783; XVI. 781. National Education in Europe, I. 745; XV. 329. Reports and Documents on Common Schools in Connecticut, I. 754, 761. Reports and Journal of Public Schools in Rhode Island, I. 755. Tribute to Gallaudet, I. 417, 759. Memoir of Ezekiel Cheever, I. 297, 769. Reformatory Schools and Education, III. 551, 819. Military Schools and Education, XII. 3-400. Naval and Navigation Schools, XV. 17, 65. Competitive Examination, XI. 103. Educational Aphorisms, VIII. 7; XIII. 7, 717. German Universities, VI. 9; VII. 49, 201. Books for the Teacher, XIII. 447. German Educational Reformers, XIII. 448. American Text-books, XIII. 209, 401, 628; XIV. 753; XV. 539. English Pedagogy, XVI. 467; Object Teaching and Primary Instruction in Great Britain, 469. Pestalozzi and Pestalozzianism, VII. 284, 502. National and State Educational Associations, XVI. 311; American College Education, 339. Standard Publications, XVI. 797; Progressive Development of Education in the United States, XVII; Educational Land Grants, XVII.
Barnard, J. School-days in 1689, I. 307.
Barnard, J. G. Treatise on the Gyroscope, III. 537; IV. 529; V. 298.

Burney, H. H. Schools of Ohio, **II**, 531.
Barrow, Isaac. Education defined, **XI**, 13.
Basedow, and the Philanthropinum, **V**, 487-520.
Bateman, N. Educational Labors, **XVI**, 165.
Bates, S. P. On Liberal Education, **XV**, 155. Memoir, **XV**, 682.
Bates, W. G. On Training of Teachers, **XVI**, 453.
Becker, K. L. Study of Language, **XII**, 460.
Beecher, Miss C. E. Physical Training, **II**, 399. Western Education, **XV**, 274.
Beecher, Henry W. School Reminiscences, **XVI**, 135.
Bell, Andrew, and the Madras System, **X**, 467.
Benedict, St., and the Benedictines, **XVII**.
Beneke, F. E. Pedagogical Views, **XVII**.
Bernhardt. Teachers' Conferences, **XIII**, 277.
Berranger. Training of Orphan Children, **III**, 736.
Bingham, Caleb. Educational Labors, **V**, 325.
Bishop, Nathan. Public Schools of Boston, **I**, 458. Girls' High School of Boston, **XI**, 263. Plans of Providence School-houses, **XI**, 582. Memoir, **XVII**.
Blockman, Dr. Pestalozzi's Poor School at Neuhoff, **III**, 585.
Boccaccio, and Educational Reform in Italy, **XII**, 418.
Bodleigh, Sir T. On Travel, **XV**, 380.
Bolingbroke. Genius and Experience, **XI**, 12.
Booth, Rev. J. Popular Education in England, **III**, 252, 265. Competitive Examination, **III**, 257.
Borgi, Jean, and Abandoned Orphans, **III**, 583.
Botta, V. Public Instruction in Sardinia. **III**, 513; **IV**, 37, 479.
Bowen, Francis. Life of Edmund Dwight, **IV**, 5.
Braidwood, J. Education of Deaf-mutes, **III**, 348.
Brainerd, T. Home and School Training in 1718, **XVI**, 331.
Braun, T. Education defined, **XIII**, 10.
Breckenridge, R. J. Schools of Kentucky, **II**, 488.
Brinsley, J. Consolations for Grammar Schools, **I**, 311.
Brockett, L. P. Idiots and their Training, **I**, 593. Institutions and Instruction for the Blind, **IV**, 127.
Brooks, Charles. Best Methods of Teaching Morals, **I**, 336. Education of Teachers, **I**, 587.
Brooks, K. Labors of Dr. Wayland, **XIII**, 771.
Brougham, Lord. Life and Educational Views, **VI**, 467. Education and the State, **XIII**, 722. Training of the Orator, and Value of Eloquence, **XVI**, 187.
Brown, Thomas. Education defined, **XIII**, 13.
Brownson, O. A. Education defined, **XIII**, 12.
Buckham, M. H. English Language in Society and School, **XIV**, 343. Plan of Study, **XVI**, 595.
Buckingham, J. T. Schools as they were, **XIII**, 129.
Bulkley, J. W. Teachers' Associations, **XV**, 185.
Burgess, George. Thoughts on Religion and Public Schools, **II**, 562.
Burke, Edmund. Education defined, **XI**, 17.
Burrowes, T. H. Reports on Pennsylvania Schools, **VI**, 114, 556. History of Normal Schools in Pennsylvania, **XVI**, 195.
Burton, W. District-school as it was, **III**, 456. Memoir, **XVI**, 330.

Bushnell, Horace. Early Training, **XIII**, 79. Pastimes, Plays, and Holidays, **XIII**, 93. Homespun Era of Common Schools, **XIII**, 142. The State and Education, **XIII**, 723.
Buss, J., and Pestalozzianism, **VI**, 293.
Byron, Lady. Girls' Reformatory School, **III**, 785.
Cady, L. F. Classical Instruction, **XII**, 561.
Caldwell, Charles. Education in North Carolina, **XVI**, 109.
Calhoun, W. B. Memorial on Nor. Sch., **XVI**, 86.
Calkins, N. A. Object Teaching, **XII**, 633.
Carlyle, T. Education defined, **XIII**, 13. The State and Education, **XIV**, 406. Reading, **XVI**, 191. University Studies, **XVII**.
Carpenter, Mary. Reformatory Education, **III**, 10, 785.
Carpenter, W. B. Physical Science and Modern Languages in Schools, **XVII**.
Carter, J. G. Life and Services, **V**, 409. Essay on Teachers' Seminaries, **XVI**, 71. Memorial, **XVI**, 80.
Cecil, Sir William. Advice to his Son, **IX**, 161.
Channing, W. E. Teachers and their Education, **XII**, 453. End of Education, **XIII**, 15.
Chauveau, P. J. O. Education in Lower Canada, **II**, 728.
Cheever, Ezekiel. Memoir and Educational Labors, **XII**, 531.
Cheke, Sir John. **III**, 24.
Chesterfield, Lord. Advice to his Son, **XVII**.
Choate, Rufus. The Peabody Institute, **I**, 239.
Christian Brothers, System of. **III**, 347.
Cicero. Cited, **VIII**, 13, 14, 43, 79; **X**, 133, 151, 167, 194-196; **XII**, 409.
Clajus, and the German Language, **XI**, 408.
Clark, H. G. On Ventilation, **XV**, 787.
Clark, T. M. Education for the Times, **II**, 376.
Claxton, T. First Manufacturer of School Apparatus, **VIII**, 253.
Clay, John. Juvenile Criminals, **III**, 773.
Clerc, Laurent. **III**, 349.
Clinton, DeWitt. Education of Teachers, **XIII**, 341
Cocker, E. Methods of Arithmetic, **XVII**.
Coggeshall, W. J. Ohio System of Public Schools **VI**, 81, 532.
Colburn, Dana P. Memoir and Educational Work **XI**, 289.
Colburn, Warren. Educational Work, **II**, 194.
Cole, David. On Classical Education, **I**, 67.
Coleridge, D. St. Marks' Normal College, **X**, 531.
Coleridge, S. T. The Teacher's Graces, **II**, 102.
Colet, John. Educational Views and Influence, **XVI**, 657.
Collis, J. D. Endowed Grammar Schools of England, **VIII**, 256.
Colman, Henry. Agricultural School at Grignon **VIII**, 555.
Comenius, Amos. Educational Labors, **V**, 257-298. Orbis Pictus, **VI**, 585.
Confucius. Cited, **VIII**, 10, 11; **X**, 132, 167.

Coote, Edward. The English Schoolmaster, I. 309.

Courteilles, Viscount de, and the Home Reformatory, III. 572, 647, 704.

Cousin, V. School System of Holland, VIII. 598. School Law of Prussia, IX. 382. Normal Schools, XIII. 282.

Coutts, Miss Burdett. Prize Scheme for Teaching Common Things, II. 708.

Cowdery. M. F. Moral Training, XVI. 323.

Cowley, A. Plan of Philosophical College, XII. 651.

Cowper, William. The Tirocinium, or Review of Schools, VIII. 469. Discipline, VIII. 489.

Crabbe, George. Schools of the Borough, IV. 582; III. 461.

Crosby, Alpheus. Massachusetts Schools, II. 508.

Currie, James. Methods of Early Education, IX. 229-293.

Curtin, A. G. Schools of Pennsylvania, II. 541.

Cuvier, Baron. Schools of Holland, VIII. 597, 607.

Dana, J. D. Science and Scientific Schools, II. 349.

Dante, and the Revival of Education in Italy, VII. 418.

Darlington, W. Schools as they were, XIII. 741.

Dawson, J. W. Natural History in its Educational Aspects, III. 428.

Day, Henry N. English Composition. XVI. 641.

Day, Jeremiah. On Schools as they were, XVI. 126.

Degerando, Baron. Monitorial Methods, X. 465.

De La Salle, Abbe. Memoir, and System of Christian Schools, III. 437.

De Laspe. Method and Motive of Instruction, VIII. 180.

Delille, James. The Village Schoolmaster, III. 153.

Demetz, M. Agricultural Colonies, I. 611; III. 572, 667.

De Morgan. Arithmetics and their Authors, XVII.

Dick. Bequest, I. 392.

Diesterweg. Methods of Teaching, IV. 233, 505. School Discipline and Plans of Instruction, VIII. 616. Intuitional and Speaking Exercises, XII. 411.

Dinter, G. F. Memoir and Educational Labors, VII. 153; XIV. 738. Defense of Catechetical Method, IX. 377.

D'Israeli, I. Influence of Books and Authors, II. 226.

Doane, G. W. The State and Education, XV. 5.

Dole, Isaiah. Requirements in an English Lexicographer, III. 161. Mary Lyon, X. 649.

Donaldson, J. W. University Teaching, XVI. Competition Tests, XVII. German and English Scholarship compared, XVII.

Ducpetiaux, M. Reports on Reform Schools, III. 677, 597, 599, 604, 716, 749.

Duffield, D. B. Education a State Duty, III. 81.

Dunn, H. Organization and Instruction of the Borough Road Schools, X. 381-459.

Dunnell, M. H. Report on the Schools of Maine, II. 495.

Dwight, Edmund. Memoir IV. 5.

Dwight, Francis. Educational Labors. V. 803

Dwight, Mary. Art Education, II. 409, 587; III. 467; IV, 171; V. 305.

Dwight, Timothy, as an Educator, V. 567.

Eaton, H. School-houses of Vermont, XI. 510.

Eberhard, J. J. Rural Reformatory School at Casa, III. 599.

Edgeworth, Maria. Extract from Practical Education, XII. 602.

Edson, T. Warren Colburn and his System of Arithmetic, II. 294.

Edwards, N. W. Report on Schools of Illinois, II. 479.

Edwards, Richard. Memoir of Tillinghast, II. 568. Normal Schools, XVI. 271.

Elgin, Lord. Education in the United States and Canada, III. 239.

Eliot, Samuel. Arnold as a Teacher, IV. 535.

Eliot, S. A. Educational Benefactions of Boston, VIII. 522; IX. 606. History of Harvard College, IX. 129.

Elyot, Sir Thomas. The Governour, XVI. 483.

Emerson, G. B. Educational Labors, V. 417. Memorial on State Superintendent, V. 652. Memorial on Normal Schools, XVI. 93. Life of Felton, X. 265. Plan of School-houses, IX. 542.

Epictetus. Cited, VIII. 11, 42; X. 132, 168.

Erasmus. Educational Views, IV. 729; XVI. 681.

Euclid, and the Method of Geometry, VIII. 155.

Everett, Alexander H. Normal Schools, XVI. 89.

Everett, Edward. Uses of Astronomy, II. 604. John Lowell and the Lowell Lectures, V. 437. Influence of Harvard, V. 531. Boston Library, VII. 266, 365. Female Education, IX. 635; XII. 721. Extracts from Addresses—Public Schools Fifty Years Ago—College Life—Common Schools and Colleges —Conditions of a Good School—Science and Popular Education—Moral Education—Popular Education—VII. 343; XV. 14. Life of Thomas Dowse, IX. 355.

Faraday, M. Claims of Natural Science in a Liberal Education. XVII.

Felbiger, J. L. Educational Labors in Austria, IX. 600.

Fellenberg. Principles of Education, III. 594; X. 81; XIII. 11, 523.

Felton, C. C. Characteristics of American Colleges, IX. 112. Memoir and Extracts, X. 265.

Fenelon. Memoir and Educational Views, XIII. 477.

Feuerbach, L. Intuition and Thinking in Education, XII. 422.

Fichte. On Learning by Heart, XII. 416. Physical Culture, VIII. 192. Cited, VIII. 29, 620.

Fletcher, J. Borough Road Normal School, X. 435-465.

Fliedner. Institution for Deaconesses at Kaiserswerth, III. 487.

Follenius, Karl. Relations to Karl Ludwig Sand, VI. 111, 125.

Forbes, E. Educational Uses of Museums. IV. 789

Fowle, W. B. Memoir and School Improvements, **X**, 600.
Francké, A. H. His Views and Labors, **V**, 441.
Franklin, B. His Interest in Higher Education, **VII**, 268; **VIII**, 251; **X**, 283.
Friesen, F., and the German Gymnastics, **VIII**, 197.
Froebel, and the Kindergarten System, **II**, 449; **IV**, 257, 793.
Fuller, Thomas. The Good Schoolmaster, **III**, 155.

Gallaudet, T. H. Life and Services, **I**, 425. Education of Teachers, **X**, 16.
Galloway, Samuel. Teachers' Institute, **XV**, 401. Memoir, **XVI**, 583.
Gammell, W. Memoir of Nicholas Brown, **III**, 291.
Gardner, Francis. Boston Latin School, **XII**, 553.
Garfield, J. A. Department of Education, **XVII**.
Gerard-Groote, and the Hieronymians. **IV**, 623.
Gesner, J. M. Educational Views, **V**, 741; **VI**, 583.
Gibbs, J. W. Philological Contributions, **II**, 198; **III**, 101-194.
Gilfillan. The Scotch School-dame, **III**, 456.
Gillespie, W. M. Mathematical Methods of the Ecole Polytechnique, **I**, 533; **II**, 177.
Gilman, D. C. Scientific Schools of Europe, **I**, 315. Higher Special Schools of France, **II**, 93.
Gladstone, W. E. The Classics in a Liberal Education, **XVII**.
Goethe. Educational Views, **VIII**, 20, 619, 648; **X**, 51, 161, 199, 225, 617, 621.
Goldsmith. Essay on Education, **XIII**, 347. The Village Schoolmaster, **III**, 158.
Goodrich, S. G. Schools as they were, **XIII**, 134.
Goodwin, F. J. Norwich Free Academy, **III**, 195.
Gordon, John. Normal Schools of Scotland, **X**, 583.
Gottsched, J. C. German Grammar, **XI**, 447.
Gould, B. A. An American University, **II**, 265-293.
Graser. System of Instruction, **VI**, 575.
Gray, Thomas. Alliance of Education and Government, **VIII**, 287. Ode on Eton College, **VIII**, 285.
Green, L. W. Normal Schools for. Kentucky, **III**, 217.
Green, S. S. Educational Duties of the Hour, **XVI**, 229. Object Teaching, **XVI**, 245.
Gregory, J. M. The Problem of Education, **XIV**, 431-5. Memoir, **XV**, 643.
Grimke, T. S. Plan of Study, **II**, 230.
Grimm, the Brothers. **XI**, 454.
Grimshhaw, A. H. Schools of Delaware, **II**, 474.
Griscom, John. Memoir and Educational Labors, **VIII**, 324.
Grote, J. Education defined, **XI**, 18.
Guilford, Nathan. Educational Labors, **VIII**, 289.
Guizot. Ministry of Public Instruction in France, **XI**, 254, 357. The State and Education, **XIII**, 718.
Gulliver, J. P. Norwich Free Academy, **II**, 665.
Guts-Muths. System of Physical Training, **VIII**, 191. Training of the Senses, **VIII**, 207.

Haddock, C. B. School-houses in New Hampshire, **IX**, 512.

Hale, R. Continental Reformatories, **III**, 642, 744.
Hale, Sir Matthew. Plan of Study, **XVII**.
Hall, E. E. Life of Edward Everett, **VII**, 325.
Hall, S. R. Educational Labors, **V**, 373. Teachers' Seminary at Andover **V**, 386.
Hall, W. On Schools as they were, **XVI**, 127.
Halsey, L. J. Life of Philip Lindsley, **VII**, 9.
Hamann, J. G. Educational Views, **VI**, 247.
Hamilton, J., and the Hamiltonian Method, **VI**, 586.
Hamilton, Sir W. Education defined, **XI**, 18; **XIII**, 13. On Mathematics, **XVII**.
Hammill, S. M. School Government, **I**, 123.
Hammond, C. On N. England Academies, **XVI**, 403.
Harnisch. Cited, **VIII**, 58. Plan of Instruction for Annaberg Orphan House, **VIII**, 437.
Harris, James. Education a Growth, **XI**, 16.
Hart, J. S. Study of the Anglo-Saxon, **I**, 33-66. Memoir and Views, **V**, 91.
Hartlib. Plan of College of Husbandry in 1681, **XI**, 191, 649. Memoir, **XII**, 649.
Haskins, G. F. Reformatory School at Rome, **III**, 580.
Haupt. The Burschenschaften of the German Universities, **VII**, 161.
Haüy, V., and the Instruction of the Blind, **III**, 477; **IV**, 130.
Haven, Joseph. Mental Science as a Study, **III**, 125.
Hawley, Gideon. Memoir and Labors, **XI**, 94.
Hedge, N. On Schools as they were, **XVI**, 738.
Hedge. On University Reform, **XVII**.
Hegius. Educational Views, **IV**, 723.
Helps, Arthur. Learning and Doing, **XI**, 18.
Henfrey, A. Study of Botany, **XVII**.
Henry, Joseph. Philosophy of Education, **I**, 17.
Heutschel, E. Singing, **VIII**, 633; Drawing, **X**, 59.
Herbert, J. F. Pedagogical Views, **XVII**.
Herder. Life and Educational Views, **VI**, 195.
Herschel, Sir J. F. W. On Reading, **XVII**.
Heyder, W. Address at Jena in 1607, **VI**, 56.
Hickson, E. H. The State and Education, **XIII**, 718.
Hill, M. D. Preventive Treatment of Crime, **III**, 766.
Hill, Thomas. True Order of Studies, **VI**, 190, 449; **VII**, 273, 491. Powers to be Educated, **XIV**, 81. Didactics in Colleges, **XV**, 177.
Hillard, G. S. Public Library of Boston, **II**, 203. The State and Education, **XV**, 14.
Hillhouse, James A. Education and Literature in a Republic. **XVII**.
Hintz, E. Natural History, **IV**, 241.
Hobbs, Thomas. Knowledge and Experience, **XI**, 14.
Hodgins, J. G. Popular Education in Canada, **I**, 186
Holbrook, Josiah. The Lyceum System, **XIV**, 535 Educational Labors, **VIII**, 229.
Holls, G. C. Family Reformatories, **IV**, 824.
Honcamp. Instruction in Reading, **IV**, 234; Language, **XII**, 482.
Hood, Thomas. The Irish Schoolmaster, **IV**, 183.
Hooker, J. Study of Botany in Schools, **XVI**, 403.
Hooker, Richard. Knowledge of and Obedience to Law, **XI** 13

Hoole, C., and Object Teaching in 1658, **XII**. 647.
Old Art of Teaching, **XVII**.
Hopkins, Mark. Memoir and Educational Publications, **XI**. 225. Extracts—Education—Self-education—Female Education—Academies—Medical Science—Theological Education—Objections to Colleges—Taste and Morals—**XI**. 225-231.
Hornberg, T. Thoughts on the Education of Girls, **VIII**. 319.
Hovey, C. E. Memoir and Labors, **VIII**. 94.
Howe, S. G. Laura Bridgman's Education, **IV**. 383. Summary of Labors, **XI**. 389.
Hubbs, P. K. Schools of California, **II**. 467.
Hubbard, J. O. Normal Schools in New York, **XIII**. 345.
Humphrey, Heman. Normal Schools, **XII**. 655. Schools as they were, **XIII**. 125.
Huntington, F. D. Unconscious Tuition, **I**. 141. Public Prayers in Colleges, **IV**. 22.

Ickelsamer, V., and the German Language, **XI**. 402.
Ingraham, J. Plan of Primary School-house, **X**. 719.

Jackson, W. L. Schools of Virginia, **II**. 557.
Jacobs, F. Method of Teaching Latin, **VI**. 612.
Jacotot, I., and his Method, **VI**. 295; **XII**. 604.
Jahn, F. L. German Turning System and Physical Education, **VII**. 196; **XV**. 229.
Jameson, Mrs. Social Position and Occupations of Woman, **III**. 495.
Jarvis, E. Misdirected Education and Insanity, **IV**. 591.
Jay, John. Education and the State, **XV**. 13.
Jefferson, T. The State and Education, **XV**. 12.
Jerome, St. On Female Education, **V**. 593.
Jewell, F. S. Teaching as a Profession, **XV**. 579.
John of Ravenna. Educational Views, **VII**. 435.
Johnson, Samuel. Thoughts on Education and Conduct, **XIII**. 359.
Johnson, W. R. Educational Labors, **V**. 799.
Julius, Dr. Normal Schools in Prussia, **XVI**. 89.

Kant. Cited, **V**. 504; **VIII**. 28, 48; **X**. 135, 137, 191, 641; **XIII**. 13.
Kay, J. P. Training of Parochial Schoolmasters, **IX**. 170.
Kay, Joseph. Subjects and Methods of Primary Instruction, **VIII**. 416. Position of Prussian Teachers, **XI**. 169. Normal Schools in Saxony, **XIII**. 524.
Keenan, P. J. Monitorial System in Ireland, **X**. 462; **XIII**. 150. School Organization, **XIII**. 145.
Kepler. Estimate of Euclid, **VIII**. 159.
Kingsbury, John. Young Ladies' High School at Providence, **V**. 16.
Kingsley, J. L. Discourse on Yale College, **V**. 541.
Klüpfel. History of Tübingen University, **IX**. 57.
Knight, Charles. Economical Science, **IX**. 105.
Knighton, W. Educational Lectures, **X**. 573.
Krug. Cited, **VIII**. 23, 60; **X**. 122, 123, 133.

Krüsi. Life and Educational Labors, **V**. 161-186.
Kuratli, M. Reform School at Bachtelen, **III**. 590.

Lactantius. Cited, **X**. 168.
Lalor, J. Nature and Objects of Education, **XVI**. 33-64.
Lancaster, Joseph, and Monitorial Schools, **X**. 355.
Landor, W, S. Roger Ascham and Lady Jane Grey, **III**. 39.
Lange, R. Educational Labors, **IV**. 726.
Lathrop, J. Boston Association of Teachers, **XV**. 530.
Leach, Daniel. Public Schools of Providence, **I**. 468. Plan of School-houses, **IX**. 563.
Leibnitz. Cited, **VIII**. 57; **X**. 133, 134, 168.
Leigh, Lord. Reformatory Results of Mettray, **III**. 731.
Lewis, Dio. The New Gymnastics, **XI**. 531; **XII**. 665.
Lewis, Tayler. Methods of Teaching Greek and Latin, **I**. 285, 489.
Lieber, F. The Cooper Institute, **I**. 652. History of Atheneums, **II**. 735.
Lindsley, Philip. Memoir and Views of Education, **VII**. 26.
Ling, H., and the Swedish Gymnastics, **XV**. 296.
Lloyd, Robert. The School Usher, **III**. 160.
Locke, John. Views on Education, **VI**. 209. Thoughts on Education, **XI**. 461; **XIII**. 548; **XIV**. 305. School of Labor, **III**. 577.
Locke, W. Ragged Schools, **III**. 779.
Longstreet. School Scene in Georgia, **XVI**. 121.
Lord, A. D. Plan of School-house, **IX**. 502. Educational Labors, **XVI**. 607.
Lothrop, S. K. W. Lawrence and the Academies of New England, **II**. 33.
Lovell, John. Eulogy on Peter Faneuil, **IX**. 604.
Loyola, and his Society and System, **V**. 213; **XIV**. 453.
Lubinus. Grammatical Instruction, **VI**. 581.
Luther. Views on Education, **IV**. 421-449. Physical Culture, **VIII**. 190. Cited, **VIII**. 15, 78, 356; **X**. 137, 141, 151, 163, 183, 191.
Lycurgus, and Education among the Spartans, **XIV**. 611.
Lyell, Sir Charles. Physical Science in a Liberal Education, **XVII**.
Lyon, Mary. Principles of Mt. Holyoke Seminary, **X**. 670.
Lytton, Sir E. B. Address at School Festival, **III**. 259.

Macaulay, Lord T. B. The State and Education, **XIII**. 721; **XIV**. 403. Competitive Examinations for East India Service, **XVII**.
Madison, James. The State and Education, **XV**. 12.
Mansfield, E. D. The Military Academy at West Point, **XIII**. 17-48.
Marcel, C. Conversational Method, **XI**. 21, 330.
March, F. A. Study of English Language, **XVI**. 599.
Marion, General. On Free Schools, **XVI**. 119.

Mann, Horace. Teachers' Motives, **XIV**, 277. College Government, **III**, 65. Special Training a Prerequisite to Teaching, **XIII**, 507. Methods of Education in Germany, **VIII**, 382. Results of Normal Schools in Prussia, **VIII**, 361. Analysis of Reports, **V**, 623. Plan of District School-house, **IX** 642. Estimate of S. G. Howe, **XI**, 389. Education defined, **XIII**, 16. The State and Education, **XIII**, 724; **XV**, 13. Normal Schools, **XVI**, 100.
Mason, S. W. Physical Exercise in Schools, **XIV**, 61.
Masson, D. College and Self-education, **IV**, 262.
Milton's Home, School, and College Training, **XIV**, 159-190.
Mathews, J. D. Report on Schools of Kentucky, **II**, 493.
May, S. J. Life and Views of Cyrus Peirce, **IV**, 275. Educational Labors, **XVI**, 141.
Mayhew, Ira. School-houses of Michigan, **IX**, 515. Educational Labors, **XV**, 651.
McElligott, J. N. Debating as a Means of Educational Discipline, **I**, 495.
Meierotto. Method of Teaching Latin, **VI**, 609. Physical Culture, **VIII**, 191.
Meiring. On the Hamiltonian System, **VI**, 502.
Melancthon. Life and Educational Services, **IV**, 741-764.
Memminger, C. G. Schools of South Carolina, **II**, 553.
Mill, John Stuart. State and Education, **XIII**, 721. University Education, **XVII**,
Mills, Caleb. Report on Schools of Indiana, **II**, 480.
Milton. Treatise on Education, **II**, 61. Education defined, **XI**, 12. The State and Education, **XIII**, 719. His Home, School, and College Training, **XIV**, 159.
Molineux, E. L. Physical and Military Exercises in Schools a National Necessity, **XI**, 513.
Montaigne. On Learning and Education, **IV**, 461.
Montucla. Elements of Euclid, **VIII**, 156.
More, Sir Thomas. The State and Education, **XIII**, 719. Education of his Children, **XVII**.
Morrison, T. Manual of School Management, **IX**, 294. Oral Lessons, **IX**, 321.
Moscherosch. Cited, **VIII**, 71; **X**, 190, 198.
Moseley, Canon. Tripartite System of Instruction, **IX**, 316. English Training Colleges, **X**, 543-670.
Mulcaster, R. Positions, **XVII**.
Muller, Max. French and German in Public Schools, **XVII**.

Neander, Michel. Educational Labors, **V**, 599.
Niebuhr, B. S. Letter to a Student, **XVI**, 215.
Niebuhr, J., and Pestalozzi, **VII**, 289.
Niemeyer. Cited, **VIII**, 52, 56, 61, 67, 71; **X**, 118.
Nieuvenhuysen, and the Society for the Public Good in Holland, **XIV**, 641.
Nissen, H. Public Schools in Norway, **VIII**, 295.

Oberlin, John Friedrich. The Practical Educator, **V**, 505; **XVII**.
Oelinger, Albert, and the Study of German, **XI**, 406.

Olmsted, Dennison. Democratic Tendencies of Science, **I**, 164. Ideal of a Teacher; Timothy Dwight **V**, 567.
Osgood, S. G. Address at Dedication of School-house, **XIII**, 848.
Overberg, B. Educational Views, **XIII**, 365.
Owen, R. Natural History in Public Schools, **XVII**.

Page, D. P. Memoir and Processes of Teaching, **V**, 819. Education defined, **XIII**, 14.
Paget, J. Physiology, **XVII**, 119.
Paley, Dr. Education defined, **XI**, 15.
Palmerston, Lord. Popular Education, **II**, 712.
Park, Prof. The School of Locality, **XVI**, 331. Memoir of B. B. Edwards, **XIV**, 381.
Parr, Samuel. Principles of Education, **XI**, 17.
Pattridge, Alden. Educational Views, **XIII**, 54, 683.
Pattison. On Prussian Normal Schools, **XVI**, 393.
Paulet. System of Monitorial Instruction, **X**, 464.
Payson, T. Boston Association of Teachers, **XV**, 533; **X**, 464.
Peabody, George. Public Library of Baltimore, **III**, 226. Educational Benefactions, **XVII**.
Peel, Sir R. Study of Classics, **XVII**.
Peet, H. P. New York Institution for the Deaf and Dumb, **III**, 347. Memoir, **III**, 366.
Peirce, B. K. Reformatory for Girls, **XVI**, 652.
Peirce, Cyrus. Ideal of Education, **IV**, 285. Normal Schools, **IV**, 306.
Perkins, G. R. Labors in Normal Schools, **XIII**, 544.
Perry, Gardner. On School-houses, **IX**, 520.
Perry, W. F. Schools of Alabama, **II**, 465.
Pestalozzi. Life and Educational System, **III**, 401; **IV**, 65. Pestalozzi and the Schools of Germany, **IX**, 343. Pestalozzi, Fellenberg, and Wehrli, **X**, 81. Poor School at Neuhof, **III**, 585. His Assistants and Disciples, **VII**, 285. Hundredth Birthday, **V**, 503. Publications by and relating to, **VII**, 513. Selections from his Publications, **VII**, 519-722. Evening Hours of a Hermit, **VI**, 169. Leonhard and Gertrude, **VII**, 519. Christopher and Alice, **VII**, 665. His Account of his Educational Experience and Methods, **VII**, 671.
Petrarch, and Education in Italy, **VII**, 424.
Petty, Sir W. Plan of a Trades School, 1647, **XI**, 199.
Peurbach, G. Method of Arithmetic, **VIII**, 170.
Phelps, W. F. Normal Schools, **III**, 417. Educational Labors, **V**, 7.
Philbrick, J. D. On the National Teachers' Association, **XIV**, 49. Extracts from Reports, **II**, 261. Report on Schools of Connecticut, **II**, 469. Plans of School-houses, **X**, 740; **XVI**, 701.
Phillips, J. H. Schools of New Jersey, **II**, 317.
Picket, A. Teachers' Association, **XV**, 493.
Pierce, Benjamin. On a National University, **II**, 88.
Pierpont, J. Public High School for Girls, **XIII**, 244.
Pitt, Earl of Chatham. Studies and Conduct, **XVII**.
Plato. Cited, **IV**, 166; **VIII**, 11, 43, 76-78; **X**, 141, 157, 162, 167, 170, 194; **XI**, 104, 105; **XII**, 409; **XIII**, 8.

Plutarch. Views of Education, **XI**, 99-110. Cited, **VIII**, 77; **X**, 118-195.
Poggius, and Education in Italy, **VII**, 442.
Porter, J. A. Plan of an Agricultural School, **I**, 329.
Porter, Noah. Essay on Educational Reform in Connecticut, **XIV**, 244. Norwich Free Academy, **III**, 200.
Potter, Alonzo. Consolidation, &c., of American Colleges, **I**, 471. Moral and Religious Instruction, **II**, 169. School Houses in New York, **IX**, 507. Normal Schools, **XIII**, 344. What and How to Read, **II**, 215. Memoir, **XVI**, 599.
Pullicino, and Education in Italy, **II**, 721.
Pythagoras. Cited, **VIII**, 11, 12, 38, 43; **X**, 132, 162, 166; **XI**, 109; **XIII**, 8, 81.

Quincy, Josiah. Girls' High School in Boston, **XIII**, 297. Phillips' Academy in 1778, **XIII**, 740.
Quincy, Josiah, Jr. School Policy of Boston, **XII**, 706.
Quintilian. Views of Education, **XI**, 3.

Rabelais, and his Educational Views, **XIV**, 147.
Ramsauer. Memoir, **VII**, 301. Life at Hofwyl, **IV**, 84, 119.
Ramsden. The Heart of a Nation, **XI**, 17.
Rumusat. Circular to Teachers, adopted by Guizot, **XI**, 278.
Randall, S. S. On Francis Dwight, **V**, 809. Josiah Holbrook. Educational Labors, **XIII**, 227. New York Normal School, **XIII**, 532.
Raphall, H. L. Education among the Hebrews, **I**, 243.
Ratich. Life and Educational Methods, **V**, 229; **XI**, 418. On Teaching Latin, **VI**, 586.
Raumer, Karl von. History of Education, q. v. under SECTION I. German Universities, **VI**, 9; **VII**, 47, 160. Essays on University Reform, **VII**, 200.
Raumer, Rudolf. Instruction in the German Language, **XI**, 155, 419-429; **XII**, 460-527.
Ravaisson, F. Instruction in Drawing, **II**, 319.
Reid, D. B. College of Architecture, **II**, 629.
Reisch, Gregorius. Margarita Philosophica, **XVII**. Roman System of Measures, **XVII**.
Rendu, Eugen. Public Instruction in France and Prussia, **II**, 337.
Reuchlin, and German Educators of the Fifteenth Century, **V**, 65.
Rice, V. M. Schools of New York, **II**, 518.
Richard, W. F. Methods in the National Schools of England, **X**, 501-540.
Richards, Z. Discipline, **I**, 107. The Teacher an Artist, **XIV**, 69.
Richter, J. P. Cited, **VIII**, 27, 50, 618; **X**, 119-199.
Rickoff, A. J. National Bureau of Education, **XVI**, 299.
Rider, Captain. On System of Navigation Schools, **XV**, 67.
Rosenkrantz. Present Age to the Educator, **XII**, 425.
Rosmini, A. Philosophy of Pedagogy, **IV**, 491.

Ross, William. Cathechetical Method, **IX**, 308.
Ross, W. P. Education among the Cherokees, **I**, 120
Rousseau, and his Educational Views, **V**, 459-486 Education defined, **XIII**, 11.
Rush, Benjamin. The State and Education, **XV**, 13
Ruskin, John. Material of Education, **XI**, 19.
Russell, William. Principles and Methods of Intellectual Education, **II**, 113, 317; **III**, 47, 311; **IV**, 109. Moral Education, **IX**, 19-48. National Organization of Teachers, **XIV**, 7. Educational Labors of Lowell Mason, **IV**, 141. Recollections of Josiah Holbrook, **VIII**, 339. Legal Recognition of Teaching as a Profession, **X**, 297.
Russell, W. H. Plan of Gymnasium, **IX**, 534.
Ruthardt, J. C. Method of Teaching Latin and Greek, **VI**, 600.

Sarmiento, D. F. The Schoolmaster's Work, **XVI**, 65. Basis of U. S. prosperity, **XVI**, 533. Educational Labors, **XVI**, 593.
Schmid, Joseph, and Pestalozzi, **VII**, 297.
Schmidt. Definition of Education, **XIII**, 9.
Schottelius, J. G. Philological Labors, **XI**, 429.
Schwartz. Cited, **VIII**, 34, 53; **X**, 164.
Sears, Barnas. Schools of Massachusetts, **II**, 498.
Sears, E. I. Henry Lord Brougham, **V**, 467. Memoir.
Sedgwick, C. M. What and How to Read, **II**, 215.
Seguin, E. Treatment and Training of Idiots, **II**, 145.
Seneca. Cited, **VIII**, 12-68; **X**, 135-196; **XII**, 409.
Seton, S. S. Extracts from Manual, **XIII**, 853.
Shea, J. G. Catholic Institutions in the U. S., 435.
Shearman, F. W. Schools in Michigan, **II**, 510.
Sheldon, E. A. Object Teaching, **XIV**, 93.
Shenstone, William. The Schoolmistress, with Annotations, **III**, 449.
Shurtleff, N. B. Boston Latin School, **XII**, 559.
Shuttleworth, Sir J. K. Educational Progress in England, **III**, 245. Vehrli, **III**, 392. Training Schools, **IX**, 171-200.
Sidney, Sir H. On Conduct, **XV**, 378.
Simonson, L. Cadet System in Switzerland, **XIII**, 603.
Simpson, J. Education defined, **XIII**, 13.
Slade, William. Education at the West, **XV**, 274.
Smith, Adam. The State and Education, **XIII**, 720
Smith, B. B. Visit to Radleigh School, **IV**, 803.
Smith, Elbridge. Norwich Free Academy, **III**, 208.
Smith, Goldwin. History, **XVII**, 119.
Smith, H. B. The Dutch Universities, **I**, 387.
Smyth, Sidney. Objects of Education, **XIII**, 12.
Snell, E. S. The Gyroscope, **II**, 701.
Socrates. Cited, **IV**, 156; **VIII**, 77; **X**, 167, 187; **XI**, 61, 62, 103, 107. Methods of Philosophy, **X**, 375.
South, R. Educational Views, **XVII**.
Southey, Robert. The State and Education, **XIII**, 719. Views of Home Education, **XVI**, 433. Conduct and Knowledge, **XVI**, 223.
Spencer, Herbert. Thoughts on Education, **XI**, 485-512; **XIII**, 372-400.
Spencer, J. C. Education of Teachers, **XIII**, 342

Sprague, W. B. Influence of Yale College, **X**, 681.
Spurzheim. Mutual Instruction, **X**, 611. Education defined, **XIII**, 11.
Stanley, Lord. Lyceums and Popular Edu., **III**, 241.
Stephens, L. Normal Schools of Prussia, **VIII**, 368.
Stewart, Dugald. Objects of Education, **XIII**, 13.
Stifler, Michael, and Algebraic Signs, **XVI**.
Stiles, W. H. Education in Georgia, **II**, 477.
Stow, David. Gallery Training Lessons, **IX**, 413.
Stowe, C. E. Life and Labors, **V**, 586. Educational Wants of Ohio, **V**, 588. Primary Instruction in Germany, **VIII**, 371. Teachers' Seminary, **XV**, 688.
Sturm, J. Life and Educational Labors, **IV**, 167, 401.
Sullivan, O. Teaching the Alphabet, **XII**, 601. Premiums for Knowledge in Com. Things, **X**, 93.
Swett, John. Educational Labors, **XVI**, 625, 790.
Swift, J. On Manners, **XVII**.

Tafel, L. The Hamiltonian System, **VI**, 591.
Tappan, H. P. Educational Development in Europe, **I**, 247-268. Educational Labors, **XIII**, 452.
Tarbox, I. N. Statistics of New England Colleges, **I**, 405. American Education Society, **XIV**, 367.
Tasso. Memoir and Educational Views, **XVII**.
Temple, F. Literature and Science, **XVII**.
Tenney, Jonathan. Schools of New Hampshire, **II**, 511. Memoir, **XVI**, 761.
Tentleben, K. von, and Society of Usefulness, **XI**, 424.
Thaer, August, and Gymnastics, **VIII**, 197.
Thayer, G. F. Letters to a Young Teacher, **I**, 357; **II**, 103, 391, 657; **III**, 71, 313; **IV**, 219, 450; **VI**, 435; **VIII**, 81. Chauncey Hall School. **XIII**, 851.
Thayer, S. Competitive Examination, **XV**, 58.
Thibaut. On Purity in Music, **X**, 635.
Thompson, A. Industrial School, **III**, 780.
Tice, J. H. Public Schools of St. Louis, **I**, 348.
Tillinghast, Nicholas. As an Educator, **II**, 508. On Normal Schools, **XVI**, 453.
Timbs, John. Endowed Schools of England, **VIII**, 261. The Hornbook, **XII**, 687.
Tixier, J. School Dialogues, **XVI**, 445.
Tobler, J. G. Methods of Teaching, **V**, 210.
Town, Salem. Schools as they were, **XIII**, 737.
Trask, A. B. Town School of Dorchester, **XVI**, 105.
Trench, R. English Language, **XVII**.
Trotzendorf, V. F. Educational Views, **V**, 107.
Turk, R. C. W. von. **V**, 155.
Turner, Sydney. Reformatory Schools, **III**, 772.
Tyndall. Study of Physics, **XVII**.

Vail, T. H. Methods of Using Books, **II**, 215.
Vassar, M. Plan of Vassar Female College, **XI**, 55.
Vehrli, Hofwyl and Kruitzlingen, **III**, 389; **X**, 81.
Verplanck, J. C. Memoir of D. H. Barnes, **XIV**, 513. Scientific Knowledge and Business, **V**, 116.
Vinci, Leonardo di. Drawing, **II**, 425.

Wadsworth, James. Labors of Education, **V**, 395.
Watts, Isaac. Improvement of the Mind, **II**, 215.
Webster, Daniel. Normal Schools, **I**, 590. Free Schools, **I**, 591. Education defined, **XIII**, 14.
Wayland, Francis. Objects and Methods of Intellectual Education, **XIII**, 801. Dedicatory Address at Pawtucket, **VIII**, 843. Educational Labors and Publications, **XIII**, 771. Extracts on Method of Recitation—System of University Education—System of Public Schools for a City—The Library in Popular Education—Theological Education—Moses Stuart—Dr. Nott—Thomas K. Arnold—**XIII**, 776.
Webster, Noah. Schools as they were, **XIII**, 123.
Weld, Theodore D., and Manual Labor, **XV**, 234.
Wells, W. H. Life and Educational Labors, **VIII**, 529. Teachers' Conferences, **XIII**, 272. Teaching English Grammar, **XV**, 241. Exercises on Retiring from Chicago High School, **XIV**, 811.
Wessel, John. Educational Views, **IV**, 714.
Whately, Archbishop. Annotations on Bacon, **XIII**, 103. Education defined, **XI**, 18.
Whewell, W. Education defined, **XI**, 11. School Studies and University Examinations, **XVII**.
White, E. E. National Bureau of Edu., **XVI**, 177.
White, H. R. The Village Matron, **III**, 460.
White, S. H. National Bureau of Edu., **XV**, 180.
Wichern, T. H. Reformatory Education, **III**, 5, 603.
Wickersham, J. P. Education as an Element of Reconstruction of the Union, **XVI**, 283.
Wilbur, H. B. On Object Teaching, **XV**, 189.
Wilderspin, S. Infant School, **IX**, 531; **XIII**, 163.
Wiley, C. H. Schools of North Carolina, **II**, 527.
Willard, Mrs. Emma. Female Education, **VI**, 125. Female Association, **XV**, 612.
Willm, J. The Monitorial System, **X**, 466. Teachers' Libraries, **XIII**, 293, 298.
Wimmer, H. Public Instruction in Saxony, **V**, 350; **IX**, 201. Educational Intelligence, **III**, 272; **IV**, 243, 793. On Real Schools of Austria, **III**, 275.
Winthrop, R. C. Free Schools, **I**, 645.
Wise, Henry A. Schools of Virginia, **II**, 557.
Wiseman, Cardinal. Education of the Poor, **XVII**.
Wohlfarth, J. F. F. Pedagogical Treasure Casket, **VIII**, 8-80; **X**, 116-290.
Wolf, T. A. Educational Views, **VI**, 260.
Wolsey, Cardinal. Plan for Grammar School, **VII**, 487.
Woodridge, W. Suggestions on School Improvements, **XV**, 609. Reminiscences of Female Education prior to 1801, **XVI**, 137.
Woodbridge, W. C. Life and Educational Labors, **V**, 51. Education defined, **XIII**, 16.
Woolsey, T. D. Historical Discourse on Yale College, **V**, 546. Norwich Free Academy, **III**, 197.
Wordsworth, W. State and Education, **XIII**, 719.
Wotton, Sir Henry. Survey of Educ., **XV**, 123-143.
Wyatt, Sir T. On Conduct. **XV**, 376.
Wykeham, and Winchester College, **VIII**, 261.

Young, Samuel. Schools of New York, **IX**, 505.
Young, T. U. Infant School Teaching, **XII**, 155.

Zeller, C, H. Teachings of Experience for Christian Schools, **III**, 386. Memoir, **VII**, 305.
Zoroaster. Cited, **X**, 167.
Zschokke. Cited, **VIII**, 21, 30, 51; **X**, 142-198.

III. STUDIES AND METHODS; SCHOOL ORGANIZATION AND DISCIPLINE.

A B C-shooters, **V.** 90, 603; books, **XII.** 593.
Absence, **II.** 444, 504; **V.** 631; **XV.** 293.
Academy, plan for, **XVI.** 403.
Accuracy, **XIII.** 515.
Acquisition, **XIII.** 512.
Acting plays, **IV.** 175; **VII.** 503; **XIV.** 474.
Activity, independent, **VIII.** 617; **XIII.** 13, 376.
Adult education, **I.** 634; **VIII.** 230; **XVI.** 343.
Advice to Students on Studies and Conduct, **XIII.** 193; **XV.** 377; **XVI.** 186, 216, 223. Lord Bacon, **XVI.** 186; Sir Thomas Bodleigh, **XV.** 381; Lord Brougham, **XVI.** 186; Carlyle, **XVI.** 191; Sir Matthew Hale, **XVII**; Niebuhr, **XVI.** 216; Sir H. Sidney, **XV.** 379; Southey, **XVI.** 233; Vail, **II.** 215; Whately, **XIII.** 106; Wyatt, **XV.** 377.
Algebra, **II.** 177.
Alphabet, Modes of Teaching. **XII.** 593.
Amusements, **III.** 42; **V.** 449; **X.** 256; **XIII.** 93; **XIV.** 474.
Analysis and Analytic Method, **II.** 122, 133; **IV.** 505; **VIII.** 169; **IX.** 205.
Anger, **XI.** 482, 504.
Anglo-Saxon Laugunge, **I.** 33; **XVI.** 568.
Anthropology, **XIII.** 327.
Aphorisms on Studies and Conduct, **XV.** 376; Subjects of Instruction, **X.** 141; Discipline **X.** 187; Early Training. **XIII.** 79.
Appetites, **X.** 137; **XIII.** 512, 578; **XVI.** 53.
Aptness to teach, **XIII.** 762.
Archery, **III.** 41; **XVI.** 496.
Architectural Game, **XI.** 27.
Arithmetic, Currie, **IX.** 247; Hill. **VI.** 454; Gillespie, **I.** 539; Raumer, **VIII.** 170; Richards, **X.** 534.
Art—as a Study, by Miss A. M. Dwight, **II.** 409, 587; **III.** 467; **IV.** 191; **V.** 305.
Art and Science, by Dana, **II.** 349; Raumer, **X.** 218.
Attendance, Barnard, **XV.** 293.
Ball-frame, **IX.** 255; **XI.** 24.
Basedow's Methods, **V.** 487.
Beans in Arithmetic, **VI.** 454.
Beating of Children, **IV.** 156, 165; **V.** 509; **XI.** 479.
Bible, **II.** 613; Arnold, **IV.** 443; Locke, **XII.** 471; **XIV.** 308; Luther, **IV.** 443; Raumer, **VII.** 402; **VIII.** 104; Whately, **XIII.** 108.
Bifurcation, **XII.** 47.
Biographical Method in History, **IV.** 514, 577.
Biology, **XIII.** 392.
Bipartite Organization, **XIII.** 150.
Birch, **III.** 462; **V.** 500.
Blackboard or surface, **V.** 499; **X.** 600; **XII.** 648; **XIII.** 32.
Blocks in Geometry, **VI.** 451.
Books, Value of, **II.** 205, 215; **X.** 158; **XIII.** 788; **XVI.** 191.
Book-learning, **II.** 561; **VII.** 267, 366; **XIII.** 837.
Borough-road School Methods, **X.** 381.
Botany, **VII.** 296; **VIII.** 126; **IX.** 77, 109; **X.** 640; **XI.** 46.

Boy-tutors, **XVI.** 227.
Burgher, or Citizens' School, **VIII.** 414; **IX.** 210, 384; **XI.** 248; **XII.** 520.
Benschenschaft, **VII.** 80, 91, 165.
Calisthenics, **II.** 405.
Catechism on Methods, from Diesterweg. **IV.** 233, 505.
Catechetical Method, W. Ross, **IX.** 367.
Character, **X.** 129; **XIII.** 571.
Chemistry, **V.** 712; **VII.** 277; **VIII.** 065; **XI.** 210; **XIII.** 391.
Childhood, **IV.** 424; **V.** 467; **VII.** 382; **XI.** 483; **XII.** 629; **XVI.** 193.
Chiding, **XIII.** 559.
Church-cross-row, **XVII.** 195.
Christianity in Schools, **I.** 251; **II.** 567, 693; **IV.** 527, 572; **V.** 77; **XIII.** 118, 287, 325.
Christmas Festival, **X.** 260; **XIII.** 95.
Chronological Method, **IV.** 515.
City Influence, **III.** 323. **VII.** 33, 240; **VIII.** 143; **XV.** 309.
Classical Instruction, by Ascham, **XI.** 70; I. Cady, **XII.** 561; David Cole, **I.** 67: Erasmus, **IV.** 729; T. Lewis, **I.** 285; Raumer, **VII.** 471; Sturm, **IV.** 169; Woolsey, **VII.** 487.
Collective Teaching, **X.** 395.
Common Things, by Lord Ashburton, **I.** 629; Morrison, **IX.** 321; Stow, **IX.** 413; Specimen Lessons, **X.** 105, 575; **IX.** 349.
Competitive Examination, by Barnard, **XIV.** 108; Booth, **III.** 267.
Common Sense, **V.** 476; **XIII.** 599.
Composition, **III.** 331; **VIII.** 387; **X.** 415; **XI.** 122; **XII.** 494; **XIV.** 363; **XVI.** 641.
Compulsion in attendance, **XI.** 266; in study, **VII.** 213; **XIII.** 373.
Conduct, **IV.** 161; **X.** 141; **XIII.** 79; **XV.** 123, 378; **XVI.** 191.
Conversation, **XI.** 106, 339; **XIII.** 556; **XIV.** 360; **XV.** 152; **XVI.** 682.
Conversational Method, by Marcel, **XI.** 106, 339.
Constructive Method, by Abbenrode, **IV.** 507.
Corporal Punishment, Bell, **X.** 486; Diesterweg, **XIII.** 619; Erasmus, **XVI.** 680; Goldsmith, **XIII.** 352; Johnson, **XIII.** 363; Locke, **XIII.** 563; Austria, **XVI.** 614, 690; England, **III.** 157.
Country Training, **III.** 323: **V.** 472; **X.** 641; **XIII.** 141; **XV.** 303.
Counters, **VIII.** 182
Courage, **IX.** 41; **X.** 57; **XIII.** 584; **XVI.** 57.
Crime and Education, **IV.** 579; **VI.** 311, 494; **XI.** 77.
Curiosity. **II.** 118; **V.** 477; **XIII.** 119, 572.
Debating, by J. M. Elligott. **I.** 495.
Discipline, by Diesterweg, **VIII.** 619; Locke, **XIII.** 557; Hamill, **I.** 122; Spencer, **XI.** 498; Thayer, **VI.** 435; **XIII.** 831; Dorchester School in 1645, **XVI.** 106; Hopkins Grammar School, 1684, **IV.** 710.
Drawing, by Hentschel, **X.** 59; Ravaison, **II.** 419.

English Language and Literature, by Buckham, **XIV.** 343; **XVI.** 556; Day, **XVI.** 641; Gibbs, **II.** 193; **III.** 101; Hart, **I.** 33; Felton, **X.** 284; March, **XVI.** 502; Wells, **XV.** 145.
Fagging in English Schools, **IV.** 509; **V.** 80; **XV.** 107.
French Language, **XV.** 772.
German Language, **XI.** 155, 400; **XII.** 460.
Geography—Methods of Teaching, by Abbenrode, **IV.** 505; Currie, **IX.** 209; Dunn, **X.** 421; Hill, **VII.** 275; Key, **IX.** 186; Mann, **VIII.** 390; Marcel, **XI.** 35; Pestalozzi, **X.** 150; Phelps, **IX.** 62; Raumer, **VIII.** 3; Thayer, **VIII.** 81.
Geometry, Huxelow, **V.** 512; Diesterweg, **IV.** 239; Euclid, **VIII.** 155; Gillespie, **I.** 541; Hill, **VI.** 191, 449; Raumer, **VIII.** 153; Spencer, **XIII.** 383.
Geology, **IV.** 785; **VI.** 238; **VII.** 71, 293; **VIII.** 241; **XI.** 46.
Gradation of Schools, **II.** 455.
Greek Language, **XII.** 561; **I.** 284, 482.
Grouping Method in History, **IV.** 515.
Gymnastics, Lewis' System, **XI.** 531; **XII.** 665.
History, Method in, by Abbenrode, **IV.** 512; **XII.** 665; Arnold, **IV.** 565; Basedow, **V.** 503; Hill, **VI.** 184; **VII.** 490; Marcel, **XI.** 41; Niemeyer, **X.** 156; Raumer, **VIII.** 101; **X.** 641; Richter, **X.** 154; Whately, **XIII.** 119.
Intellectual Training, by Eliot, **XVI.** 488; Fellenberg, **III.** 594; Goldsmith, **XIII.** 347; Hill, **VI.** 180; Krüsi, **V.** 187; Lalor, **XVI.** 40; Locke, **XIV.** 305; Milton, **II.** 79; Montaigne, **IV.** 161; Pestalozzi, **VII.** 512; Quintilian, **XI.** 3; Raumer, **VIII.** 81; Rousseau, **V.** 459; Russell, **II.** 112; Spencer, **XI.** 484; **XIII.** 372; Wayland, **XIII.** 801.
Infant Schools and Instruction, Currie, **IX.** 228; Froebel, **II.** 449; **IV.** 237; Home and Colonial Society, **XIII.** 78; Marcel, **XI.** 21; Prussian Schools, **VIII.** 371; Raumer, **VII.** 381; Young, **XIV.** 105.
Intuitional Instruction, **IV.** 233; **XII.** 411.
Italian Language, **VII.** 434, 459.
Itinerating Schools, **VIII.** 996.
Jesuit System of Schools, **V.** 212; **XIV.** 455.
Kindergarten, **IV.** 237.
Lacedamonian System, **III.** 85; **XIV.** 612.
Lancasterian System, **X.** 402.
Latin Language, by Acquaviva, **XIV.** 462; Arnold, **IV.** 564; Asham, **XI.** 70; Bates, **XV.** 155; Comenius, **VI.** 585; Erasmus, **IV.** 729; Gesner, **V.** 744; **VI.** 583; Hamilton, **VI.** 586; Herder, **VI.** 207; Hoole, **XVII.** 225; Jacotot, **VI.** 595; Jacobs, **VI.** 612; Locke, **XIV.** 311; Luther, **IV.** 44; Melancthon, **IV.** 755, 764; Meierotto, **VI.** 583, 600; Meiring, **VI.** 592; Milton, **II.** 79; Montaigne, **IV.** 473; **VI.** 584; Ratich, **V.** 234; **VI.** 586; Raumer, **VI.** 581; **VII.** 471; Rousseau, **V.** 473; Rutbardt, **VI.** 600; Sturm, **IV.** 169; **VI.** 581; Tafel, **VI.** 591; Textor, **XV.** 444; Trapp, **VI.** 261; Vossius, **VI.** 582; Wolf **VI.** 268; Woolsey, **VII.** 487.
Latin Pronunciation, **XV.** 171.
Lectures and University Teaching, Barnard, **V.** 775;
Johnson, **XIII.** 363; Masson, **IV.** 271; Raumer, **VII.** 201, 213; Vaughn, **IV.** 271; Wolf, **VII.** 487.
Liberal Education and Studies, Bates, **XV.** 155; Everett, **VIII.** 364; Felton, **X.** 281.
Madras System, **X.** 467.
Manners, Hopkins, **XI.** 930; Locke, **VI.** 213; **XIII.** 531; Montaigne, **IV.** 469; Thayer, **II.** 103; Plutarch, **XI.** 106.
Mathematics, French Polytechnic system, **I.** 533.
Memory, **II.** 385; **IV.** 171, 201, 721; **V.** 678; **VI.** 464, 602; **VII.** 279; **X.** 126; **XII.** 416; **XIV.** 87, 321, 469; **XVII.** 230.
Mental Arithmetic, **II.** 301; **VIII.** 385, 459.
Mental Science, by J. Haven, **III.** 125.
Methods, Essays on, by Currie, **IX.** 229; Diesterweg, **IV.** 233, 505; Dunn, **X.** 391; Morrison, **IX.** 294; Raumer, **VIII.** 101; Richards, **X.** 505; Ross, **IX.** 367; Spencer, **XIII.** 372; Thayer, **III.** 313; **IV.** 219, 450.
Military Exercises in School, by Molineux. **XI.** 513.
Monitorial System, English National Schools, **X.** 503; Irish National Schools, **XIII.** 150.
Moral Education, Brooks, **I.** 336; Cowdery, **XVI.** 323; Fellenberg, **III.** 595; Lalor, **XVI.** 48; Locke, **XI.** 473; **XIII.** 548; Russell, **IX.** 19; Spencer, **XI.** 496.
Music, or Singing, **VIII.** 633; **IX.** 267; **XVI.** 38.
Mutual Instruction, Bell, **X.** 401; De Gerando, **X.** 405; Fowle, **X.** 611; Keenan, **X.** 462; Lancaster, **X.** 402.
Mother Tongue, **III.** 327; **IV.** 473; **V.** 235, 246, 253; **VI.** 197, 201; **VII.** 375; **XI.** 458; **XII.** 464; **XIV.** 343; **XVI.** 340.
Motives to Study, Lyton, **III.** 295; Mann, **XIII.** 518; **XVI.** 279; Rousseau, **V.** 477; Spencer, **XIII.** 377; Thayer, **VI.** 435.
Natural Science, **IV.** 445; **VIII.** 123; **X.** 145; **XV.** 95; **XVI.** 599.
Number, Early Sessions In, **II.** 132; **V.** 188; **VII.** 698; **IX.** 247, 467; **XI.** 24.
Natural History, Dawson, **III.** 428.
Natural Consequences of Actions, the Law of Discipline, Spencer, **XI.** 498.
New Gymnastics, **XI.** 531; **XII.** 665.
Object Teaching, Bacon, **V.** 674, 680; Calkins, **XII.** 633; Comenius, **V.** 680; Halm, **V.** 696; Hecker, **V.** 693, 696; Henzky, **V.** 694; Hoole. **XII.** 647; Gesner, **V.** 748; Greene, **X.** 245; Locke, **VI.** 220; Marcel, **XI.** 21; Oswego System, **XII.** 604; **XIV.** 93; Pestalozzi, **V.** 76; Ratich, **V.** 689; Semler, **V.** 691; Sheldon, **XIV.** 93; Spencer, **XIII.** 378; Wilbur, **XV.** 189.
Oral Teaching, Barnard, **V.** 777; Currie, **IV.** 104; Masson, **V.** 270; Marcel, **XI.** 31, 330; Morrison, **IX.** 303, 321; Wolf. **VI.** 272; Vaugh, **IV.** 271.
Penmanship, Everett, **IV.** 452; **XII.** 556; Mulhausen, **X.** 524; Niebuhr, **XVI.** 207; Raumer, **X.** 626; Thayer, **IV.** 450.
Perception and Perceptive Faculties, Bacon, **XII.** 42; Hill, **XIV.** 86; Marcel, **XI.** 21; Raumer, **VIII.** 207; Russell, **II.** 113, 316; Spencer, **XIII.** 396.

Physical Education, Aphorisms, **VIII.** 75; Aristotle, **XIV.** 140; Ascham, **III.** 41; Bandow, **V.** 510; Beecher, **II.** 399; Comenius, **V.** 281; Currie, **XI.** 233; Elyot, **XVI.** 490, Fellenberg, **III.** 596; Gutsmuths, **VIII.** 191; Jahn, **VIII.** 190; Lalor, **XVI.** 34; Locke, **XI.** 462; Lorinser, **VIII.** 187; Luther, **IV.** 448; **VIII.** 190; Lycurgus, **XIV.** 620; Mann, Mason, **XIV.** 61; Milton, **II.** 83; Montaigne, **IV.** 465; Pestalozzi, **VIII.** 192; Plutarch, **XI.** 105; Quintilian, **XI.** 118; Rabelais, **XIV.** 149; Raumer, **VIII.** 185; Rousseau, **V.** 475, **VIII.** 185; Spencer, **XI.** 485; Trotzendorf, **V.** 112; Vehrli, **III.** 390, 394; English Public Schools, **XV.** 105.

Pictures in School-books, **IV.** 509; **V.** 506, 512; **VI.** 585; **XII.** 647.

Picturing-out Method, **IX.** 413, 424.

Pleasure in Study and Work, **VI.** 464; **XIII.** 386, 488, 587.

Pleasure-grounds of Knowledge, **XIII.** 121; **XVI.** 438.

Play-state of Childhood, **XIII.** 93.

Physiology, **V.** 499, 512; **XI.** 49; **XVI.** 44.

Plays and Pastimes, **V.** 284; **X.** 259; **XI.** 490; **XIII.** 93, 539, 594; **XIV.** 476.

Poetry, Study of, **II.** 82; **III.** 329; **VI.** 220, 226, 467, 517; **VIII.** 226; **X.** 161; **XI.** 509; **XIII.** 117; **XVI.** 47.

Political Science, **II.** 82; **III.** 82; **V.** 513; **IX.** 105; **XI.** 214; **XIV.** 135, 326.

Posture in Devotion, **IV.** 29; **VIII.** 631.

Pouring-in Method, **V.** 819.

Powers to be Educated, Hill, **XIV.** 84.

Practicality, **IV.** 477; **V.** 480; **X.** 129, 414; **XIII.** 13, 103, 812.

Praise, **VIII.** 618; **XVI.** 62.

Prayers in Colleges, **II.** 662; **IV.** 23; **V.** 515.

Precocity, **V.** 473, 749; **XI.** 492, 508.

Prize Schemes, **I.** 629; **II.** 708; **III.** 249, 255; **V.** 226; **VI.** 287.

Printing-press, uses of to Boys, **IX.** 636.

Private Schools, **II.** 719; **VI.** 213; **XIII.** 553.

Progression, **XVI.** 643.

Progressives of the 16th Century, **VI.** 463.

Promotion by merit, **XIII.** 667; **XV.** 92.

Pronunciation of English, **IV.** 226; **XIV.** 354; of Greek and Latin, **IV.** 226; **XV.** 171.

Public Schools in England, **VIII.** 257; **XV.** 81; **XVI.** 501, 567.

Public Schools and Private Schools, **XI.** 114; **XIII.** 361; **XV.** 323.

Punctuality, **II.** 659; **V.** 520.

Pupil-Teachers, **IV.** 191; **X.** 385, 504.

Puzzling Pupils, **XIV.** 313.

Quadriennium, **XIV.** 172.

Quadrivium, **I.** 254; **VI.** 21.

Quick-wits, **XI.** 58.

Questions for Examining a School, **I.** 686; **X.** 449.

Ratio Studiorum, of the Jesuits, **XIV.** 462.

Reaction, Law of, **XI.** 493, 502.

Real Schools, **VI.** 248; **V.** 661, 674, 691; **VIII.** 508; **IX.** 247; **XIV.** 425; **XV.** 440, 767.

Reading, Methods of Instruction, Currie, **IX.** 273, 277; Dunn, **X.** 399; Harwich, **VIII.** 431; Honcamp, **IV.** 234; Lloyd, **IV.** 225; Locke, **VI.** 219, **XIV.** 304; Morrison, **IX.** 307; Olivier, **V.** 508; Prinsen, **VIII.** 612; Quintilian, **XI.** 120; Raumer, **X.** 624; **XII.** 473; Thayer, **IV.** 218; Wilbur, **XV.** 201.

Reasoning with Children, **V.** 471; **XIII.** 562.

Reflection and Reflective Faculties, Marcel, **XI.** 33; Russell, **IV.** 198, 309.

Religion and Religious Instruction, Acquaviva, **XIV.** 471; Arnold, **IV.** 559; Bible, **X.** 167; Basedow, **V.** 501, 513; Brooks, **I.** 336; Burgess, **II.** 562; Currie, **IX.** 284; Cousin, **XIII.** 287; Comenius, **V.** 226; Cowdery, **XVI.** 323; Dunn, **X.** 427; Fellenberg, **XIII.** 325; Fisher, **X.** 180; Hegel, **X.** 171; Hoole, **XVII.** 238; Huntington, **IV.** 23; Krüsi, **V.** 195; Lalor, **XVI.** 49; Lindsley, **VII.** 35; Locke, **XIV.** 308; Luther, **X.** 183; Niemeyer, **X.** 132, 173, 177, 184; Pinto, **X.** 170; Pestalozzi, **X.** 175, 182; Potter, **II.** 154, 162; Pythagoras, **X.** 167; Randall, **II.** 156; Raumer, **VII.** 401; **X.** 241; Richards, **X.** 512; Socrates, **X.** 169; Thayer, **II.** 71; Zcbokke, **X.** 169, 176.

Religion in Public Schools of Baden, **X.** 206; Bavaria, **VI.** 281; **VIII.** 501; England, **IV.** 559, 573; **X.** 513; **XV.** 103; **XVI.** 670; Greece, **XII.** 574; Holland, **XIV.** 642, 693; Hanover, **XV.** 426, 769; Ireland, **XI.** 137, 152; Jesuit Schools, **XIV.** 471; Prussia, **VIII.** 420; Scotland, **IX.** 222.

Requisitions and Prohibitions, **XIII.** 851.

Rewards in School, **VI.** 212, 435; **XI.** 480.

Rote-learning, **V.** 247, 474; **VI.** 465; **VII.** 405; **XII.** 416; **XIII.** 113, 373.

Rules for School Attendance, **XIV.** 816; Good Behavior, **VIII.** 613; **X.** 438; **XIII.** 171, 549, 851; Hopkins' Grammar School, **IV.** 710; Dorchester School, **XVI.** 106.

Science in Schools, **I.** 164, 514; **II.** 66, 81, 349, 447; **III.** 147, 265; **IV.** 757; **V.** 671, 779; **VI.** 233, 448; **XIII.** 309.

Science and Art, **I.** 102, 315, 388; **II.** 715; **X.** 218.

Simultaneous Method, **IX.** 299.

Socratic Method, **IX.** 375; Currie, **IX.** 283.

Spelling, Dunn, **X.** 409; Richards, **X.** 517; Thayer, **III.** 312.

Studies, True Order of, Hill, **VI.** 180, 449; **VI.** 273, 491; Spencer, **XIII.** 374.

Synthetical Method, **IV.** 504.

Synchronistical Method in History, **IV.** 515.

Text-books, Catalogue of American, **XIII.** 208, 401, 627; **XIV.** 601, 753.

Topical Method in Geography, **VIII.** 82.

Tripartite Organization, **IX.** 316; **XIII.** 149.

Turners and Turning System, **VII.** 92; **VIII.** 189.

Unconscious Tuition, **I.** 141.

Utility of Studies, **II.** 386; **V.** 479; **XV.** 101.

Virtue, **V.** 494; **VIII.** 10; **X.** 167; **VIII.** 550.

Will, **V.** 511, 671; **IX.** 37; **V.** 137; **XIV.** 472, 617.

Writing and Reading, **IV.** 234; **VII.** 694; **XII.** 477.

Writing and Drawing, **VIII.** 383.

IV. TEACHERS; NORMAL AND MODEL SCHOOLS; TEACHERS' INSTITUTES.

The School and the Teacher in English Literature, **III**, 155, 449; **IV**, 183; **VIII**, 283; **XVI**, 432.
Legal Recognition of Teaching as a Profession; Memorial, **X**, 297-308.
The Teacher as an Artist, by Z. Richards, **XIV**, 69.
The Teacher's Motives, by Horace Mann, **XIV**, 277.
Essentials to Success in Teaching, **I**, 561.
Letters to a Young Teacher, by G. F. Thayer, **I**, 357; **II**, 103, 391, 657; **III**, 71, 313; **IV**, 219, 450; **VI**, 435; **VIII**, 81.
Lectures to Young Teachers; Intellectual Education, by W. Russell, **II**, 113, 317; **III**, 47, 321; **IV**, 199, 309. Moral Education, **IX**, 19.
Special Training a Pre-requisite to Teaching, by H. Mann, **XIII**, 507.
Teachers and their Education, by W. E. Channing, **XII**, 453.
Professional Training of Teachers, **XIII**, 269.
Didactics as a Department in Colleges, by T. Hill, **XV**, 177.
German Views upon Female Teachers, **IV**, 793.
Teachers' Conferences and other Modes of Professional Improvement, **XIII**, 273.
Teachers' Institutes in Wisconsin, **VIII**, 673. In Different States—Historical Development, **XV**, 387. Connecticut, 387; New York, 395; Ohio, 401; Rhode Island, 405; Massachusetts, 412.
School for Teachers, by W. R. Johnson, **V**, 799.
Teachers' Seminaries, by C. E. Stowe, **XV**, 688.
Relation of Normal Schools to other Institutions, by W. F. Phelps, **III**, 417.
Historical Development of Normal Schools in Europe and America, **XIII**, 753-770.
Germany and other European States—Number, Location and Results of Normal Schools, **VIII**, 360; Professional Training of Teachers in Anhalt, **XV**, 345; Austria, **XVI**, 345; Baden, **X**, 212; Bavaria, **VI**, 289; Belgium, **VIII**, 593; Brunswick, **XV**, 453; France, **XIII**, 281; Greece, **XII**, 579; Hanover, **XV**, 419; Hesse-Cassel, **XV**, 439; Hesse Darmstadt, **XIV**, 416; Holland, **XIV**, 501, 647; Lippe Detmold, **XV**, 475; Mecklenburg, **XV**, 464, 472; Nassau, **II**, 444; Prussia, **XI**, 165; Russia, **XII**, 727; Sardinia, **III**, 517; Saxony, **V**, 353; Switzerland, **XIII**, 313.
Great Britain. Training Colleges in England and Wales, **X**, 349. Normal Schools of the British and Foreign School Society, **X**, 435. Normal and Model Schools of the Home and Colonial Society, **IX**, 449. St. Mark's Training College for Masters of the National Society, **X**, 531. Battersea Training School for Parochial Schoolmasters, **IX**, 170. Chester Diocesan Training College, **X**, 553. Normal Schools for Training Schoolmistresses, **X**, 571; Normal Schools at Edinburgh and Glasgow, **X**, 583. Irish System of Training Teachers, **XI**, 136.
France. Normal Schools and Training, **XIII**, 281. Normal Schools of the Christian Brothers, **III**, 437.

Holland. Normal School at Haarlem, **XIV**, 501.
Prussia. Provisions for Education and Support of Teachers, **XI**, 165-190. System of Normal Schools, **XIV**, 191-240. Seminary School at Weissenfels, **VIII**, 455; **XIV**, 219. Dr. Julius on, **XVI**, 29. Regulations of 1854, **XVI**, 305.
Normal Schools in Switzerland, **XIII**, 313-440.
Normal and Model Schools of Upper Canada, **XIV**, 483.
United States—Documentary History of Normal Schools—Adams, **I**, 589; Bache, **VIII**, 360; Barnard, **X**, 24, 40; Bates, **XVI**, 453; Brooks, **I**, 587; Barrowes, **XVI**, 195; Calhoun, **XVI**, 80; Carter, **XVI**, 77; Channing, **XII**, 453; Clinton, **XIII**, 341; Dwight, **IV**, 16; Edwards, **XVI**, 271; Emerson, **XVI**, 93; Everett, **XIII**, 758; Gallaudet, **X**, 16; Hall, **V**, 386; **XVI**, 75; Humphrey, **XII**, 655; Julius, **XVI**, 89; Johnson, **V**, 798; Lindsley, **VII**, 35; Mann, **V**, 646; **VIII**, 360; Olmsted, **V**, 369; Peirce, **IV**, 305; Phelps, **III**, 417; Putnam, **I**, 588; Sears, **XVI**, 471; Stephens, **VIII**, 368; Stowe, **XV**, 688; Tillinghast, **I**, 67; Webster, **I**, 590; Wickersham, **XV**, 221.
Chapter in the History of Normal Schools in New England; Charles Brooks, **I**, 587.
California. State Normal School, **XVI**, 628.
Connecticut. History of State Normal School, **X**, 15-58. History of Teachers' Institutes, **XV**, 387.
Illinois. State Normal University at Bloomington, **IV**, 774.
Kentucky. State Normal School, **III**, 217.
Maine. State Normal School, **XVII**.
Maryland. State Normal School, **XVII**.
Massachusetts. State Normal School at Bridgewater, **V**, 646; **XVI**, 595. At Barre; Everett's Address, **XIII**, 758. At Westfield, **XII**, 652. Teachers' Seminary at Andover, **V**, 386. History of Teachers' Institutes, **XV**, 387.
New Jersey. State Normal School, **III**, 221. Its Aims, by D. Cole, **V**, 835. Farnum Preparatory School, **III**, 307.
New York. State Normal School at Albany, **XIII**, 341, 531. History of Teachers' Institutes, **XV**, 395. Training School at Oswego, **XVI**, 230. Normal School at Brockport, **XVII**.
Ohio. History of Teachers' Institutes, **XV**, 401. Normal Schools in, **XVII**.
Pennsylvania. Professional Training of Teachers, **XIV**, 721. Normal School at Millersville, **XV**, 221. Philadelphia Normal School for Female Teachers, **XIV**, 727. **XVI**, 195. Normal School at Mansfield, **XVII**.
Rhode Island. Education of Teachers, **XI**, 282. History of Teachers' Institutes, **XV**, 405.
Vermont. Teachers' Seminary in 1823, **XVI**, 146. State Normal Schools, **XVII**.
Wisconsin. Teachers' Institutes, **VIII**, 673. Normal Schools, **XVII**.

V. STATE AND NATIONAL SYSTEMS.

Educational Statistics, **I.** 640–651.
Anhalt. System of Public Instruction, **XV.** 344.
Austria. System of Public Instruction, **IX.** 589. Educational Statistics, **III.** 275; **IV.** 257; **XVI.** 5, 337, 609; **XVII.** 127.
Baden. System of Public Instruction; Primary, **X.** 201. Secondary, **XI.** 233. Seminary for Orphans at Beuggen, **III.** 383.
Bavaria. System of Public Instruction, **VI.** 273, 571; **VIII.** 491. Educational Statistics, **I.** 625.
Belgium. System of Public Instruction, **VIII.** 581.
Brunswick. System of Public Instruction, **XV.** 447.
Canada. History and System of Public Instruction in Upper Canada, by J. G. Hodgins, **I.** 186. Statistics of Education in Upper Canada, **XIII.** 649. Educational Institutions in U. and L. Canada, **II.** 728.
Denmark. System of Public Instruction, **XIV.** 625.
England. Historical Sketch of Elementary Instruction, **X.** 323. British and Foreign School Society and Borough Road Schools, **X.** 371–459. National Society for Promoting the Education of the Poor, **X.** 409–574. Home and Colonial Infant and Juvenile Society, **IX.** 449. Lord John Russell's Scheme of National Education, **I.** 638. Ashburton Prizes for Teaching Common Things, **I.** 629; **X.** 93. Miss Coutts' Prizes, **II.** 708. Public Endowed or Foundation Schools, **IV.** 807; **VIII.** 257; **XV.** 81–117. Appropriations to Education, Science, and Art, **I.** 385; **II.** 348; **X.** 347.
France. System of Public Instruction, **VI.** 293; **IX.** 481–412. Guizot's Ministry of Public Instruction, **XI.** 254, 357. Statistics of Education, **IV.** 257. Expenditures for Public Instruction, **II.** 337, 717.
Free Cities; Frankfort, Hamburg, Bremen, and Lübeck. System of Public Instruction, **XV.** 333.
Germany. History and Course of Primary Instruction, **VIII.** 348–402. Real Schools, **V.** 689–714. Educational Intelligence, **III.** 273; **IV.** 245.
Greece. System of Public Instruction, **XII.** 571–592. Statistics of Education, **I.** 628.
Hanover. System of Public Instruction, **IV.** 250; **XV.** 415, 752.
Hesse Cassel. System of Public Instruction, **XV.** 431.
Hesse Darmstadt. Public Instruction, **XIV.** 409–430.
Holland. System of Public Instruction, **IV.** 801; **VIII.** 595; **XIV.** 495, 641–720. Proposed Revision of System, **II.** 719. Statistics of Public Schools, **I.** 401. Scheme of Christian Education adopted at Dort, 1618, **V.** 77.
Honduras. Condition of Education, **II.** 236.
India. Progress of Education, **II.** 727.
Ireland. Elementary Education, **XI.** 133–154. System of National Education, **III.** 272; **IV.** 363. National Schools. **XIII.** 145. Educational Appropriations, **I.** 390; **II.** 348, 716. Endowed Grammar and English Schools, **XV.** 721.
Italy. Institutions for Public Instruction, **II.** 721. History of Education, **VII.** 413.

Lippe-Detmold and Schaumburg Lippe. System of Public Instruction, **XV.** 473, 576.
Luxemburg and Limberg. System of Public Instruction, **XIV.** 664.
Mecklenburg. System of Public Instruction, **XV.** 459. Ignorance in, **III.** 278.
Nassau. System of Public Instruction, **II.** 444.
New South Wales. Statistics of Education, **I.** 639.
Norway. System of Public Instruction, **VIII.** 295.
Portugal. System of Public Instruction, **XVII.**
Prussia. History and Statistics of Public Instruction, **IV.** 245; **VIII.** 403–434; **IX.** 569. Expenditures for Public Instruction in Prussia and France, **II.** 337. Public Schools of Berlin, **VIII.** 440. Frederic William Gymnasium and Real Schools of Berlin, **V.** 699. Burgher School at Halle, **VIII.** 434. Higher Burgher School of Potsdam, **VIII.** 457.
Russia. National Education, **XII.** 725
Sardinia. System of Public Instruction, **III.** 513; **IV.** 37, 479.
Saxony. System of Public Instruction, **V.** 350. Secondary Instruction, **IV.** 251. Burgher School, **IX.** 201 Early School Code, **VI.** 432.
Scotland. Elementary Education, **IX.** 215. Parochial School System, **II.** 716; **VII.** 319.
Spain. Public Instruction, **XVII.**
Sweden. Public Instruction, **II.** 720; **XVI.** 639.
Turkey. System of Education, **II.** 725.
Wurtemburg. Early School Code, **VI.** 426. System of Public Instruction, **XVII.**
United States. Official Exposition of Common Schools, **II.** 257, 465–561. School Funds and Public Instruction in the several States, **I.** 371, 447. Statistics of Population, Area, and Education in 1850, **I.** 364. Statistics of Public Instruction in Cities and large Towns, **I.** 458. Educational Movements in the several States, **I.** 234, 641; **II.** 257, 452, 734; **IV.** 824. Plan of Central Agency for Advancement of Education, by H. Barnard, **I.** 134. National Bureau of Education, **XV.** 180. Lord Elgin on the American School System, **III.** 239. Education among the Cherokees, by W. P. Ross, **I.** 120. Schools as they were Sixty Years ago, **XIII.** 123, 737; **XVI.** National Department of Education, **XVII.** 49. Constitutional Provision, **XVII.** 81. Educational Land Policy, **XVII.** 65.
Alabama. School Statistics, **I.** 368, 371; **II.** 464. Constitutional Provision, **XVII.**
Arkansas. Statistics, **I.** 368, 371.
California. **XVI.** 625. Statistics, **I.** 372; **II.** 467.
Connecticut. History of Common Schools, by H Barnard, **IV.** 657; **V.** 114; **XIII.** 725; **XIV.** 244; **XV.** 275; **XVI.** 333. History of the School Fund, **VI.** 367–415. Henry Barnard's Labors, **I.** 669. Public Schools and other Educational Institutions, **XI.** 305. Free Academy and School Movements in Norwich, **II.** 665; **III.** 191. Statistics, **I.** 372; **II.** 469. Constitutional Provision, **XVII.**

Delaware. Statistics, **I.** 368, 373; **II.** 474.
Florida. Statistics, **I.** 367, 374.
Georgia. **I.** 368, 374; **II.** 477.
Illinois. **I.** 368, 375; **II.** 479.
Indiana. **I.** 368, 375; **II.** 480.
Iowa. **I.** 368, 374; **II.**
Kansas. **XVII.**
Kentucky. **I.** 368, 377; **II.** 488.
Louisiana. **I.** 368, 377; **II.** 473.
Maine. **I.** 368, 378; **II.** 495.
Maryland. **I.** 368, 378.
Massachusetts. Doctrine of Free Schools, **XV.** 15. Analysis of Horace Mann's Reports, **V.** 623. School Superintendence; Memorial of American Institute of Instruction, **V.** 653. Legal Recognition of Teaching as a Profession; Memorial of Worcester County Teachers' Association, **X.** 297. **I.** 368, 379; **II.** 499.
Michigan. **I.** 368, 447; **II.** 510.
Minnesota. **I.** 368.
Mississippi. **I.** 368, 447.
Missouri. **I.** 368, 448.
Nebraska. **XVII.**
Nevada. **XVII.**
New Hampshire. **I.** 368,'448; **II.** 510.
New Jersey. **I.** 368, 449; **II.** 517.
New York. **I.** 368, 449; **II.** 518
North Carolina. **I.** 368, 451; **II.** 527. Schools as they were in 1794, **XVI.** 1.
Ohio. System of Common Schools, by W. T. Coggeshall, **VI.** 81, 532; **I.** 368, 451; **II.** 531.

Oregon. **I.** 368; **XVII.**
Pennsylvania. History of Common Schools, **VI.** 107, 555; **I.** 368, 452; **II.** 541.
Rhode Island. **I.** 368, 454; **II.** 544. Labors of Henry Burnard, **I.** 723.
South Carolina. **I.** 368, 455; **II.** 553. Marion on Free Schools for, **XVI.** 119.
Tennessee. **I.** 368, 455.
Texas. **I.** 368, 445.
Vermont. **I.** 368, 466.
Virginia. **I.** 368, 457; Gov. Wise on Education, **II.** 557.
West Virginia. **XVII.**
Wisconsin. **I.** 368, 457.
District of Columbia. **XVII.**
Cities. Statistics of Population, **I.** 479. Gradation of Schools for, **XV.** 316, 309. Reports on, **I.** 458.
Boston: Edward Everett and the Boston Schools, **I.** 642. Latin Grammar School of Boston, **XII.** 529. Girls in the Public Schools of Boston, **XIII.** 243. Dedication of the Everett School House, **IX.** 633. Report of N. Bishop, **I.** 458. School Houses in, **XVI.** 701.
Chicago High School, by W. H. Wells, **III.** 531. Retirement of Mr. Wells, **XIV.** 811.
Cincinnati; Woodward High School, **IV.** 520.
New York City. Public School Society, **XV.** 489.
Philadelphia High School, by J. S. Hart, **I.** 93. Report on Public Schools, **I.** 465.
Providence: Report on, **I.** 468.
St. Louis System of Public Instruction, **I.** 348.

VI. SECONDARY, INTERMEDIATE AND ACADEMICAL SCHOOLS.

Anhalt. Gymnasiums and Higher Schools, **XV.** 346.
Austria. System and Statistics of Secondary Instruction, **IX.** 598. **XVI.** 465. **XVII.** 127.
Baden. System of Sec. Instruction, **XI.** 233-253.
Bavaria. Secondary Schools, **VIII.** 491-521.
Belgium. Secondary Schools, **VIII.** 587.
Brunswick. Classical Schools, **XV.** 456.
Canada. Secondary Schools, **XIII.** 649.
Denmark. Outline of System and Statistics, **XIV.** 625.
England. Public or Foundation Schools, **VIII.** 257; **XV.** 81. Mr. Sewall's School at Radleigh, **IV.** 803. St. Mary's College at Winchester, **XVI.** 501. St. Paul's School in London, **XVI.** 667. Eton College, **XVII.**
France. Lyceums and Secondary Schools, **VI.** 294. Statistics of Secondary Education in 1843, **IX.** 400. Secondary Instruction under Guizot's Ministry, **XI.** 357. Schools of Preparation for the Polytechnic School, **XII.** 47.
Free Cities. Gymnasiums and Secondary Institutions, **XV.** 339.
Greece. Secondary Schools, Gymnasiums, &c., **XII.** 581.
Hanover. Real Schools and Girls' High School, **IV.** 250. Secondary Instruction, **XV.** 753-781.
Hesse-Cassel. Secondary Institutions, **XV.** 435.

Hesse-Darmstadt. Classical, Real, Trades, and Higher Female School Systems, **XIV.** 419.
Holland. Secondary Schools, **XIV.** 654.
Ireland. Endowed Grammar and English Schools, **XV.** 721.
Mecklenburg. Secondary Schools, **XV.** 465.
Nassau. Secondary Education, **II.** 445.
Norway. Burgher, Real, and Learned Schools, **VIII.** 301.
Prussia. Statistics of Secondary Instruction, **II.** 341; **IV.** 247. Higher Institutions of Berlin, **V.** 699. Secondary Education, **IX.** 569.
Sardinia. Secondary Instruction, **III.** 518; **IV.** 37.
Saxony. Real and Classical Schools, **V.** 354; **IV.** 251. Secondary Education, **IX.** 201.
United States. Historical Development of Incorporated Academies, **XVI.** 403. Statistics of Academies, &c. in 1850, **I.** 368; Lawrence Academy, Groton, Mass., **I.** 49. Williston Seminary, Easthampton, Mass., **II.** 173. Norwich Free Academy, Norwich, Conn., **II.** 665; **III.** 190. Public High School in Chicago, **III.** 531. Woodward High School in Cincinnati, **IV.** 520. Phillips Academy, Andover, Mass., **VI.** 73. Phillips Academy, Exeter, N. H., **VI.** 76. Boston Latin School, **XII.** 529. Public Grammar Schools of Philadelphia, **XIII.** 818.

CLASSIFIED INDEX OF BARNARD'S AMERICAN JOURNAL OF EDUCATION. 33

VII. UNIVERSITY AND COLLEGE EDUCATION.

Signification of the term University, IX, 49-56.
University Honors, VIII, 313.
University Studies and Teaching, Raumer, VII. 201.
Classical Education. Erasmus' Views, IV, 729. David Cole upon, I, 67. Discussion before the American Association, I, 86. S. P. Bates, XV, 155. Speaking and Writing Latin, Raumer, VII, 471.
College Education and Self-Education, IV, 262.
Prayers in Colleges, by F. D. Huntington, IV, 23.
College Code of Honor, by Horace Mann, III, 65.
Authorities upon the History of Universities, and Academical Degrees, II, 747; VII, 49; IX, 56.
Canada. University and Colleges of Upper and Lower Canada, II, 728; VII, 188; XIII, 649.
England. Government Grants in 1856, II, 348. Oxford Commemoration, II. 234. Expenses in Eton College in 1560, IV, 259. University for Legal Education, I, 386. Working Men's College, I, 389.
France. University and Colleges, VI, 296.
Germany. German Universities in the Sixteenth Century, from Raumer, V, 535. History of German Universities, from Raumer, VI, 9-65; VII, 47-152. Student Societies in German Universities, VII, 160. Essays on the Improvement of German Universities, from Raumer, VII, 200-251. Statistics, I, 401.
Greece. The Otho University, XII, 591.
Holland. Condition of the Universities, I, 397.
Ireland. Queen's Colleges and University, IX, 579.
Prussia. Receipts and Expend. of Universities, II, 338.
Russia. Universities, I, 381.

Sardinia. University Education, IV, 43.
Saxony. University of Leipsic, V, 362.
Scotland. University of Edinburg, IV, 821.
Wurtemburg. University of Tübingen, IX, 57.
United States. Characteristics of American Colleges, by C. C. Felton, IX, 122.
Improvements Practicable in American Colleges, by F. A. P. Barnard, I, 175, 260.
Consolidation and other Modifications of American Colleges, by Alonzo Potter, I, 471.
An American University, by B. A. Gould, II, 265-293. By A. D. Bache, I, 477. By an Alabamian, III, 213. Discussion, I, 86.
Society for the Promotion of Collegiate and Theological Education at the West, I, 235; XV. 261.
Statistics of New England Colleges in 1855-6, I, 405.
Harvard University. History, IX, 129. Grants and Donations to, IX, 139-165. Progress under Pres. Felton, X, 293. Museum of Zoölogy, IX, 613.
Yale College. History, V, 541-566, Elihu Yale, V, 715. List of Deceased Benefactors, X, 693. Department of Philosophy and the Arts, I, 459. Influence of, by F. A, P. Barnard, V, 723; by W. B. Sprague, X, 681.
Illinois College. History, I, 225.
Transylvania University, Kentucky, III, 217.
Cumberland University, Tennessee; History, IV, 765.
University Convocation of New York, XV, 502.
St. John's College, Maryland, Charter, XVI. 549. Report on Reorganization, XVI, 539.

VIII. SCHOOLS OF SCIENCE AND ARTS; MUSEUMS, &C.

Democratic Tendencies of Science, D. Olmsted, I, 164.
Progress of Science in the United States, I, 641.
Science and Scientific Schools, by J. D. Dana, II, 349.
Schools of Science and Art, X, 216.
Physical Science. By H. J. Anderson, I, 515-532.
Scientific Schools in Europe, by D. C. Gilman, I, 315.
Department of Science and Art, Eng., II, 233, 715.
Higher Special Schools of Science and Literature in France, by D. C. Gilman, II, 93.
Special Instruction in Science and Art in France, IX, 405.
Polytechnic Schools. At Paris, VIII, 661; XII, 51-130. Le Verrier's Report upon Mathematical Study preparatory to the Polytechnic School of Paris, I, 533-550; II, 177-192. Conditions for Admission, XIII, 678. Polytechnic Institute at Vienna, VIII, 670. Polytechnic School at Carlsruhe, XI. 209. Polytechnic School at Zürich, XI, 218. Polytechnic Schools of Bavaria, VIII, 510.
Russia. Schools of Special Instruction, I, 382.
Lawrence Scientific School at Cambridge, I, 216.
Scientific Department in Yale College, I, 359.
Cooper Scientific Union, New York, I, 652; IV. 526.
Industrial School at Chemnitz, III, 252; IV. 798.
School of Mines at Freyburg, Saxony, IX, 167.

Drawing; Report of a French Commission, II, 419.
Art Education, by Miss M. A. Dwight, II, 409-587; III, 467; IV, 191; V. 305.
On a College of Architecture, by D. B. Reid, II, 629.
Dudley Observatory, II, 593. Uses of Astronomy, by E. Everett, II, 605-628.
United States Coast Survey. I, 103.
Geological Hall and Agricultural Rooms of New York, IV, 785.
British Museum, VIII, 314. British Museum of Practical Geology, VI, 239. Museum of Comparative Zoölogy at Harvard, IX, 613. Educational Uses of Museums, by Prof. E. Forbes, IV, 785.
Institute of Agriculture and Forestry at Hohenheim, VIII, 564. At Tharand, Saxony, IV, 797.
Agricultural Education in France, VIII, 545-563. In Ireland, VIII, 567-580.
Plan of Agricultural School, by J. A. Porter, I, 329.
Hartlib's Plan of a College of Husbandry, XI, 191.
Mechanics' Institutes in England, I, 388; II, 712.
Plan of a Trade School, by Sir W. Petty, 1647, XI, 199.
Industrial Training of Poor, X, 81. Industrial Schools in England, I, 653. Ireland, I, 545. Belgium, I, 384; VIII, 588. Bavaria, VIII, 510. Nassau, II. 446. Saxony, IV, 252, 798. Wurtemburg, IV, 799.

IX. MILITARY AND NAVAL EDUCATION.

Physical and Military Exercises in Public Schools a National Necessity, by E. L. Molineux, **XI**, 513.
Military Schools and Education in England, **IV**, 808; **XIV**, 523. France, **I**, 626; **XII**, 7-274. Holland, **XIV**, 241. Prussia, **XII**, 275-399; **VIII**, 437. Russia, **I**, 383; **XIV**, 503. Switzerland, **XIII**, 689-710. Sardinia, **XIII**, 455. Austria, **XIII**, 409-446, 711. Persia, **II**, 727.
United States; Military Academy at West Point, **XIII**, 17-48. Regulations for Admission, **XIII**, 659. Report of Visitors, 1863, **XIII**, 661; **XV**, 51. On the Conditions for Admission, by H. Barnard, **XIV**, 103-127. Military Academy at Norwich, Vt., **XIII**, 65. Eagleswood Military Academy, at Perth Amboy, N. J., **XIII**, 471.
Naval and Navigation Schools in England, **XIV**, 627; **XV**, 65.
French Naval School at Brest, **XII**, 263.
United States Naval Academy; Report of Visitors, 1864, **XV**, 17-50.

X. PREVENTIVE AND REFORMATORY EDUCATION.

Education a Preventive of Misery and Crime, by E. C. Tainsch, **XI**. 77.
Crimes of Children and their Prevention, **I**, 345.
Publications on Reformatory Education, **III**, 812.
Family Training and Agricultural Labor in Reformatory Education, **I**, 609-624.
Crime, Pauperism, and Education in G. Brit., **VI**, 311.
Preventive and Reformatory Education, **III**, 561-818. Reform Schools in England, **III**, 753. In Ireland, **III**, 807. In Scotland, **III**, 801. In France, **III**, 653. In Holland, **III**, 619. In Italy, **III**, 580. In Switzerland, **III**, 591.
Reformatory Establishment of Dusselthal Abbey, Prussia, **II**, 231.
Prison for Juvenile Criminals, Isle of Wight, **III**, 19.
Wichern and the Rauhe Haus, **III**, 5, 10, 603; **IV**, 824.
Agricultural Reform Schools in Belgium and France, **III**, 621-736.
Agricultural Colonies of France, particularly Mettray, **I**, 609; **III**, 653.
Reformatory Education in the United States, **IV**, 824; Statistics of State and City Reform Schools in the United States, **III**, 811; **VIII**, 339.
State Industrial School for Girls, at Lancaster, Mass., **IV**, 359; **XVI**. 652.
Mode of Improving Factory Population, **VIII**, 305.
Special Training of Women for Social Employments, **III**, 485.
International Philanthropic Congress at Brussels, **II**, 236; **III**, 231.
Industrial Training of the Poor, **I**, 384, 635; **II**, 446; **III**. 585; **IV**, 252, 798; **X**, 81.

XI. EDUCATION FOR DEAF-MUTES, BLIND AND IDIOTS.

Statistics of the Deaf, Dumb, Blind, Insane, and Idiotic in the U. S. in 1850, **I**, 650.
Statistics of the Deaf and Dumb Institutions in the United States, **I**, 444.
American Asylum for the Deaf and Dumb, **I**, 440.
N. Y. Institution for the Deaf and Dumb, **III**, 347.
Institutions and Instruction for the Blind, by L. P. Brockett, **IV**, 127.
Valentine Haüy and the Instruction of the Blind, **III**, 177; **IV**, 130.
Account of Laura Bridgman, by S. G. Howe, **IV**, 383.
Idiots and Institutions for their Training, by L. P. Brockett. **I**, 593.
Origin of Treatment and Training of Idiots, by E. Seguin, **II**, 145.
New York Asylum for Imbeciles at Syracuse, **IV**, 416.
Butler Hospital for the Insane, at Providence, R. I., **III**, 309.
Insanity as the Result of Misdirected Education, by E. Jarvis, **IV**, 591.

XII. MORAL AND RELIGIOUS EDUCATION; DENOMINATIONAL SCHOOLS.

Thoughts on Religion and Public Schools, by George Burgess, **II**, 562.
Christianity in Education, from Raumer, **VIII**, 216.
Religious Instruction, from Raumer, **VII**, 401.
Religious and Moral Instruction in Public Schools; Discussion by the American Association, **II**, 153.
Importance and Methods of Moral Training, by G. F. Thayer, **III**, 71.
Best Methods of Moral Teaching, by C. Brooks, **I**, 336.
Moral and Mental Discipline, by Z. Richards, **I**, 107.
Formation of Moral Character, the Main Object of Schools, by M. F. Cowdery, **XVI**, 353.
Moral Education, by W. Russell, **IX**, 19-48; Fellenberg, **III**, 595; Krüsi, **V**, 193; Lalor. **XVI**, 48; Locke, **XI**, 473; **XIII**, 548; Spencer, **XI**, 496.
Aphorisms on Religious and Moral Training, **X**, 166; **XII**. 407.
Prayers in Colleges, by F. D. Huntington, **IV**, 23.
Catholic Educational Establishments in the United States, **II**, 435.
The Hieronymians; from Raumer, **IV**, 622.
Jesuits and their Schools, **XIV**, 455-482. From Raumer, **V**, 213; **VI**, 615.
The Christian Brothers, (Freres Chrétiens,) **III**. 437.

CLASSIFIED INDEX OF BARNARD'S AMERICAN JOURNAL OF EDUCATION. 35

XIII. EDUCATION AND SCHOOLS FOR FEMALES.

Aphorisms upon Female Education, **XIII**, 232.
Views of German Authorities, **XIII**, 495.
St. Jerome—Letter to Læta on the Education of her Daughter, **V**, 593.
E. Everett, Female Education, **IX**, 635; **XII**, 721.
Education of Girls, from Raumer, **X**, 227, 613.
Mental Education of Women, by C. McKeen, **I**, 567.
Training of Women for Social Employments, **III**, 485.
Sisters of Charity—Mrs. Jameson, **III**, 493.
Female Adult Education in Ireland, **I**, 634.
School for Girls in Paris, **I**, 594.

Girls in the Public Schools of Boston, **XIII**, 243.
Female Colleges in the State of Ohio, **XIII**, 267.
New York Grammar School for Girls, **I**, 408. Packer Collegiate Institute for Girls, **I**, 579. Young Ladies' High School, Providence, R. I., **V**, 14. Troy Female Seminary, **VI**, 145. Mt. Holyoke Female Seminary, **X**, 670. Bailey's Young Ladies' High School, Boston, **XII**, 435. Ohio Female College, College Hill, **XIII**, 503. Girls' High School, Charleston, S. C., **XIII**, 620. Vassar College, **XI**, 55. **XVII.**

XIV. PHYSICAL EDUCATION.

Aphorisms and Suggestions upon Physical Training, **VIII**, 75.
Physical Education; by Raumer, **VIII**, 185. By Locke, **XI**, 462. By Lalor, **XVI**, 34. By Spencer, **XI**, 485.
Health of Teachers, by Miss C. E. Beecher, **II**, 399.
Physical Exercises, by S. W. Mason, **XIV**, 61.
New Gymnastics, by Dio Lewis, **XI**, 531; **XII**, 665.

Physical and Military Exercises in Schools a National Necessity, by E. L. Molineux, **XI**, 513.
Plays, Pastimes, and Holidays of Children, by Horace Bushnell, **XIII**, 93.
Progressive Development of Physical Culture in the United States, **XV**, 231.
Military Gymnastic School at Vincennes, France, **XII**, 265.

XV. SUPPLEMENTARY, SELF AND HOME EDUCATION.

Hints on Reading; Selections from Authors, by T. H. Vail, **II**, 215.
Advice to Students and Young Men on Education, Studies, and Conduct, **XV**, 377; **XVI**, 187, 216, 223.
Pestalozzi—Address on Christmas Eve, **VII**, 701. On New Year's, **VII**, 712. Paternal Instructions, **VII**, 722.
Home Education; Labors of Rev. W. Burton, **II**, 333.
College and Self-education, by D. Masson, **IV**, 262.
Lowell Lectures, **V**, 439.
Mechanics' Institutes, **VIII**, 250.
Origin of Lyceums, **VIII**, 249. The American Lyceum, **XIV**, 535-558.

Lyceums, Mechanics' Institutes and Libraries in England, **I**, 388; **II**, 712; **III**, 241-272.
Statistics of Libraries in Europe, **I**, 370; **II**, 214. In the United States in 1850, **I**, 369.
Libraries for Teachers in France, **XIII**, 293. Economic Library, England, **III**, 271.
Astor Library, **I**, 648. Boston Public Library, **II**, 203; **VII**, 252. Baltimore Public Library, **III**, 226. Worcester Free Public Library, **XIII**, 606. Providence Atheneum, **III**, 308. Lawrence Library for Factory Operatives, **I**, 649.
Management of Libraries—Edward's Library Manual, **II**, 210.
Books of Reference, **VIII**, 315.

XVI. EDUCATIONAL ASSOCIATIONS.

Association for Educational Purposes, by H. Barnard, **XIV**, 366; **XV**, 819.
American Association for the Advancement of Education, **I**, 3-136, 234; **XV**, 267.
American Association for the Advancement of Science, **III**, 147.
American Association for the Supply of Teachers, **XV**, 237.
American Common School Society, **XV**, 247.
American Education Society, **XIV**, 367.
American Institute of Instruction, **II**, 19, 234. Index to Lecturers and Subjects, **II**, 241. Memorial on State School Superintendence, **V**, 653. Biographical Sketches of Presidents, **XV**, 211.
American Lyceum, **XIV**, 535.
American School Society, **XV**, 118.
American Social Science Association, **XVI**, 391.

American Sunday School Union, **XV**, 705
American Women's Educational Asso., **XV**, 273.
Baltimore County and City Association, **XV**, 377.
Board of National Popular Education, **XV**, 271.
Boston Associated Instructors of Youth, **XV**, 527.
British and Foreign School Society, **X**, 371-459.
College Delegates (New England) Association, **XVII**.
Guild of Schoolmasters, **XV**, 337.
Home and Colonial Infant and Juvenile Society, **IX**, 449-486.
Literary and Scientific Convention; New York, 1830, **XV**, 221.
National Associations, **XV**, 237, 823.
National Association (England) for Promotion of Social Science, **IV**, 818.
National Convention and Association of Superintendents of Schools, **XVI**, 389.

National Organization of Teachers, by W. Russell, **XIV**, 7.
National Teachers' Association; Proceedings, **XIV**, 5-92, 593. Its Nature and Objects, by J. D. Philbrick, **XIV**, 49.
National Society (England) for Promoting the Education of the Poor, **X**, 499-474.
National Society of Science, Literature, and Arts, **XV**, 61.
New York (City) Society of Teachers, **XIV**, 807; **XV**, 491. Teachers' Associations, **XV**, 495.
New York University Convocation, **XV**, 502.
North-Western Educational Society, **XV**, 275.
Public School Society of New York, **XV**, 489.
Society for the Diffusion of Useful Knowledge, **XV**, 239.
Society for Promoting Manual Labor in Literary Institutions, **XV**, 231.
Society for the Promotion of Collegiate and Theological Education at the West, **I**, 235; **XV**, 261.
State Convention of County Superintendents; New York, **XV**, 505.
TEACHERS' ASSOCIATIONS in France, **XIII**, 293.
General Assembly of German Teachers, **IV**, 258.
United Association of Schoolmasters, Eng., **III**, 202.

Teachers' Conferences and other Modes of Professional Improvement, **XIII**, 273.
Western Literary Institute and College of Professional Teachers, **XIV**, 730.
Middlesex County (Conn.) School Association, **XIV**, 397; **XV**.
State Teachers' Associations, Educational Societies and Conventions—Alabama, **XVI**, 375. Arkansas, **XVI**, 381. California, **XVI**, 785. Connecticut, **XV**, 393. Delaware, **XVI**, 369. Florida, **XVI**, 381. Georgia, **XVI**, 358. Illinois, **XVI**, 149. Indiana, **XVI**, 765. Iowa. **XVI**, 745. Kansas, **XVI**, 385. Kentucky, **XVI**, 352. Louisiana, **XVI**, 382. Maine, **XVI**, 777. Maryland, **XVI**, 377. Massachusetts, **XV**, 507. Michigan, **XV**, 633. Minnesota, **XVII**, Mississippi, **XVI**, 381. Missouri, **XVI**, 365. New Hampshire, **XVI**, 751. New Jersey, **XVI**, 729. New York, **XVI**, 340, 477. North Carolina, **XVI**, 361. Ohio, **VI**, 532. Oregon, **XVI**, 383. Pennsylvania, **XV**, 647. Rhode Island, **XIV**, 559. South Carolina, **XVI**, 364. Tennessee, **XVI**, 357. Texas, **XVI**, 373. Vermont, **XV**, 617. Virginia, **XVI**, 172. Wisconsin, **XIV**, 583; **XVII**, District of Columbia, **XVI**, 380. West Virginia, **XVI**, 383.

XVII. PHILOLOGY AND BIBLIOGRAPHY.

Philological Contributions, by J. W. Gibbs, **II**, 198; **III**, 101-124.
English Language in Society and the School, by M. H. Buckham, **XIV**, 343.
Study of the Anglo-Saxon, or the Relation of the English to other Languages, by J. S. Hart, **I**, 33.
Dictionary of the English Language; Requirements in a Lexicographer, by Isaiah Dole, **III**, 161.
Modern Greek Language, by S. G. Howe, **II**, 193.
Latin Language, from Raumer, **VII**, 471.
Early Illustrated School Books, **XIII**, 205. Primers and Hornbooks, **VIII**, 310. A B C Books and Primers, **XII**, 593.

Books of Reference, **VIII**, 315.
American Text Books—Catalogue of Authors and Books, **XIII**, 209, 401, 626; **XIV**, 601, 751; **XV**, 539.
Educational Literature—Book Notices, **I**, 415; **II**, 256, 737, 739; **IV**, 261, 272, 831; **V**, 318; **IX**, 351; **XI**, 319; **XIII**, 223, 652; **XV**, 400.
Statistics of Newspapers and Periodicals in the United States in 1850, **I**, 651.
Educational Periodicals of America, **I**, 413, 656. Complete List, **XV**, 383.
English Educational Journals, **I**, 414. French, **I**, 413. German, **I**, 413. Italian, **IV**, 802.

XVIII. SCHOOL ARCHITECTURE.

Defects in School Constructions, **IX**, 487.
Principles and Practical Illustrations of School Architecture, by Henry Barnard, **IX**, 487; **X**, 695; **XI**, 563; **XII**, 701; **XIII**, 817; **XIV**, 778; **XV**, 782; **XVI**, 701.
District Schools, or for Children of every age. Plan by H. Mann, **IX**, 540; by G. B. Emerson, 542, 548; by H. Barnard, 550, 553, 555; by R. S. Burt, 556; by T. A. Teft, 559; by A. D. Lord, 562; by D. Leach, 563.
Primary and Infant Schools. General Principles, **X**, 695. Playground and Appliances, **X**, 697. Schoolroom, by Wilderspein, **X**, 699; by Chambers, 702; by British and Foreign School Society, 705; by National Society, 706; by Committee of Council on Education, 710; by Dr. Dick, 714; by J. Kendal, 715; by J. W. Ingraham, for Boston Primary

Schools, 718; by J. D. Philbrick, 740; by New York Public School Society, 750; in Providence, **XI**, 583.
Baltimore Female High School, **V**, 198; Cincinnati Hughes High School, **XIII**, 623; Boston Latin School, **XII**, 551; Woodward High School, **IV**, 522; Chicago High School, **III**, 537; High School, Hartford, **XI**, 606; Public High School, Middletown, **XI**, 612; New York Free Academy, **XIV**, 788; Providence Public High School, **XI**, 597; Norwich Free Academy, **II**, 606; St. Louis High School, **I**, 348.
Seminaries for Girls. Packer Collegiate Institute, Brooklyn, **I**, 581; Richmond Female College, **I**, 231; Public Grammar School for Girls in New York, **I**, 408; Providence Young Ladies' High School, **V**, 14; Vassar College, **XVII**.

CLASSIFIED INDEX OF BARNARD'S AMERICAN JOURNAL OF EDUCATION. 37

Union and Graded Schools—Plans, Elevations, &c., X, 563–612; XII, 701. Union School, Ann Arbor, Mich., VIII, 91. Public Floating School, Baltimore, V, 201. Haven School Building, Chicago, XIII, 610. Newberry Public School, Chicago, VI, 515. Putnam Free School, Newburyport, Mass., XIII, 616. Public Schools No. 20 and No. 33, New York City, VI, 524. School Houses in Philadelphia, XIII, 817. Graded School, Simcoe, U. C., VIII, 679. Union Public School, Ypsilanti, Mich., IV, 780. Norwich Central School, II, 699. Grammar Schools—Plans. Lincoln Grammar School, Boston, VI, 518. Dwight Grammar School, Boston, IV, 769. Fifteenth Ward (N. Y.) Public Grammar School for Girls, I, 409. Central High School, Philadelphia, I, 92; XIII, 831. Grammar, Providence, XI, 528, 594. Prescott Grammar, XVI, 711.
Normal Schools—Plans, Elevations, &c. Illinois State Normal School, IV, 774. New Jersey State Normal School, III, 220. Massachusetts State Normal School at Westfield, XII, 653. New York State Normal School, XIII, 539. Philadelphia City Normal Schools, XIV, 737. Girls' High Normal School, Charleston, S. C., XIII, 620. Normal and Model Schools at Toronto, U. C., XIV, 488. Oswego Training School, XVI, 213. New Britain, X, 51. Bridgewater Normal School, XVI, 466. Framingham, XVI, 469. Salem, XVI, 470.
Public Library, Boston, VII, 252. Cooper Scientific Union, N. Y., I, 652. Dudley Observatory, Albany, I, 594. Yale College in 1764, V, 722. American Asylum for the Deaf and Dumb, Hartford, Ct., I, 440. New York Institution for the Deaf and Dumb, III, 346. New York Asylum for Imbeciles, Syracuse, IV, 416. N. Y. State Geological Hall, IV, 781. Harvard Hall, V, 530. Yale College, 1764, V, 722.

Apparatus for Physical Exercise, IX, 530; XI, 530; XII, 677; for illustration, XIV, 569.
Blackboard and wall-surface, IX, 546, 563; X, 739; XVI, 575. Crayons, how made, XVI, 574.
Dedicatory Exercises and Addresses, III, 193; IX, 633; XIII, 836; V, 648; XII, 655; XIII, 534; XVI, 453; I, 645, 647.
Drawing-room and Desks, X, 554; XIV, 795; XVI, 722.
Furniture for Schools, IX, 551; X, 754; XII, 6–7; Defective Construction, IX, 492, 518; XI, 537; Chase's Adjustable Desk, XIII, 656; Mott's Revolving Seat, X, 563.
Library of Reference, I, 739; IX, 545.
Location and Playground, IX, 402, 503, 507, 510, 527, 542; X, 731.
Privies and Facilities for Cleanliness, IX, 520, 539; X, 728; XI, 607; XIII, 853.
Warming, IX, 546, 552; X, 705, 727; XI, 584, 598; XII, 832; XVI, 579, 713.
Ventilation in American Dwellings, V, 35. In School Houses, IX, 563, 547, 568; X, 724; XIII, 612, 832, 858; XIV, 801; XV, 782; XVI, 716, 727.
Ornamentation, X, 731; Mrs. Sigourney on, 732; Salem High School, XIV, 804; IX, 543.
Specifications, Terms of, X, 733; XII, 708.
Seats and Desks, Arrangement of, IX, 551; XI, 583; XIII, 656; Octagonal Plan, XVI, 728; Barnard's plan, with division, X, 760, 761.
Size of building, XVI, 716.
Stand, movable, for blackboard, XVI, 709.
Furnaces, XVI, 579, 582; Hot-water apparatus, XVI, 713.
Rules for Care of School-house, XIII, 851, 857; for use of Furnaces, XV, 803; setting furnace, XVI, 584.

XIX. EDUCATIONAL ENDOWMENTS AND BENEFACTORS.

Land Grants of the Federal Government for Educational Purposes, to 1854, I, 202; XVII, 65.
List of Benefactions to Harvard University, IX, 139.
List of Deceased Benefactors of Yale College, X, 693.
Boston Educational Charities, VIII, 528; IX, 606.
Individual Benefactors. Samuel Appleton, XII, 403. J. J. and W. B. Astor, I, 638. Joshua Bates, VII, 270. John Bromfield, V, 521. Nicholas Brown, III, 289. Peter Cooper, IV, 526. Thomas Dowse, III, 284; IX, 355. Mrs. Blandina Dudley, II, 593. Edmund Dwight, IV, 5. Peter Faneuil, IX, 603. Paul Furnum, III, 397. John Green, XIII, 606. John Harvard, V, 523. Edward Hopkins, IV, 668. John Hughes, IV, 520. William Lawrence, II, 33. John Lowell, V, 427. Theodore Lyman, X, 5. James McGill, VII, 188. S. J. North, VI, 104. George Peabody, I, 237; II, 642; III, 226. T. H. Perkins, I, 551. Miss Caroline Plummer, XIII, 73. John and Samuel Phillips, VI, 66. Henry Todd, IV, 711. Stephen Van Rensselaer, VI, 223. Matthew Vassar, XI, 53. James Wadsworth, V, 389. David Watkinson, IV, 837. Samuel Williston, II, 173. William Woodward, IV, 520. Elihu Yale, V, 715.

XX. MISCELLANEOUS.

The Gyroscope, or Mechanical Paradox, II, 238. Explanation of the Gyroscope, by E. S. Snell, II, 701. Treatise upon the Gyroscope, by Maj. J. G. Barnard, III, 537; IV, 529; V, 290.
Lowe's Printing Press, IX, 636.
Stereoscope, Educational Uses of, IX, 632.
Museum of Zoölogy, IX, 61.

Indexes. Vol. I, ix.–xix.; II, 749; III, 819; IV, 839; V, 851; VI, 317, 623; VII, 723; VIII, 681; IX, 637; X, 763; XI, 613; XII, 731; XIII, 865; XIV, 817; XV, 829; XVI, 791.
General Index to Vols. I. to V., V, 857.
Classified Index to Vols. I. to XVI., XVII, 17–40.

XXI. EDUCATIONAL BIOGRAPHY AND LIST OF PORTRAITS.

BIOGRAPHICAL SKETCHES.

Abbot, Benjamin, **VI**, 80.
Abbott, Gorham D., **XVI**, 600.
Agricola, Rudolph, **IV**, 717.
Adelung, J. C., **XI**, 451.
Alcott, W. A., **IV**, 629.
Alcott, A. B., **XVI**, 130.
Allen, C. H., **XIV**, 396.
Allen, F. A., **XV**, 681.
Allen, W., **X**, 365.
Alexander, de Villa Dèi, **IV**, 726.
Andrews, I. W., **XVI**, 605.
Acquaviva, Claudius, **XIV**, 462.
Andrews, L., **XVI**, 604.
Appleton, Samuel, **XII**, 403.
Aristotle, **XIV**, 131.
Arey, Oliver, **XV**, 484.
Arnold, Thomas K., **IV**, 545.
Astley, J., **IV**, 165.
Ascham, Roger, **III**, 23.
Aventinus, **XI**, 163.
Bailey, Ebenezer, **XII**, 429.
Baker, W. M., **XVI**, 166.
Baker, W. S., **X**, 592.
Baldwin, Theron, **XV**, 261.
Barnard, F. A. P., **V**, 753.
Barnard, Henry, **I**, 659,
Barnard, John, **I**, 307.
Barnes, D. H., **XV**, 513.
Basol, Marquise de, **III**, 510.
Basedow, T. B., **V**, 487.
Basedow, Emile, **V**, 491.
Bateman, Newton, **XVI**, 165.
Bates, J., **VII**, 270.
Bates, S. P., **XV**, 682.
Beck, T. Romeyn, **I**, 654.
Beecher, Miss C. E, **XV**, 250.
Benton, A. R., **XVI**, 775.
Bell, Andrew, **X**, 467.
Bild, **V**, 66.
Bingham, Caleb, **V**, 325.
Bishop, Nathan, **XVI**,
Blewett, B. T., **XVI**, 431.
Bodiker, J., **XI**, 437.
Boccaccio, **VII**, 422.
Boyd, E. J., **XV**, 645.
Braidwood, J., **III**, 348.
Bridgman, Laura, **IV**, 383
Brainerd, J., **XVI**, 331.
Borgi, Jean, **I**, 583.
Bromfield, John, **V**, 521.
Brooks, Charles, **I**, 581.
Brougham, Lord, **VI**, 467.
Brown, J. Horace, **XV**, 764.
Brown, Nicholas, **III**, 291.
Buckingham, J. T., **XIII**, 129.
Buckley, J. W., **XIV**, 28.
Burrowes, T. H., **VI**, 107, 555.

Burtt, Andrew, **XV**, 679.
Burton, Warren, **II**, 333.
Busch, **V**, 727.
Butler, Caleb, **II**, 54.
Butler, J. D., **XVII**,
Butler, Cyrus, **III**, 310.
Buss, Johannes, **V**, 293.
Caldwell, C., **XVI**, 109.
Calhoun, W. B., **XV**, 212.
Cæsarius, J., **IV**, 2 5.
Carlton, Oliver, **XV**, 523.
Carter, James, **V**, 337.
Carter, J. G., **V**, 407.
Cecil, Sir W., **IV**, 161.
Cheever, Ezekiel, **I**, 297; **XII**, 530.
Cheke, Sir John, **IV**, 163.
Chrysoloras, Emanuel, **VII**, 440.
Clajus, Johannes, **XI**, 412.
Claxton, Timothy, **VIII**, 253.
Clerc, Laurent, **III**, 349.
Coburn, C. R., **XV**, 679.
Coelenius, C., **IV**, 2 5.
Coffin, J. H., **XVI**, 784.
Colburn, Dana P., **XI**, 289.
Colburn, Warren, **II**, 294.
Colet, John, **VIII**, 291; **XVI**, 405.
Comenius, **V**, 25.
Cosmo de Medici, **VII**, 445.
Conover, A. M., **XIV**, 393.
Cowley, A., **XII**, 151.
Courteilles, M. de, **III**, 704.
Corston, William, **X**, 363.
Corte, P. A., **IV**, 491.
Cowdrey, M. F., **XVI**, 589.
Craig, A. J., **XIV**, 394.
Crato, **V**.
Cross, M. K., **XVI**, 751.
Cruikshank, J., **XV**, 485.
Crozet, Claude, **XIII**, 31.
Curtis, Joseph, **I**, 655.
Curtis, T. W. T., **XV**, 607.
Dante, **VII**, 418.
Davies, Charles, **XV**, 479.
Davis, Wm. Van L., **XV**, 675.
Day, J., **XVI**, 126.
Denman, **XV**, 395.
Denzel, B. G., **VII**, 315.
Delillee, J., **III**, 158.
Dewey, Chester, **XV**, 477.
Dewitt, G. A., **V**, 17.
Diesterweg, **VII**, 312.
Dick, James, **I**, 392.
Dinter, **VII**, 153.
Donatus, **XVII**,
Dowse, Thomas, **III**, 284; **IX**, 355.
Dringenberg, Louis, **V**, 65
Dudley, Mrs. E., **II**, 598.

Dunnell, M. H., **XVI**, 783.
Duncan, Alexander, **III**, 311.
Dwight, Edmund, **IV**, 5.
Dwight, F., **V**, 803.
Dwight, Theodore, **XIV**, 558.
Dwight, Timothy, **V**, 567.
Eaton, Theophilus, **I**, 298; **V**, 30.
Ebrardt, U., **XI**, 160.
Edson, H. K., **XVI**, 750.
Edwards, B. B., **XIV**, 381.
Edwards, Richard, **XVI**, 169.
Elyott, Sir Thomas, **XVI**, 483.
Emerson, G. B., **V**, 417.
Erasmus, **IV**, 729.
Ernesti, I. A., **V**, 750.
Everett, Edward, **XII**, 325.
Faneuil, P., **XI**, 603.
Farnum, Paul, **III**, 397.
Farnham, G. L., **XV**, 483.
Faville, O., **XVI**, 750.
Fellenberg, E., **III**, 591.
Felton, C. C., **X**, 265.
Fenelon, **XIII**, 477.
Fisk, Wilbur, **VI**, 297.
Fliedner, T., **I**; **III**, 487.
Ford, Jonathan, **XIV**, 395.
Froebel, F., **IV**, 792
Fowle, **X**, 597.
Franklin, B., **I**, 45; **VIII**, 251.
Fuller, Thomas, **III**, 155.
Fox, **X**, 363.
Fry, Elizabeth, **III**, 508.
Frangk, Fabian, **XI**, 163.
Franke, V., 441.
Frisch, J. L., **XI**, 439.
Gall, James, **IV**,
Gallaudet, T. H., **I**, 417.
Gottsched, J. C., **XI**, 448.
Galloway, S., **XVI**, 601.
Geneintz, Christian, **XI**, 426.
George of Trebizond, **VII**, 440.
Gesner, J. M., **V**, 741.
Gerard, **IV**, 622.
Goodnow, I. T., **XVI**, 386.
Goodrich, S. G., **XIII**, 134.
Green, John, **XIII**, 600.
Grant, Miss, **X**, 656.
Gubert, John, **XI**, 42.
Greene, S. S., **XIV**, 600.
Grimm, J., **XI**, 454.
Gregory, J. M., **XV**,
Goswin, **IV**, 715.
Griscom, John, **VIII**, 325.
Guarino, **VII**, 436.
Guilford, Nathan, **VIII**, 289.
Guizot, **XI**, 254.
Hagar, D. B., **XV**, 217.

Hadden, **IV**. 164.
Hall, S. R., **V**. 373.
Hall, W., **XV**. 127.
Halm, **V**. 025.
Hamann, J. G., **VI**. 247.
Hancock, J., **XVI**. 602.
Harnisch, Wilhelm, **VII**. 317.
Hart, J. S., **V**. 91.
Harvard, John, **V**. 523.
Harvey, T. II., **XVI**. 608.
Hauberle, **V**. 509.
Haüy, V., **III**. 477.
Hawley, G, **XI**. 94.
Hazeltine, L., **XV**. 481.
Hecker, **V**. 695.
Hedges, Nathan, **XVI**. 737.
Hegius, Alexander, **IV**. 723.
Henkle, **XVI**.
Herder, **VI**. 195.
Higginson, John, **XIII**. 724.
Hillhouse, James, **VI**. 325.
Holbrook, J., **VIII**. 229; **XIV**. 558.
Hopkins, Mark, **XI**. 219
Hovey, C. E., **VIII**. 95.
Howe, S. G., **XI**. 389.
Hoole, C., **XII**. 647.
Hopkins, E., **IV**. 668.
Hoss, G. W., **XVI**. 775.
Hubbard, F., **XV**.
Hubbard, R., **V**. 316.
Huntington, **XV**. 606.
Hurty, J., **XVI**. 776.
Ickelsamer, **XI**. 402.
Ives, M. B., **V**. 311.
John of Ravenna, **VII**. 435.
Johnson, Samuel, **VII**. 461.
Johnson, Walter R., **V**. 781.
Jones, R. D., **XV**. 481.
Kelly, Robert, **I**. 655; **X**. 313.
Kempis, Thomas à, **IV**. 626.
Kingsbury, John, **V**. 9.
Kneeland, John, **XV**. 526.
Krachenberger, **V**. 79.
Krüsi, Hermann, **V**. 161.
Kyrle, John, the "Man of Ross," **II**. 654.
Ladd, J. J., **XIV**. 592.
Lancaster, Joseph, **X**. 355.
Lange, Rudolph, **IV**. 726.
Lawrence. Abbot, **I**. 205.
Leo X., **VII**. 454.
Lewis, Samuel, **V**. 727.
Lindsley, Philip, **VII**. 9.
Locke, John, **VI**. 209.
Long, W., **XVI**. 497.
Lord, A. D., **XVI**. 607.
Lowell, John, **V**. 427.
Loyola, Ignatius, **XIV**. 455.
Lycurgus, **XIV**. 611.
Lyman Theodore, **X**. 5.
Lyon, Mary, **X**. 649.

Lawrence, Amos, **XVII**.
Lawrence, William, **II**. 33.
May, Samuel J., **XVI**. 141.
McDonough, John, **II**. 736.
McGill, James, **VII**. 188.
McJilton, J. N., **XVII**.
McKeen, Joseph, **I**. 655.
McMynn, **XIV**. 391.
Mann, Horace, **V**. 611.
Marks, D., **V**. 64.
Marvin, J. G., **XVI**. 626.
Mason, Lowell, **IV**. 141.
Mayhew, Ira, **XV**. 641.
Medici, Lorenzo di, **VII**. 445.
Melancthon, Philip, **IV**. 741.
Micyllus, **IV**. 464.
Mildmay, Sir W., **IV**. 164.
Mirandola, Picus di, **VII**. 449.
Milton, John, **XIV**. 159.
Morhof, **XI**. 436.
Morse, Augustus, **XV**. 608.
Mowry, William A., **XIV**. 592.
Nagali, **VII**. 300.
Neander, **V**. 509.
Niederer, **VII**. 289.
North, Edward, **XV**. 486.
North, S. J., **VI**. 104.
Northend, C., **XV**. 220.
Oberlin, **XVII**.
Oelinger, **XI**. 406.
Olivier, **V**. 508.
Olmsted, Denison, **V**. 367.
Orbilius, **III**. 157.
Orcutt, **XV**. 630.
Overberg, **XIII**. 365.
Page, D. P., **V**. 811.
Parish, A., **XV**. 523.
Partridge, A., **XIII**. 49, 683.
Peabody, George, **I**. 328; **XVII**.
Peabody, S. H., **XIV**. 395.
Pease, Calvin, **XV**. 631.
Peckham, J., **XVI**. 743.
Peers, B. O., **XVI**. 147.
Peet, H. P., **III**. 365.
Peirce, C., **IV**. 275.
Pelton, J. C., **XVI**. 626.
Perkins, T. H., **I**. 551.
Pestalozzi, **III**. 401.
Phelps, W. F., **V**. 827.
Petrarch, **VII**. 424.
Philbrick, J. D., **XIV**. 32.
Philelphus, **VII**. 441.
Phillips, John, **VI**. 75.
Phillips, S., **VI**. 66.
Pickard, J. L., **XIV**. 392.
Picket, Aaron, **XV**. 393.
Picket, Albert. **XVII**.
Picus, J, **VII**. 449.
Pierce, J. D., **XV**. 640.
Plamann, **VII**. 309.
Platter, Thomas, **V**. 79.

Plummer, Caroline, **XIII**. 73.
Poggius, **VII**. 442.
Politian, **VII**. 445.
Pomeroy, E. C., **XV**. 486.
Potter, Alonzo, **XVI**. 599.
Powell, W. H., **XVI**. 167.
Pradt, J. B., **XIV**. 394.
Putnam, D., **XV**. 646.
Radwin, Florentius, **IV**. 623.
Ramsauer, J., **VII**. 301.
Randall, S. S., **XIII**. 227.
Ratich, **V**. 229.
Ray, J., **XVI**. 603.
Raumer, **IV**. 149.
Redfield. W. C., **IV**. 833.
Reuchlin, **V**. 67.
Rice, V. M., **XV**. 391.
Richards, Z., **XIV**. 23.
Richard, C. S., **XVI**. 764.
Richardson, M., **XV**. 605.
Rickoff, A. J., **XIV**. 24.
Ripley, E. L., **XV**. 645.
Robbins, T., **III**. 279.
Rousseau, V. 459.
Russell, W., **III**. 139.
Rytwise, J., **XVI**. 682.
Sams, **XVI**. 602.
Sanborn, E. D., **XVI**. 762.
Sandinus, **VII**.
Sapidus, **V**. 66.
Sarmiento. **XVI**. 593.
Sargano, **VII**. 435.
Sawyer, H. E., **XVI**. 763.
Scheurl, C., **XI**. 161.
Schmidt, **VII**. 297.
Seymour, D., **X**. 321.
Sheldon, E. A., **XV**. 484.
Sheldon, W. E., **XV**. 525.
Sherwin. T., **VIII**. 461.
Shottelius, **XI**. 429.
Sill, D. M. B , **XV**. 645.
Slade, W., **XV**. 250.
Simler, **V**. 66.
Smith, Sir Thomas, **IV**. 165.
Spicer, A. C., **XV**. 392.
Standish, J. V. N., **XVI**. 165.
Stearns, **XV**. 524.
Sticler, **XI**. 435.
Stoddard, J. V., **XV**. 480.
Stone, A. P., **XV**. 219.
Stowe, C. E., **V**. 586.
Strong, E. F., **XV**. 607.
Sturm, **IV**. 167.
Swett, J., **XVI**. 790.
Tappan, H. P., **XIII**. 451.
Taylor, J. O., **XV**. 248.
Thayer, G. F., **IV**. 613.
Tenney, J., **XVI**. 761.
Thayer, Sylvanus, **XVII**.
Thomasius, J., **V**. 742.
Thompson, J, B., **XV**. 487.

Thompson, Z., **I.** 654.
Tillinghast, N., **I.** 655.
Tobler, J. G., **V.** 205.
Todd, Henry, **IV.** 711.
Trotzendorf, **V.** 107.
Valentine, T. W., **XV.** 482.
Valla, **VII.** 443.
Van Rensselaer, **VI.** 223.
Vassar, M., **XI.** 53.
Vehrli, **III.** 389.
Vetrier, **XVI.** 665.
Vitellius, **XVI.** 669.
Vittorino, **VII.** 436.
Von Turk, **V.** 155.

Wadsworth, J., **V.** 389.
Warton, J., **XVI.** 511.
Wayland, F., **XIII.** 771.
Watkinson, D., **IV.** 837.
Welch, A. S., **XV.** 642.
Weld, T, **XV.** 234.
Wells, F. D., **XVI.**
Wells, W. H., **VIII.** 529.
Werner, G., **IV.** 799.
Wessel, **IV.** 714.
Weston, E. P., **XVI.** 784.
White, E. E., **XVI.** 606.
Wickersham, J. P., **XVI.** 282.
Wichern, **III.** 5.

Willard, Mrs. Emma, **VI.** 125.
Wimpheling, **V.** 65.
Wines, E. C., **IX.** 9.
Wolf, F. A., **VI.** 260.
Woodbridge, W. C., **V.** 51.
Woodbridge, W., **XVI.** 136.
Woodman, J. S., **XVI.** 761.
Woolworth, S. B., **XV.** 498.
Wotton, Sir Henry, **XV.** 123.
Wright, L., **II.** 176.
Wykeham, William of, **XVI.** 497.
Yale, Elihu, **V.** 716.
Zeller, **VII.** 305.
Zerbolt, Gerard, **IV.** 625.

PORTRAITS.

Abbott, Gorham D., **XVI.** 600.
Alcott, W. A., **IV.** 629.
Allen, F. A., **XV.** 622.
Andrews, I. W., **XVI.** 605.
Appleton, Samuel, **XII.** 1.
Arnold, Thomas, **IV.** 545.
Bailey, Ebenezer, **XII.** 401.
Baker, W. S., **XIV.** 401.
Baldwin, Theron, **XV.** 269.
Barnard, F. A. P., **V.** 753.
Barnard, Henry, **I.** 1.
Bateman, N., **XVI.** 166.
Bates, S. P., **XV.** 1.
Bishop, N., **XVII.**
Blewett, B. G., **XVI.** 432.
Brooks, Charles, **I.** 587.
Brown, Nicholas, **III.** 291.
Bulkley, J. W., **XIV.** 28.
Burrowes, T. H., **VI.** 107.
Camp, D. N., **XV.** 605.
Carter, J. G., **V.** 407.
Coburn, C. R., **XV.** 679.
Colburn, D. P., **XI.** 289.
Colburn, Warren, **II.** 294.
Davies, Charles, **XV.** 479.
Dowse, Thomas, **IX.** 355.
Dwight, Edmund, **IV.** 1.
Dwight, Francis, **V.** 803.
Edwards, Richard, **XVI.** 167.
Emerson, G. B., **V.** 417.
Everett, E., **VII.** 325.
Farnum, Paul, **III.** 307.
Faville, O., **XVI.** 759.
Felton, C. C., **X.** 265.
Fisk, Wilbur, **VI.** 297.
Fowle, W. B., **X.** 597.
Gallaudet, T. H., **I.** 417.
Galloway, S., **XVI.** 601.
Garfield, James A., **XVII.** 1.
Goodnow, I. T., **XVI.** 387.
Green, John, **XIII.** 606.
Greene, S. S., **XIV.** 609.
Gregory, J. M., **XV.** 643.

Griscom, John, **VIII.** 325.
Hagar, D. B., **XV.** 517.
Hall, S. R., **XV.** 5.
Hart, J. S., **V.** 91.
Haüy, V., **III.** 477.
Hazeltine, L., **XV.** 481.
Henkle, William D., **XVI.** 432.
Hillhouse, James, **VI.** 325.
Holbrook, Josiah, **VIII.** 1.
Hopkins, Mark, **XI.** 219.
Hovey, C. E., **XIII.** 94.
Howe, S. G., **XI.** 321.
Johnson, W. R., **V.** 781.
Kelley, Robert, **X.** 313.
Kingsbury, John, **V.** 9.
Lawrence, Abbott, **I.** 137.
Lawrence, William, **II.** 1.
Lewis, Samuel, **V.** 727.
Lindsley, Philip, **VII.** 9.
Lord, A. D., **XVI.** 607.
Lyman, Theodore, **X.** 1.
Lyon, Mary, **X.** 609.
McCarty, H. D., **XVI.** 388.
McGill, James, **VII.** 188.
McJilton, J. N., **XVII.**
McMynn, J. G., **XIV.** 391.
Mann, Horace, **V.** 611.
Mason, Lowell, **IV.** 141.
Mayhew, Ira, **XV.** 641.
North, E., **XVII.**
North, S. J., **VI.** 104.
Northend, Charles, **XVI.** 510.
Olmsted, Denison, **V.** 367.
Orcutt, Hiram, **XV.** 630.
Page, D. P., **V.** 811.
Parish, A., **XV.** 523.
Partridge, Alden, **XIII.** 657.
Peabody, George, **II.** 642.
Peckham, Isaiah, **XVI.** 743.
Peet, H. P., **III.** 366.
Peirce, Cyrus, **IV.** 275.
Perkins, T. H., **I.** 551.
Pestalozzi, **IV.** 65.

Phelps, Mrs. A. Lincoln, **XVII.**
Phelps, W. F., **V.** 827.
Philbrick, J. D., **XIV.** 32.
Phillips, Samuel, **VI.** 66.
Pickard, J. L., **XIV.** 129.
Potter, Alonzo, **XVI.** 1.
Randall, S. S., **XIII.** 227.
Ray, I., **XVI.** 603.
Richards, Z., **XIV.** 23.
Rickoff, A. J., **XIV.** 24.
Russell, William, **III.** 139.
Ryerson, E., **XVII.**
Sarmiento, D. F., **XVI.** 593.
Sawyer, H. E., **XVI.** 763.
Scammon, Jos. T., **XVII.**
Sears, B., **XVII.** *
Sheldon, E. A., **XV.** 484.
Sheldon, W. E., **XV.** 525.
Sherwin, Thomas, **VIII.** 461.
Silliman, Benjamin, **XVII.**
Standish, J. V. N., **XVI.** 165.
Stoddard, J. F., **XV.** 675.
Stone, A. P., **XV.** 519.
Stowe, C. E., **V.** 586.
Swett, John, **XVI.** 790.
Tappan, H. P., **XIII.** 449.
Thayer, Sylvanus, **XVII.**
Thayer, G. F., **IV.** 613.
Tillinghast, N., **II.** 568.
Van Rensselaer, Stephen, **VI.** 223.
Vassar, Matthew, **XI.** 1.
Wadsworth, James, **V.** 389.
Watkinson, David, **XVII.**
Wayland, Francis, **XIII.** 1.
Wells, D. F., **XVI.** 749.
Wells, W. H., **VIII.** 529.
Weston, E. P., **XVI.** 783.
Whitford, W. C., **XVII.**
Wichern, J. H., **III.** 1.
Wickersham, J. P., **XV.** 677.
Willard, Mrs. Emma, **VI.** 1.
Wines, E. C., **IX.** 9.
Woolworth, S. B., **XV.** 385.

www.ingramcontent.com/pod-product-compliance
Lightning Source LLC
Chambersburg PA
CBHW022111160426
43197CB00009B/979